Glob Inequality

Global Inequality
Patterns and Explanations

Edited by
David Held and Ayse Kaya

First published in 2007 by Polity Press

Reprinted 2007

Polity Press
65 Bridge Street
Cambridge CB2 1UR, UK

Polity Press
350 Main Street
Malden, MA 02148, USA

ISBN-10: 0-7456-3886-4
ISBN-13: 978-07456-3886-7
ISBN-10: 0-7456-3887-2 (pb)
ISBN-13: 978-07456-3887-4 (pb)

A catalogue record for this book is available from the British Library.

Typeset in 10.5 on 13 pt Swift
by Servis Filmsetting Ltd, Manchester
Printed and bound in Great Britain by MPG Books Ltd, Bodmin, Cornwall.

For further information on Polity, visit our website: www.polity.co.uk

Contents

Notes on Contributors

David Dollar is World Bank Country Director for China and Mongolia, based in Beijing. He has a PhD in economics from New York University and a BA in Chinese language and history from Dartmouth College. He has spent 30 years studying and advising developing economies in Asia, including Bangladesh, China, India, Mongolia, South Korea, Taiwan, Thailand and Vietnam. Before joining the World Bank he taught economics at UCLA and at the Chinese Academy of Social Sciences in Beijing. Since joining the World Bank in 1989 he has spent half his time writing on globalization in the research department and half working on the Bank's operational programmes in Asia.

Gøsta Esping-Andersen teaches at Universitat Pompeu Fabra, Barcelona. His research is centred on issues related to social inequality, social policy and stratification. His most recent books include *Why We Need a New Welfare State* (2003) and *Social Foundations of Postindustrial Economies* (1999) and has a forthcoming book *Households, Employment and Fertility*. He received the 2005 APSA Enduring Contribution Award.

Nancy Fraser is the Henry A. and Louise Loeb Professor of Philosophy and Politics at the New School for Social Research. She is the author of *Redistribution or Recognition? A Political-Philosophical Exchange*, with Axel Honneth, (2003); *Justice Interruptus: Critical Reflections on the 'Postsocialist' Condition* (1997); *Feminist Contentions: A Philosophical Exchange*, with Seyla Benhabib, Judith Butler and Drucilla Cornell, (1994); and *Unruly Practices: Power, Discourse, and Gender in Contemporary Social Theory* (1989). Her current research is on post-Westphalian democratic justice.

James K. Galbraith holds the Lloyd M. Bentsen Jr Chair in Government/Business Relations at the Lyndon B. Johnson School of Public Affairs, the University of Texas at Austin. He is Senior Scholar at the Levy Economics Institute and Chair of Economists for Peace and Security. His books on inequality are *Created Unequal: The Crisis in American Pay*, Free Press (1998) and *Inequality and Industrial Change: A Global View*, co-edited with Maureen Berner, Cambridge (2001).

David Held is Graham Wallas Professor of Political Science at the London School of Economics and Political Science (LSE). Among his books are *Democracy and the Global Order* (1995), *Global Covenant* (2004), *Models of Democracy* (third edition, 2006). He is the co-author of *Global Transformations* (1999) and *Globalization and Anti-Globalization* (2002); and editor or co-editor of *Prospects for Democracy* (1993), *Cosmopolitan Democracy* (1995) and *Re-Imagining Political Community* (1998).

Ravi Kanbur is T. H. Lee Professor of World Affairs, International Professor of Applied Economics and Management, and Professor of Economics at Cornell University. He has previously taught at various universities including Cambridge, Oxford, Essex, Princeton and Warwick. He has also served on the senior staff of the World Bank, including as the Chief Economist for Africa.

Ayse Kaya is a researcher and a PhD candidate at the London School of Economics and Political Science (LSE). Her PhD examines the different ways in which the USA and the EU attempt to shape globalization, utilizing US–EU trade disputes at the World Trade Organization (WTO) as case studies. She is the former manager of the Ralph Miliband Programme at the LSE.

Branko Milanovic is Lead Economist in the World Bank Research Department's unit dealing with poverty, income distribution and household surveys; Senior Associate at the Carnegie Endowment for International Peace in Washington; Adjunct Professor at the School for Advanced International Studies at Johns Hopkins University, Washington. He writes on methodology and empirics of inequality; poverty and social policy in transition economies, and globalization and inequality. His recent publications include *Income and Influence: Social Policy in Emerging Market Economies*, co-authored with Ethan Kapstein, Upjohn (2003); 'True World Income Distribution 1988 and 1993: First Calculations Based on Household Surveys Alone', *Economic Journal*, 112 (476), 2002; and *Income, Inequality and Poverty During the Transition from Planned to Market Economy*, World Bank (1998). His new book *Worlds Apart: Measuring International and Global Inequality*, Princeton University Press, came out in 2005.

Thomas W. Pogge, since receiving his PhD in philosophy from Harvard, has been teaching moral and political philosophy and Kant at Columbia University. His recent publications include *Freedom from Poverty as a Human Right*, edited, Oxford (forthcoming); *Global Institutions and Responsibilities*, edited with Christian Barry, Blackwell (2005); *Real World Justice*, edited with Andreas Follesdal, Springer (2005); *World Poverty and Human Rights*, Polity (2002); and with Sanjay Reddy 'How *Not* to Count the Poor', in Sudhir Anand and Joseph Stiglitz (eds), *Measuring Global Poverty*, Oxford (forthcoming) and at www. socialanalysis.org. Thomas Pogge is Editor for Social and Political Philosophy for the *Stanford Encyclopedia of Philosophy* and a member of the Norwegian Academy of Science. His work was supported, most recently, by the John D. and Catherine T. MacArthur Foundation, the Princeton Institute for Advanced Study, All Souls College (Oxford), the National Institutes of Health (Bethesda) and the Australian Research Council. He is currently Professorial Fellow at the ANU Centre for Applied Philosophy and Public Ethics.

Bob Sutcliffe is the author of *100 Ways of Seeing an Unequal World*, Zed Books (2001). He has taught development and international economics in the UK, the USA, Nicaragua and Spain and now lives in the Basque Country.

Grahame F. Thompson is Professor of Political Economy at the Open University. His long-term research interests include the nature of network forms of governance and the international system. Thompson is currently engaged in researching the fate of the categories of borders, territories and jurisdictions in debates about globalization, and the meaning of 'global corporate citizenship'.

Anthony J. Venables is Professor of International Economics at LSE and Chief Economist in the UK Department for International Development. He has published extensively in the areas of international trade and spatial economics, including work on trade and imperfect competition, economic integration, multinational firms and economic geography. His publications include: *The Spatial Economy: Cities, Regions and International Trade*, with M. Fujita and P. Krugman, MIT Press (1999), and *Multinationals in the World Economy*, with G. Barba Navaretti, Princeton (2004).

Robert H. Wade is Professor of Political Economy at LSE. His research has focused on the question of why some countries and regions are rich and many others so poor. He has followed this theme in fieldwork sites ranging from Pitcairn Island, Tuscany, India, South Korea,

Taiwan, to the World Bank. More recently he has concentrated on how the structure of the world economy and the agency of the G7 states help to explain the reproduction of the dizzyingly steep world hierarchy of income and wealth; and on the possibilities of 'open economy' industrial policy.

Editors' Preface

Most of the chapters in this book are revised versions of the Ralph Miliband Lectures on Global Inequalities: Dimensions and Challenges, given at the London School of Economics and Political Science (LSE) in 2004–5. Contributions by other distinguished authors, and an Introduction, have been added to the collection in order to provide the reader with a more comprehensive exploration of this important topic.

The nature and form of global inequalities raises questions of crucial significance. At stake is the contemporary character of the global order and its capacity to promote economic development, prosperity and social justice. The chapters in this book provide a broad range of views on global inequalities – how to conceive them, how to measure them, how to interpret historical trends, how to draw out implications for policy within-nation-states and across borders. We think that presenting these diverse perspectives in the same book contributes to a vital public debate about the nature and future of global economic change.

The Ralph Miliband programme honours the memory of Ralph Miliband, who taught at the LSE from 1949 to 1972, and is funded through a generous bequest of a former LSE PhD student, who was inspired by Ralph Miliband's critical vision. This bequest has made the lecture series possible, and we are grateful to all those who supported the initiative; in particular, we wish to thank Michael Cox, Anne Philips, Marion Kozak, Chun Lin, David Miliband, Edward Miliband, Henrietta Moore and Salome Van Jaarsveld.

D. H. and A. K.

Acknowledgements

The author and publishers are grateful to the following for permission to reproduce copyright material:

Blackwell Publishing for permission to reproduce figure 9.1 from Ravi Kanbur and Xiaobo Zhang, 'Fifty Years of Regional Inequality in China: A Journey through Central Planning, Reform and Openness', *Review of Development Economics*, 9, no. 1 (Feb. 2005), pp. 87–106: figure 2, 'Trends of regional inequality'.

Centre for Economic Policy Research for permission to reproduce figure 8.2 from M. Weisbrot, D. Baker and D. Rosnik, 'The Scorecard on Development: 25 years of Diminished Progress', Centre for Economic Policy Research, Sept. 2005.

HM Treasury, for permission to reprint figure 8.8 from 'Global Europe: Full Employment Europe', chart 5, p. 6, Oct. 2005.

New Left Review for permission to reprint chapter 11 from Nancy Fraser, 'Reframing Justice in a Globalizing World', *New Left Review*, 36 (Nov.–Dec. 2005), pp. 69–88. First delivered as a 2004 Spinoza Lecture at the University of Amsterdam, the text was revised at the Wissenschaftskolleg zu Berlin in 2004–5, then delivered as a Miliband Lecture at the London School of Economics in March 2005.

Oxford University Press Journals for permission to reprint chapter 4 from David Dollar, 'Globalization, Poverty and Inequality since 1980', *World Bank Research Observer*, 20 (2005), pp. 1–31.

Palgrave Macmillan for permission to reproduce figure 8.1 from A. Freeman, 'Globalization: Economic Stagnation and Divergence', in A. Pettifor (ed.), *Real World Economic Outlook* (2003): figure 16.1, p. 153.

Springer Science and Business Media for permission to reproduce figure 8.3 from R. J. Barro, 'Inequality and Growth in a Panel of Countries', *Journal of Economic Growth*, 5 (2000), pp. 5–32: figure 4, p. 25.

Every effort has been made to trace all copyright holders, but if any have been inadvertently overlooked, the publishers will be pleased to include the necessary credits in any subsequent reprint or edition.

Abbreviations

CEO	Chief Executive Officer
FDI	foreign direct investment
GDI	Gross Domestic Income
GDP	Gross Domestic Product
ILO	International Labour Organization
IMF	International Monetary Fund
MNC	multinational corporation
NBER	National Bureau of Economic Research
OECD	Organization for Economic Cooperation and Development
PPP	purchasing power parity
TRIPS	Trade-Related Aspects of Intellectual Property Rights
UN	United Nations
UNDP	United Nations Development Programme
UNICEF	United Nations Children's Fund
UNIDO	United Nations International Development Organization
UNU-WIDER	United Nations University-World Institute for Development Economics Research
UTIP	University of Texas Inequality Project
WDI	World Development Indicators
WHO	World Health Organization
WTO	World Trade Organization

1

Introduction

David Held and Ayse Kaya

THERE is powerful evidence to illustrate contemporary global disparities. Today about 2,742 million people live without access to
adequate sanitation and more than 830 million people are seriously
undernourished (UNDP 2004, p. 129).[1] The difference in the average life
expectancy between a low-income and a high-income country is 19
years (UNDP 2005, p. 25). The richest 10 per cent of the world's population receive approximately half of the world's income (Milanovic,
chapter 2 below).[2] Rich countries' agricultural subsidies amount to
more than 10 times the aid to Africa (Benn 2005). A recent study found
the average CEO of the companies that comprise the Standard & Poor's
(S&P) 500 made 212 times the wages of the average worker in the USA
(*WSJ* 21 January 2006). Such inequalities have motivated many protest
movements – ranging from the objections of developing-country farmers against the World Trade Organization (WTO), to rock stars with a
mission to address poverty in Africa, to non-governmental organizations' efforts to promote 'fair trade'. Embedded in these reactions has
been not just a cry against inequalities but also a conviction that globalization underlies global disparities.

Has globalization affected inequality? This is a tough question to
answer. On the standard liberal view, often heard in the mass media and
in the international financial institutions, economic globalization
stimulates growth and development around the world. Openness to
trade and investment boosts growth and growth raises standards of
living. As income levels rise, poverty is reduced and the economically
marginalized begin to prosper. In accounts of this kind, a catch up or
convergence story is often assumed whereby poorer countries which
open their markets and liberalize are expected to grow faster and richer
so that income differentials narrow over time. A move to a market involv-
ing economic liberalization and international integration is, according
to this view, essential for the economic well-being of all; it is, as Martin
Wolf put it, 'the heart of the matter. All else is commentary' (2004, p. 144).

But is all else commentary? The links between economic globalization, economic growth, inequality and poverty are all disputed. In fact,

almost every detail of the standard liberal account has been contested, giving rise to different narratives of the benefits of globalization, the sources of inequality and poverty. At the core of some of these positions is the contention that economic globalization itself impedes development, exacerbates inequality and makes the poor worse off in many parts of the world (see Held and Koenig-Archibugi 2003).

Yet there are many good reasons for going beyond the simplicities of 'globalization good' or 'globalization bad', and this book provides some of them by focusing on the debate about globalization and its relation to inequality. For as soon as one begins to explore this matter a number of fundamental and unavoidable questions arise, such as: What is inequality? How is it to be measured? What are the contemporary levels of inequality? How do these current levels of inequality compare to the past? What is the relevance of inequality for national and global policy-making? These questions lie at the core not just of the specific controversy about the importance of inequality and possible methods of alleviating pronounced stratifications, but also at the heart of the larger debate about globalization and governance.

Answers to these questions are not self-evident, hence this volume offers a wide variety of perspectives on inequality, highlighting different aspects of the debate. As Grahame Thompson remarks in his chapter, '[A] complex phenomenon like inequality cannot be adequately described by a single measure – and that there are no simple answers to the question of whether the world is becoming more or less equal.' To comprehend contemporary patterns of global inequality, one needs to analyse different kinds of trends – such as what is happening to different regions of the world and what is happening within countries – and a number of different measurements remain at one's disposal.

This Introduction aims to provide an overview of the different chapters by analysing some of the cross-cutting themes in the book. It begins with an account of contemporary economic inequalities, emphasizing some key definitions and patterns as well as difficulties in measuring inequality. Following this, the Introduction focuses on the role of China and India in understanding global inequality. After discussing patterns of inequality, it explores the link between globalization and inequality. The Introduction ends with an account of why the contributors to this volume do or do not think inequality matters.

The State of Inequality Today: Definitions and Patterns

In chapter 2, Branko Milanovic seeks to understand contemporary levels of inequality with the help of three concepts: Concept 1,

Table 1.1 Three types of inequality
• *Unweighted international inequality (Concept 1)*: differences between countries' mean incomes as measured by their GDPs (or GDIs); population size is not taken into account.
• *Weighted international inequality (Concept 2)*: differences between countries' mean incomes as measured by their GDPs (or GDIs); population size factored into the calculations.
• *Global inequality (Concept 3)*: differences of income between the individuals of the world; includes inter-country as well as intra-country inequalities.

unweighted international inequality; Concept 2, weighted international inequality; and Concept 3, global inequality (these concepts are summarized in table 1.1 above). At the heart of these concepts is the distinction between *international* and *global* inequality. While the former identifies inequality between nations measured by the differences in their mean incomes, the latter denotes income inequality between the individuals of the world. Although other authors in the volume do not necessarily calculate global inequality in the way in which Milanovic does, they all define global inequality as income inequality between the individuals of the world, including both inter-country and intra-country inequalities.

Milanovic explains that from about 1950 to 2000 the different types of inequality have exhibited diverse trajectories. Unweighted international inequality (Concept 1) has generally been on the rise during this period with a marked upward trend since the late 1970s. On the other hand, Concept 2 inequality, weighted international inequality, has decreased particularly since around 1978 due mainly to the growth of China and to a lesser degree India. Based on household surveys from three years (1988, 1993 and 1998), Milanovic finds that global inequality (Concept 3) does not chart a clear pattern, increasing strongly between 1988 and 1993 and then displaying a minor decline from 1993 to 1998. He claims within-national inequalities 'increased almost everywhere' in the last two or so decades. Milanovic emphasizes that while global inequality remains extremely high today – around 62–66 measured in terms of the Gini Index – its direction of change remains unclear.[3]

Following Milanovic's chapter, Bob Sutcliffe examines twentieth-century inequality, emphasizing inter-country and intra-country inequalities in a wider context of changing patterns of power between countries. Sutcliffe's chapter begins by looking at total world production (world GDP), underscoring that the twentieth century has witnessed 'unequalled' levels of income growth but at the same time the highest population growth ever recorded. Sutcliffe shows that this 'unequalled' growth has been unequally distributed. For instance, in comparison to the beginning of the twentieth century, Africa's share of world GDP has declined at the end of the century. Although developing countries have seen their share decline in the first half of the century, this trend was reversed in the second half of the century particularly because of Asia's record of growth.

In analysing changes in inequality across the world, Sutcliffe offers a number of different measurements. For instance, he examines the inequality between incomes of people and households by taking the ratio of the ten poorest and the ten richest countries and their average national incomes, the '10/10' ratio (see also Milanovic). Sutcliffe explains that although such data has limitations, the 10/10 ratio declined between 1950 and 1980 but increased substantially after the 1980s. This finding highlights the growing gap between the world's very rich and very poor since the 1980s. Overall, Sutcliffe finds that although in some Asian countries inequality is lower today than it was, the gap between the rich in developed countries and the very poor in poor countries has increased remarkably and the world Gini coefficient is at a level (0.63) that now exceeds all but two (Namibia and Lesotho) of the most unequal countries by several points. Nevertheless, measuring inter-country and intra-country inequalities together, Sutcliffe's findings also show a decline in global inequality – inequality between the individuals of the world – in the last two decades of the century. (See also Dollar for similar conclusions on this particular point.)

David Dollar's chapter focuses on the way in which globalization – understood as increasing integration of world markets primarily via openness to trade and investment – has facilitated growth and hence poverty reduction. What Dollar finds unique about the current phase of globalization is the greater participation of developing countries in the world economy. Since the 1980s, but particularly in the 1990s, developing countries have in general experienced higher rates of growth than industrialized countries. Dollar recognizes the population-dependent nature of the record of economic growth of developing countries, specifically the growth of China and India, but emphasizes that these were not the only populous nations, and others, such as Vietnam and Bangladesh, have also accelerated their growth. Dollar's chapter explains how this climate of growth has generated reductions in extreme poverty,[4] leading to a decline in the number of people living on less than $1 a day. (He does acknowledge that the number of people living on less than $2 a day has increased between 1981 and 2001.) Moreover, Dollar finds a 'modest' decline in global inequality since 1980, although an increase in wage inequality (see Galbraith's chapter). While recognizing the within-country increase in inequality in certain countries, Dollar claims that this does not represent a general trend. However, because rising inequalities have occurred in populous nations, Dollar emphasizes that 'a majority of citizens of the world live in countries in which inequality is rising'. Based on these conclusions, Dollar does not find the argument convincing that increased levels of global economic integration automatically generate increased inequalities. His chapter emphasizes the necessity for further liberalization of markets across the world.

Robert H. Wade's chapter takes a different approach to Dollar's, critically assessing the record of liberal ideas, referred to as the 'Washington Consensus'[5] and their application to the developing world, Wade begins by discussing the liberal position on the question of inequality. The liberal position tends to see inequality as an inevitable result of free markets and private property rights, and as a necessary condition for 'efficiency, innovation, competitiveness'. Public policy should properly seek to remove extreme poverty and raise life expectancy of populations in poor countries. It should also seek to make the distribution of opportunities more equal. However once these issues are dealt with, it should let the distribution of income and wealth be determined by the market.

In a three-pronged criticism, Wade claims the liberals got it wrong. First, he argues empirical evidence raises serious doubts about the success of the liberal agenda. Contrary to expectations raised by the liberal argument, world growth has not accelerated even as world economic policy has shifted in a liberal direction. Average world GDP per capita growth rate has fallen in every decade since 1960 (see also Milanovic 2005 on growth figures). There are huge margins of error around the poverty numbers, and we cannot be confident that the number of people living in extreme poverty has fallen since the early 1980s. To the extent that the numbers have fallen, the fall depends entirely on China; elsewhere the numbers have risen, even according to the World Bank. The liberal claim that world income inequality has fallen thanks to globalization is based on one specific measure of (relative) income distribution. But the result again depends on China; take out China and even this measure shows widening world income inequality. Moreover, income inequality has risen by several other plausible measures.

Second, Wade discusses the negative economic, social and political repercussions of inequality both within countries and between different parts of the world, highlighting that inequality not only spurs social troubles but it is also likely to be bad for the economy. Third, Wade criticizes the liberal record for providing an inaccurate, and trivializing, account of the role of the state in development. Overall, Wade argues that the confidence with which liberal policies are prescribed does not derive from the strength of empirical evidence in their favour, but rather from the way they skew income distribution in favour of the already rich. He points to evidence which suggests that a majority of the increase in world consumption over the 1990s – a majority of the benefits of economic growth – accrued to the richest 8 per cent or so of the world's population, living mostly in the OECD countries. They have benefited magnificently from globalization, and unsurprisingly think that fuller implementation of the liberal agenda is good for the whole world.

Thomas W. Pogge discusses inequalities with an emphasis on the current global institutional structure. His chapter begins with a comprehensive overview of existing inequalities of various kinds (such as income, wealth and life chances) to demonstrate that the poor suffer from a variety of deficiencies, ranging from undernourishment, to lack of education, to lack of ability to properly participate in decision-making. Pogge defines contemporary levels of inequality as 'radical inequality'. In this age of extreme inequality, he claims 'the worse-off are very badly off', in both absolute and relative terms. Exacerbating the situation, the top and the bottom strata do not mix, leaving many people ignorant of what it means to live in poverty. The kind of poverty experienced by millions of people around the world pervades many aspects of their lives, crippling their ability to function effectively on many fronts. Finally, Pogge contends this state of 'radical inequality' can be overcome without the advantaged becoming badly off themselves.

Pogge emphasizes that although local and national factors play an important role in explaining inequalities, they do not suffice – global factors are also significant. Specifically, Pogge argues that 'global institutional rules' contribute to and sustain the extreme inequality of our age. He emphasizes such systemic causes have been neglected by those who focus on poverty only and constrain their arguments mostly to national and/or local factors. Pogge explains global rules *directly* and *indirectly* perpetuate power disparities, which in turn makes it more difficult to improve the conditions of the poor. Their direct impact can be observed, for instance, in the protectionist trade rules of developed countries, such as agricultural subsidies. The WTO permits such deviations from free trade at the expense of those in need. The global rules indirectly work against the poor because they allow illegitimate, corrupt and repressive rulers, in the name of the people they oppress, to borrow abroad, to sell national resources, to sign international treaties and to purchase the arms they need to stay in power. Pogge underlines that changing the rules to the advantage of the poor remains difficult because not only do the powerful rich continue to serve their interests at the expense of the poor but also the poor lack adequate means to participate in political decisions on the national and international levels. Pogge's arguments on why inequality matters are explored in greater detail below.

Focusing on wage inequalities, James K. Galbraith's chapter also uncovers a '*global* pattern' to changing inequalities. Galbraith bases his analysis of inequality on the dataset produced by the work of the University of Texas Inequality Project (UTIP) on UNIDO Industrial Statistics. Galbraith explains the comparability of this dataset to others, emphasizing that pay inequalities help us infer 'broader but often elusive economic distributions'. He also charts the movement of pay inequalities within countries: for instance, although an obvious pattern of change in pay inequality does not exist for the 1960s, in the 1970s the data reveals increasing inequalities in oil-importing nations and the opposite in oil exporters. Galbraith finds that from 1981 to the end of twentieth century, with some exceptions, 'inequality within countries rose relentlessly *as a global pattern.*'

Galbraith's chapter provides evidence for shifting the debate on inequality from being simply a local and microeconomic phenomenon to a global one. By combining manufacturing pay inequality and national per capita income, Galbraith finds a negative relationship between levels of inequality and pay – lower levels of income mean higher inequality and higher income levels mean lower inequality. This finding, he claims, provides proof for the existence of the essence of a Kuznets relationship.[6] Hence, it challenges the microeconomic approaches to inequality, which tend to overlook the existence of a universal element to changes in inequality. However, Galbraith under-lines that for recent years, even controlling for changes in income level, inequality has been rising. His primary conclusions highlight that in the era of liberal globalization – roughly since the 1980s – wage inequality is increasing across the world. Overall, Galbraith's position provides a critical assessment of approaches that analyse inequality only as a matter of 'policy choice, idiosyncratic to each country and its political system', arguing for the existence of a macro dynamic in the last two decades of the twentieth century.

By contrast, Grahame Thompson's contribution to this volume ques-tions the inherent assumption that there exists a global economic system and suggests economic activity continues to be concentrated nationally and regionally. Thus he does not see the quest to under-stand *global* inequality as a very viable enterprise. In challenging the 'conventional wisdom' that globalization exists, Thompson examines inequalities primarily based on an analysis by Stanley Fischer. In draw-ing upon Fischer's work, Thompson addresses the following notion: globalization has led to increased growth rates, which has in turn allowed for a convergence between the rich and the poor. Thompson's chapter first challenges the conception that the supposed era of globalization has engendered higher growth rates. On the contrary, Thompson maintains growth rates have declined since the mid-1970s. Second, Thompson focuses on the putative convergence between and amongst the 'developed' and 'less developed' countries. His conclusions emphasize that although divergence has taken place amongst the less developed countries, the developed countries have converged amongst themselves, further separating themselves from the rest.

Third, Thompson argues that economic activity – be it in the form of trade or financial integration – continues to occur primarily between developed countries. Although acknowledging the increased participation of developing countries in the world economy, Thompson finds that only a few developing countries have managed to integrate, and thus speaking of a global economy is inaccurate. In terms of financial flows and integration, Thompson explores a range of factors, such as portfolios and syndicated loans, and concludes that activities in this domain also remain sub-global. The same applies to multinational corporations (MNCs). Thompson claims economic activity has become increasingly concentrated in regional blocs, such as in Europe and East Asia. While cost and distance play crucial roles in generating economic activity on a regional, as opposed to global, basis, other factors, such as similarities in legal frameworks and language, also point to the increasing importance of regional formations. Overall, Thompson's chapter claims globalization is not the correct point of reference and proposes to examine inequalities on a domestic and regional basis.

Despite their differences, the chapters in this volume concur on the point that there exist huge variations in the economic well-being of different regions and countries of the world. Specifically, the discussions underline stratification within the developing world. For instance, Sutcliffe examines changes in inequality by examining the average incomes of continents as a percentage of the North (USA, Canada, Australia, New Zealand, Western Europe and Japan). Here he finds disparities in how continents have performed – only Asia's average income has gained as a percentage of the North. In general, Asia has performed better than other regions, particularly Latin America and Eastern Europe. The authors emphasize that the situation of Africa has become worse and remains dire. Dollar predicts that based on the slow or negative growth rates in Africa, if Asia continues to grow as it has been doing, we should expect even greater inequality in the world. Milanovic, on the other hand, emphasizes that our predictions about China (and hence the future of inequality of Asia and of global inequality in general) remain speculative. In understanding the complex patterns of inequality that emerge, all the contributions emphasize the necessity to understand what is happening to inequalities within regions and within countries.

The chapters by Ravi Kanbur and Anthony J. Venables, and Gøsta Esping-Andersen focus specifically on within-region and intra-country inequalities. Kanbur and Venables' chapter examines 'spatial inequalities'; the authors explain that such a measurement of inequality denotes 'inequality in economic and social indicators of well-being across geographical units within a country'. They summarize some of the findings of the Spatial Disparities in Human Development project by the World Institute for Development Economics Research of the United Nations University (UNU-WIDER), providing a closer look at regional differences within countries and the rural–urban divide. Regions vary on measurements such as the incidence of poverty, provision of public services and school enrolment of boys and girls. The findings of the project emphasize that up to 25 per cent of the inequalities between individuals in a country can be explained by disparities between regions. The study addresses important questions such as: Has there been rural-urban convergence in countries, and if so, which variables (for instance, school enrolment) has this convergence affected? And, how has growth affected rural and urban areas? Overall, the authors report that all the 26 countries surveyed by the project, China being one, witness high spatial inequalities and generally such inequalities exhibit an upward trend. The authors explain the existence of spatial inequalities by exploring both idiosyncratic factors, such as geography, and typical factors, such as openness to trade.

Gøsta Esping-Andersen's chapter concentrates on patterns of inequality in the developed world. Significantly, Esping-Andersen urges us to analyse the lives of people as a whole, rather than focusing on snapshots of lives utilizing measurements such as the Gini coefficient and the poverty rate. Such measurements analyse people in different stages of their life cycle and do not distinguish between 'transient' or 'persistent' low/high incomes. Moreover, instead of focusing on individuals, he proposes to analyse households, thus emphasizing the roles played by the changing participation of women in the economy as well as important demographic shifts. These demographic shifts, such as decreased fertility rates, in turn affect not only women's roles but also family structures. Esping-Andersen also emphasizes that an understanding of the welfare of individuals over the course of their lives involves more than indications of their incomes. In attaining a relatively more comprehensive sense of human welfare, one needs to examine people's mobility and, relatedly, the opportunities they face.

Esping-Andersen's chapter finds 'modest to sharp jumps in *market income* dispersion' in almost all EU countries (exceptions are France and the Netherlands) and the USA in the 1980s and 1990s. The evidence demonstrates that the position of young adult workers has declined, creating a problem of 'child poverty' when coupled with changes in family structure, such as the increase in single-parent households. On the one hand, the increasing participation of the women in the workforce and the narrowing gender gap in wages are a source for optimism. On the other hand, women's participation in the work force has disproportionately affected the relatively more educated, without really spreading its influence to less educated women. Esping-Andersen underlines how 'early childhood' profoundly affects people's life chances, pointing to studies that find greater inequality in income leads to growing divergence of parents' expenditure on children. Alongside income, 'family cultural capital' primarily determines early childhood experiences, and here the mother's education level remains very important. Generally speaking, Esping-Andersen points out how studies do not find a mother's employment has a negative impact on her children, even though other variables, such as the availability and quality of healthcare, play a role in determining this impact. While acknowledging a complex interaction of variables – such as the extent to which less educated women work – Esping-Andersen's chapter illustrates how more equal societies will be possible only if people's chances of mobility grow faster than income inequalities. The chapter illuminates the implications of wage inequality for households as well as the gender dimension of inequalities.

In the final chapter, Nancy Fraser argues that global frameworks, rather than national ones, are the appropriate reference points if humanity is to live in democratic and just societies. Fraser's arguments are analysed below in the discussion of the links between globalization and inequality.

The main themes of the volume should be clear by now, as well as points of convergence and divergence between authors. The reader may have noticed that while some authors find an increase in global inequality (Milanovic[7], Wade) between 1980 and 2000, others report a decrease during approximately the same period (Sutcliffe, Dollar). Yet other authors find different types of inequalities to be on the rise. Galbraith finds wage inequalities have risen in the era of liberal globalization; Kanbur and Venables point to exacerbations between different regions of countries; Esping-Andersen explores the complex patterns which lead to rising market income inequalities and differential life chances. Some authors focus specifically on why inequality matters greatly (Pogge, Wade), expanding upon other discussions on this matter. While Thompson challenges the idea that globalization exists and urges the reader to think in regional and national frameworks, Fraser finds a global framework necessary for addressing inequalities. Such differences in emphases introduce the reader to the varied approaches in the debate. Yet at the same time the different perspectives reveal a number of ongoing difficulties within the debate on globalization and inequality. Among these are: How can we most effectively measure inequality? Is there a causal link between globalization and inequality? Why does inequality matter?

Difficulties in Capturing Inequality: Differences and Pitfalls in Measurement

The challenge of agreeing on a single trajectory of inequality does not just stem from the fact that inequality remains a complicated issue. The difficulty of discussing inequality also arises from the differences in data sources and hence conclusions reached. Conclusively discussing global inequality would require the knowledge of the income of every individual in the world, but as this remains beyond the reach of scholars, they work with the closest approximations (see, e.g. Milanovic, Sutcliffe, and Dollar). It is worth highlighting some of the difficulties in capturing inequality as well as the differences and pitfalls in measurement.

To begin with, some chapters claim that the usefulness and reliability of some of the data remain disputable. Wade questions the World Bank's numbers, relied upon by many authors; he points out there is a 'wide margin of error' in these. Galbraith also questions the extent to which the Deininger–Squire (DS) data, utilized by the World Bank, manages to grasp inequality since it does not include year-to-year trends. Galbraith also finds this dataset particularly unsuited to testing universal movements in inequality, such as the Kuznets' relationship, because it combines different types of data, such as personal and household incomes and expenditures. Moreover, he underlines that more developed than developing countries are represented in this dataset.

Milanovic, Dollar and Pogge question the reliability of the data on China. Milanovic highlights an ongoing debate amongst experts on the accuracy of the historical data on Chinese GDP and growth rates. Dollar also draws attention to studies that find national accounts may be over-estimating growth rates in China and India. Pogge emphasizes that the estimations of the reduction of extreme poverty in China are highly disputable, given lack of information on past Chinese statistics. Dollar's chapter, on the other hand, exhibits more faith in conventional measurements of poverty. Despite their shortcomings, he indicates 'in many countries the measures are good enough to pick up large trends'. Dollar mentions that the extreme poor may be doing better than the standard measurements of their incomes suggest, since such people typically live off their own agricultural production.

Hence, the level of income of the extreme poor may be of limited relevance in gaining a sense of their welfare. However, Dollar seems to find greater uncertainty in the calculations on global inequality and acknowledges that its decline may actually be smaller than is often calculated.

Further, some authors suggest that even if the data were completely reliable, other pitfalls can present problems. Milanovic points out that although national accounts and household surveys may have distinct limitations to their usefulness, combining these two different types of data does not advance the analysis. Other authors question whether the indicators for poverty effectively measure what we are trying to capture – the conditions of the poor. For instance, Wade emphasizes that the measurements of poverty may be too arbitrary to capture the true state of the poor and that the poor's basic needs may not be met at all even if they do not fall below the official poverty line.[8] Pogge points out income itself may not tell us about the actual welfare of people, as the rich are likely to have a greater wealth than income would lead us to believe, while the opposite is true for the poor.

In addition, different measurements of inequality may yield divergent narratives on inequality. The movement of Milanovic's three concepts through time (see table 1.1 above) demonstrates this point. Sutcliffe also underlines the potential for different narratives on inequality by emphasizing that '[e]valuating poverty by the relation of the extremes often gives very different results from an integral measure like the Gini coefficient.' Moreover, as he explains, the way in which one interprets the numbers may depend on our initial disposition as to what constitutes a more equal society. Also, as mentioned above, Esping-Andersen's chapter starts from the idea that in order to properly evaluate the welfare of an individual, one needs more than just a snapshot of their lives: a dynamic assessment of their household is necessary. Hence, he also reveals how a number of stories remain embedded in the numbers. Last but not least, many authors in this volume concur on the point that how China and India are treated in the calculations profoundly affects the conclusions reached on global inequality.

The Roles of China and India in Understanding Global Inequality

Understanding China's, and to a lesser degree India's, patterns of poverty and inequality matter greatly for the debate on globalization and inequality, as the discussions of the authors in this volume make clear. While the authors agree that the contemporary era of globalization has witnessed poverty reduction in China and India,[9] thereby decreasing inter-country inequality, they do not concur on the potential causes of economic growth and poverty reduction in those countries.

Since both China and India are highly populous nations that started off very poor, the levels of reduction in poverty that followed relatively high economic growth in these countries have affected world patterns of inequality (see Sutcliffe, Milanovic, Dollar). In fact, China's effect alone has been so large that the conclusions reached about inequality depend on whether China is included in the calculations and the source of data one relies on for China. For instance, Milanovic finds that with China in the calculations, weighted international inequality (see table 1.1 above) has declined in the period from 1950–2000, but without China, 'inequality of this sort has been stable or even rising'. Similarly, Sutcliffe emphasizes that although the weighted Gini coefficient for the world charts a downward trend with China in the calculations, it exhibits a rising trend when China is excluded from the calculations (see figure 3.7 in Sutcliffe's chapter). On the same subject, Wade stresses that '[i]ncreased equality between population-weighted country incomes is the result of one – massive – case, not a general trend.'

At the same time, many authors point out that inequality within China has increased. For instance, Kanbur and Venables study the huge rural–urban inequalities in China. Overall, the contributors generally agree that the growth of China and India has contributed to a decrease in inter-country inequality, although intra-country inequality has increased in both.

Yet, the contributors provide varied explanations as to how China and India improved their conditions as such. Dollar suggests that the increased integration of China into the world economy has ushered in higher levels of growth and hence poverty reduction in that country. Alongside openness to trade and investment, Dollar mentions the important role of enhanced property rights and other reforms in the success of the Chinese economy. One can easily read from Dollar that the application of the principles of the liberal agenda has contributed most drastically to the significant strengthening of the Chinese economy.

Some authors' accounts contain contrary emphases or explanations to Dollar's. Wade urges the reader to recognize the unique position in which China reaped the benefits of greater openness to the world economy. He contends that China pursued a 'state-led capitalism' and the decline in Chinese poverty stemmed to a large degree from 'decollectivization of agriculture in the 1980s and ... the increase in government procurement prices for foodgrains in the 1990s'. Similarly to Wade, Galbraith finds that the initial stages of

Chinese economic reform did not witness a hike in inequality because agricultural reform increased the earnings of the peasantry. However, he explains that post-'open-door policy' inequalities within the country increased. Galbraith also argues that China and India did not conform to the global rises in inequality during the 'debt crisis' of the eighties due to the relatively closed capital markets both countries maintained. In this regard, Galbraith agrees with Wade that China (and India) pursued a 'state-led' capitalism. Moreover, Pogge emphasizes the reduction in severe poverty in China is 'vastly more uncertain' than reports may suggest. In addition, he points out that the splendid increase in Chinese exports came to some degree at the expense of other developing nations, and thus one cannot conclude that the other poor countries could have grown in the same way China has done.

The discussions so far reveal that the authors in this volume do not concur on the potential causes of reductions or increases in inequality and poverty. But what of globalization? Specifically, does globalization have anything to do with these issues?

Globalization and Inequality: Causal Links?

Globalization is most commonly understood in this book as the increased interdependence of the world primarily via openness to trade and investment, although some authors also emphasize the movement of people as a component of globalization. Beyond such processes, a few of the contributors understand globalization as the set of political-economic institutions and policies which contribute, if not generate, such enhanced interdependence. The discussions in this volume suggest that the link between globalization and inequality remains complicated at best and unclear at times. In their different ways, the authors tend to emphasize correlations, rather than causal links, between globalization and inequality.

Milanovic explains that the impact of globalization on inequality depends on different factors, whose interrelationship is hard to determine precisely. For instance, if globalization leads to greater economic growth in poor countries, reducing within-national inequalities, then globalization will have contributed to the reduction of inequality. Yet integration into the global economy may usher in growth without improving intra-country inequalities. Milanovic also finds globalization to have an effect on the way in which people perceive the world. He argues that with increasing exposure to fellow inhabitants of the world over time, people are more likely to become aware of global economic disparities.

Dollar suggests a link between globalization and inequality in that globalization helps economic growth and growth helps alleviate poverty. Although ruling out scientific certainty, Dollar finds persuasive the evidence on increased growth rates following the liberalization of domestic economies. Hence he regards integration of economies, despite certain dislocating impacts on domestic circumstances, to offer an opportunity to alleviate poverty. Although acknowledging the difficulties in drawing a causal link between economic integration and growth, Dollar points out that a number of important cases (China, India, Uganda and Vietnam) provide evidence that 'openness to foreign trade and investment – coupled with complementary reforms – can lead to faster growth in developing economies.' Thus, Dollar finds globaliza-tion to be associated with higher growth rates and poverty reduction. Yet, he also sees that integration is likely to play a role in increasing wage inequalities through its effects on the relatively less skilled workers.

Wade and Pogge, in different ways, both point out that the set of global institutions and policies that maintain the global political economy harbour important power disparities, which in turn create or sustain inequalities. As explained above, Wade criticizes the dom-inance of liberal ideas in major international institutions and media channels. Instead of serving the poor, these institutions serve them-selves and the interests of the powerful, who are over-represented in them in the first place. The World Bank constitutes one such example where the voting power of the affluent significantly supersedes the voice of the developing nations. Wade also sees an element of Americanization in the current form of globalization, as the American 'empire project', as he refers to it, gains the ability to affect policies of national governments elsewhere with its superior economic position and influence in international institutions. In addition, Wade under-lines (in a manner similar to Milanovic) that globalization has allowed people across the world to be more aware of each other's relative status, increasing the visibility of disparities between countries.

Pogge's arguments also link globalization and inequality by demon-strating that globalization is not neutral: as a matter of fact, it favours the rich. To begin with, as discussed above, Pogge argues that the current global economic structure, via global institutional rules, does not nurture the necessary circumstances for the improvement of the welfare of the poor. Moreover, Pogge believes the predominant intel-lectual and academic responses in global institutions serve the 'career goals' of those who recommend development policies, rather than the poor. In this way, he agrees with Wade that the pervasive way of think-ing in major global institutions, such as the WTO and the World Bank, perpetuates its own existence and a certain ideology (neoliberal convictions) without adequately delivering to the poor. Overall, the global institutions and their rules as well as dominant paradigms contribute to the persistence of inequality.

Galbraith's analysis helps elucidate elements of the connection between globalization and inequality by emphasizing that macroeconomic factors (regional and global) will impact upon countries in different ways, depending on the global position of these countries' economies. For instance, his chapter explains that when the lifting of barriers to trade and capital flows expose a previously shielded middle class to economic change, inequalities rise, and the success of foreign direct investment (FDI) in alleviating such change is likely to vary from situation to situation. Galbraith also finds that 'in the years of globalization and neoliberalism' inequality rose across the world. He attributes the global rise in pay inequality during that period to policy changes led by Ronald Reagan and Margaret Thatcher. These changes brought about an increase in interest rates and the strengthening of the dollar and the pound, while many local currencies collapsed (as in Latin America). Galbraith emphasizes that in a world where creditors gained against debtors, those countries that could export managed to do relatively well but, with the exception of a few countries, inequalities rose across the world. Even though it may not be possible to form conclusive causal links between globalization per se and inequalities, Galbraith underscores the existence of a global pattern to changes in inequality, pointing to a macro dynamic.

Thompson's chapter finds the drawing of causal links between globalization and inequality problematic because, he argues, the existence of globalization remains open to debate in the first place. Moreover, even if we were to concede the presence of a globalized economy, Thompson claims that '[g]reater trade, migration, or capital flows, have no discernable effect on the catch up of poorer countries.' To summarize briefly, he explains how the lack of catch up stems from a continued 'productivity gap'. Because capital flows have largely remained within and between rich countries and because labour mobility has remained limited to high-skilled workers from the developing world moving into the developed world, the productivity gap has not lessened to any great extent. Although trade can potentially improve the gap between the rich and the poor countries, the effects of trade on technology and the 'skill premium' have so far maintained the divergence between the two groups. Thompson's chapter illustrates how the discussions over inequality and poverty belong to a wider debate on globalization itself – it is not simply that there exist disagreements over whether globalization and inequality can be linked but there are continuing disagreements over the existence of globalization.

Kanbur and Venables' chapter also recognizes the problems of determining the precise effect of globalization – in this case, openness to trade – on rising 'spatial inequalities'. As the authors explain, trade impacts upon the national economy in different ways – it exerts pressure on inward-looking industries, but also leads to the development of new regions. The authors indicate that the studies of the UNU-WIDER's project on Spatial Disparities in Human Development find that 'trade has on balance increased spatial disparities, as new export oriented areas of economic activity have seen the most rapid economic growth.' However, 'openness to trade' was not the only variable that affected regional disparities; 'infrastructure' was also of great importance. The differences in public infrastructure, such as transportation, helped determine disparities between different regions. Hence, the uneven spread of growth within a country cannot be attributed just to trade.

Esping-Andersen's analysis finds increased 'income dispersion' across Europe and the USA, but also notes certain exceptions to this trend, emphasizing that 'a purely structural explanation' remains disputable. His chapter underscores globalization's effects to be very different from place to place on a number of variables. For instance, although the 'skills premium' has increased in general, the way in which this phenomenon translates into workers' lives shows marked variation. The workers at the low end of the European labour market have lost relatively less ground than might have been expected, possibly given policies like worker protection. In analysing mobility rates, Esping-Andersen shows that it is difficult to pinpoint a single trend and explanation. He highlights the importance of the mobility rate since, along with 'income spread', it determines 'lifetime inequality'. Although acknowledging the limitations in the extensity of the data, Esping-Andersen reports there was variation in mobility rates across Europe in the 1980s and 1990s. This finding suggests that, among other things, the national economic situation, such as the unemployment rate, plays a role in determining mobility rates. All in all, this chapter shows that one can only begin to gain a sense of trends in inequality by understanding the complex dynamics between social and economic forces.

Nancy Fraser's chapter in this volume focuses on the impact of globalization on the way in which we engage with questions of justice, understood by Fraser as 'parity of participation'. Specifically, Fraser emphasizes that globalization detracts from the 'aura of self-evidence' of the Keynesian-Westphalian (KW) framework, by exposing its inadequacies and its injustices. The KW framework addresses questions of justice within the territorial confines of the nation-state. According to Fraser, globalization has impacted the nation-state in a number of ways. First, globalization has led to events and processes across borders, challenging the control of the KW framework over its borders.

Second, globalization has engendered new actors, ranging from international organizations to transnational corporations. Third, globalization has made the emergence of 'transnational public opinion' possible. By virtue of increasing the impact of these forces on the lives of citizens within a nation-state, globalization raises new questions about justice. Fraser explains that beyond the question of 'what is a just ordering of social relations', globalization generates new dilemmas, such as who belongs to which community as well as how questions of justice can be addressed. On the one hand, as explained above, the KW framework is increasingly affected by external forces, 'offshore powers', as Fraser calls them. On the other hand, the KW framework fails to provide the necessary means and mechanisms for the non-powerful within its boundaries to represent themselves. On the contrary, in the era of globalization, Fraser maintains that the KW framework '. . . partitions political space in ways that block many who are poor and despised from challenging the forces that oppress them.' Hence as long as KW is utilized as the frame for questions of justice, it will not only be inadequate, but it will also suffer from a serious 'democratic deficit'. To redress the shortcomings of the KW framework, Fraser advocates the adoption of a 'postwestphalian theory of democratic justice.' This theory is discussed in greater detail below.

Does Inequality Matter, and Why?

In his chapter, Sutcliffe claims that commentators who find inequality unimportant usually belong to three categories. First, there are those that engage in 'inequality denial' by basically overlooking any indication that inequality has been increasing. Second, Sutcliffe finds some who engage in 'inequality displacement' by focusing on different variables, such as life expectancy, or an essentially different debate, such as the one about absolute poverty. In his final category, 'inequality embellishment', Sutcliffe includes those who regard inequality as an inevitable part of a 'benign process of economic growth'. Sutcliffe's classifications originate from his claim that rising inequalities constitute a 'stain on the record of the unequalled [twentieth] century'. If one disagrees with Sutcliffe's initial assumption that inequality matters, one is also likely to be at odds with his categories. However, whether one differs from Sutcliffe or not, his groupings capture the essence of an ongoing debate on whether inequality matters, whether it matters as much as poverty and why this might be so.

The authors in this book contribute to the understanding of the significance of inequality in a number of different ways. Some explore the implications of inequality for social justice. For example, Fraser's chapter argues that claims to justice and equal worth can be recognized only if inequalities are addressed within a global paradigm. Others explore the reasons as to why inequality matters, regardless of the justice question. Still others explore the relationship between poverty and inequality. In this respect, the book contributes to a long-running debate as to whether it is extreme poverty or inequality that matters most.

Pogge argues that inequality, and not just severe poverty, matters by discussing how the two concepts are linked. Pogge holds, as previously indicated, that high levels of inequality ensure 'global institutional rules' work to the disadvantage of the poor and serve the interests of the powerful, while also making it difficult to alter these rules. Focusing on global institutional designs, Pogge explains that inequality affects the very nature of the debate on poverty by disabling the effective participation of the poor in the governance of the global economy. Pogge also contends that as extreme inequality continues, we may be on a road of no return to reasonable levels of inequality, and economic growth may increasingly be facilitated at the expense of the poor. He emphasizes that poverty and inequality constitute not only 'a case for compassion' but also 'a question of justice'. Yet, beyond the evident moral reasons, Pogge argues 'that inequality matters because it distorts public debate and because it may well be irreversible by cutting us off, politically, from future low-inequality equilibria.' Overall, Pogge's analysis shows how inequalities can translate into and sustain power disparities.

Wade's chapter discusses the instrumental reasons as to why inequality matters, since questions of fairness or justice may remain unconvincing to some people. He explains that inequality both within and between countries may cause several kinds of negative effects. Inequality may be economically inefficient; beyond a certain level of inequality, between-country inequalities negatively impact upon world demand and hence growth. Moreover, Wade underlines the connections between inequality and certain causes of social unrest, such as crime. Taken together, Pogge's and Wade's arguments suggest that if poverty matters, so should inequality, as the associations between the two phenomena remain strong. The two authors' discussions of the relationship of poverty and inequality can be summarized as follows: (a) inequality is of significance in gaining a more comprehensive understanding of the conditions of the very poor; (b) inequality may sustain poverty as well as contribute to it; (c) inequality has negative repercussions for efforts to increase growth and reduce poverty.

Kanbur and Venables's chapter also discusses the potential negative impact of spatial inequalities on political, social and economic factors.

The authors emphasize that inequalities as such can be potential causes of wider social and political tensions, if they overlap with ethnic, racial, religious and other such differences. Economically speaking, the authors discuss how regional differences may stem from (a) natural characteristics, such as proximity to the coast, and (b) from 'efficiency gains from proximity'. Simply put, geographically advantaged regions may gain a further advantage over other regions, as firms and people concentrate in those areas. Such 'spatial agglomerations' may result from differences in growth as well as efficiency between various regions. Yet, the authors point out that these 'spatial agglomerations' may themselves not be efficient in the longer term. In this regard, the maintenance of spatial disparities can also sustain economic inefficiencies.

Dollar does not discuss whether inequality matters as such. Since Dollar's findings suggest a 'modest decline' in global inequality and do not support a general pattern of increasing within-country inequalities, inequality in his analysis remains non-problematic. Dollar's primary emphasis is on economic growth and poverty reduction, particularly in developing economies. As mentioned, although acknowledging the difficulty of establishing a conclusive causal link between openness of economies (that is integration into the world economy) and growth, Dollar regards the evidence on integration-spurred growth convincing. Beyond geographical reasons that pose hardships for countries to participate in the world economy, Dollar argues that inequalities remain inevitable as long as some countries remain non-integrated and/or they have 'weak institutions and policies'. In general, Dollar's discussions over inequality remain embedded in a wider debate about economic growth and poverty.

The study of inequality, as the above discussion emphasizes, is of significance not just because inequality relates to the question of justice but because it can also be associated with serious political, social and economic ills. Moreover, inequality can provide a benchmark for an assessment of the set of development policies adopted across the world. Increasing inequalities and deterioration in the situation of the poor may signal that governments and international institutions have failed to address issues of development adequately. The contributions in this volume, implicitly or explicitly, all judge the record of the dominant set of development policies – those endorsed by the World Bank, the IMF and other major international organizations – by assessing worldwide patterns of inequality and poverty. Those that find the divergences between the rich and poor problematic also utilize the debate on inequality to put forward proposals for ameliorating the stratifications nationally and globally.

What Can be Done about Inequality?

Some contributors to this volume advocate a revision of economic and development policies both on the national and international levels. On the national level, Wade proposes to put redistributive policies back on the agenda. He envisions that strengthened ties between civil society organizations and political parties could work towards this end. He also suggests compulsory voting could give disadvantaged groups a real voice. Governments of rich countries, Wade argues, should rethink their responsibilities and increase their efforts towards more equal societies, such as those found in Scandinavian countries. Esping-Andersen's chapter affirms that welfare state redistribution in Scandinavian countries in particular, and in the developed economies more generally, has played a role in alleviating inequalities generated by the market. The welfare state has also helped with mobility and thus people's life chances. Moreover, since the early years of children continue to be crucial for their life chances, focusing on children could be the right domestic strategy of governments. Furthermore, Esping-Andersen's analysis reveals the employment of women is likely to play a crucial role in assuaging increasing differences in household income in many parts of the developed world.

Kanbur and Venables see, in addition, a role for government to pursue more actively development strategies targeted at regional disparities. In tackling 'spatial inequalities,' these authors propose a two-tiered approach. First, the authors emphasize the necessity of removing, or lessening, barriers to the spread of economic activity – 'deconcentration' – accompanied by the strengthening of infrastructure in disadvantaged regions. Second, the authors think the state should nurture a migration-friendly environment so that population shift can occur to areas of relatively high well-being. The authors discuss how this two-pronged approach could alleviate difficulties in China.

On the international level, Milanovic envisions the creation of a global taxation authority that also distributes aid, superseding national governments and establishing a direct link between the poor of the world and the international community. He underscores the importance of national distributions in orchestrating transfers from the rich to the poor. The transfers should not only be from the rich countries to the poor ones, as is the case now, but they should also be from rich members of rich countries to those in need in the poor countries. Wade recommends a concerted effort from the G20 countries in initiating a change to the way in which the international community thinks about development goals. Specifically, he finds it necessary for developing countries to move their economies towards higher value-added activities. As discussed above, Pogge urges a change in the design of global institutions to allow the poor a real voice and participation. These authors do not suggest closed borders would be better; rather, they propose ways in which open borders should deliver more to the poor.

Fraser advocates a more radical paradigmatic shift from the national, the KW framework, to the global, offering a *theory of post-Westphalian democratic justice*. As discussed above, Fraser looks at the ways in which globalization has increased pressures on KW, exposing a '. . . widening wedge between state territoriality and social effectivity', thereby challenging KW's status as *the* political frame. Particularly, globalization has revealed that questions of justice cannot be restricted to issues concerning only the economic and cultural. It has become crucial to analyse the 'political' dimension of justice. The political dimension comprises a variety of crucial questions related to representation. For instance, the political dimension may reveal 'meta-political misrepresentation', that is whether the system structurally excludes certain groups from participation and decision-making. Fraser also illustrates how the shift to the post-Westphalian frame could democratize political participation and representation. A basic sketch of Fraser's theory is outlined in table 1.2 below.

Although some authors propose a rethink of current policies, other authors advocate an improvement or a stronger embrace of them. Dollar believes that further liberalization of markets, for both developed and developing countries, will help the poor in and of itself.

Table 1.2 Nancy Fraser's theory of post-Westphalian democratic justice	
Dimensions of justice	**Problems of justice**
Economic	**Maldistribution** Economic ordering of society prevents some people from enjoying 'full participation'
Cultural	**Misrecognition** People can also be prevented from interacting on equal terms 'by institutionalized hierarchies of cultural value that deny them the requisite standing'
Political	**Misrepresentation** 1 *Ordinary-political misrepresentation*: political rules within a nation-state may impede participation by some 2 *Misframing*: the boundaries of a community wrongly exclude some people, thereby completely removing their participation 3 *Meta-political misrepresentation*: when elites, domestic or transnational, 'monopolize the activity of frame-setting, denying voice to those who may be harmed in the process, and blocking creation of democratic fora where the latter's claims can be vetted and redressed'

He considers economic growth and the liberalization of economies as crucial factors in lifting people out of poverty and argues that an agenda of liberalization of markets and institutional reform should lie at the core of developing countries' strategies. Developed countries, on the other hand, should allow developing countries better access to their markets. Dollar does think there is a role for aid in helping certain regions, such as Africa, but he believes greater participation in economic globalization by developing countries remains the key to facilitating reductions in poverty.

The divergence between those who propose substantial changes to current development policies, like Wade and Pogge, and those who do not, like Dollar, is not simply about one side being pro-liberalization and the other side not. Rather, the disagreements centre around what kind of liberalization (gradual? state-led?) has managed to deliver what kind of opportunities (growth? poverty reduction? inequality reduction?). The disagreement focuses on how integration into world markets could better aid the poor and opportunities of all (see Held 2004; Barnett, Held and Henderson 2005). The core of the difference between the authors is about the terms and pace of global economic and political change.

What the chapters in this volume collectively demonstrate is that the debate over globalization and inequality is in fact not a struggle between those who are simply pro-globalization and those who are anti-globalization. Rather, as the complexities of the issues surrounding globalization and inequality reveal, the debate is about how the benefits of globalization can be spread to greater populations, while embedding globalization in political institutions that effectively and democratically deliver benefits to the disadvantaged. The questions are about the kind of globalized world we live in and would like to live in.

Appendix of Definitions

Purchasing power parity (PPP) PPP exchange rate is the exchange rate which allows for approximately the same bundle of goods and services to be purchased in all countries of the world. For poor countries, PPP exchange rates will tend to be smaller than the market exchange rates, reflecting lower price level in poor countries. $PPP means that the currencies were exchanged in current US dollars (see Sutcliffe's chapter). Some economists warn not only that PPP calculations remain subject to substantial margins of error but also that incomes calculated at market exchange rates, and not at PPP, are better measures of one nation's ability to purchase goods and services produced abroad (see Wade's chapter).

Gini coefficient/Index   Measures income inequality. This coefficient ranges from 0 to 1 – the higher the Gini coefficient the more unequal the society (see Milanovic, Sutcliffe in this book). The Gini Index expresses the coefficient in percentage form.

Extreme poverty   Extreme poverty is generally used to denote the level of poverty of people living on less than $1 a day ($PPP).

Kuznets curve   Named after its founder, the economist Simon Kuznets. The curve looks like an inverted U-shape, representing the changes in inequality in a country as it moves from a low-income to high-income status. Inequality initially increases and then falls as the country moves from low productivity economic activities to high productivity ones, most generally from agricultural to industrial production (see Milanovic, Sutcliffe, Galbraith, Thompson, and Esping-Andersen for a discussion).

Notes

1   2000 figures; figures for undernourishment are from 1998–2000.
2   Measured in $PPP. See the Appendix of Definitions on p. 23 for an explanation.
3   As the discussions below will make clear, there are different measurements used to explain global inequality. The Gini coefficient is one of the most common indicators of inequality.
4   See the Appendix of Definitions.
5   See Wade for a detailed discussion of the principles of the Washington Consensus. To summarize, the Consensus has stressed privatization, liberalization of domestic markets and has placed great emphasis on property rights. In its 'augmented form' the Consensus envisions the judiciary to have an increased role and financial markets to enhance their importance in the domestic economy. The ideas of the Washington Consensus, Wade claims, have been endorsed with 'little critical scrutiny' by major international institutions, such as the World Bank and the IMF, and media channels, such as the *Economist* and the *Financial Times*.
6   See the Appendix of Definitions.
7   As explained above, Milanovic's exact finding is that there was first an increase and then a decline in global inequality between 1980 and 2000.
8   See also Pogge and Reddy (2003) for a critical assessment of the World Bank's measurements of poverty, and also Pogge in this chapter, for more recent work by the authors on this subject.
9   Wade underlines that the Indian middle class benefited significantly less than the Chinese middle class from world economic growth.

References

Benn, Hilary 2005. 'Ending Unfair Subsidies is a Moral Imperative.' *Observer*, 3 July.
Barnett, Anthony, Held, David and Henderson, Caspar (eds) 2005. *Debating Globalization*. Cambridge: Polity.

Held, David 2004. *The Global Covenant: The Social Democratic Alternative to the Washington Consensus.* Cambridge: Polity.

Held, David and Koenig-Archibugi, Mathias (eds) 2003. *Taming Globalization: Frontiers of Governance.* Cambridge: Polity.

Milanovic, Branko 2005. *Worlds Apart: Measuring International and Global Inequality.* Princeton, NJ: Princeton University Press.

Pogge, Thomas W. and Reddy, Sanjay G. 2003. 'Unknown: The Extent, Distribution, and Trend of Global Income Poverty.' At www.socialanalysis.org.

UNDP 2004. *Human Development Report 2004.* New York.

UNDP 2005. *Human Development Report 2005.* New York.

Wade, Robert H. 2001. 'The Rising Inequality of World Income Distribution.' *Finance and Development*, **38** (4). At www.imf.org/external/pubs/ft/fandd/2001/12/wade.htm.

WSJ (Wall Street Journal) 2006. 'Are CEOs Worth Their Weight in Gold?' 21 January: p. A7.

Wolf, Martin 2004. *Why Globalization Works.* New Haven, Conn. and London: Yale University Press.

2

Globalization and Inequality

Branko Milanovic

Definitions and Concepts

IN our efforts to understand the state of inequality today, we need first to define the key concepts and terms. Most crucially, we need to distinguish between international and global inequality in order to avoid terminological confusion. I explore these two concepts throughout the essay. Here it suffices to say that international inequality denotes the inequality between nations, more exactly between mean incomes of nations. Global inequality (also known as 'world inequality'), on the other hand, is an inequality between individuals in the world regardless of their nation, regardless of where they live. In other words when measuring global inequality, we see the entire world as if it were one country.

In this essay I will utilize three concepts of inequality in order to explore the patterns of *international* and *global* inequality and map out changes in inequality over time. I will call these three different ways of assessing inequality Concept 1, Concept 2 and Concept 3.

Concept 1 inequality

Concept 1 measures *unweighted international inequality*. As previously explained, international inequality measures the inequality between mean incomes of different nations. This sort of inequality is captured in statements like 'the mean income in the United States is higher than the mean income in Pakistan'. In measuring this inequality, we generally rely on national accounts, that is Gross Domestic Income (GDI) of the countries. We compare the GDIs of countries to each other to grasp Concept 1 inequality. Because populations of countries are left out, Concept 1 is unweighted international inequality. Notice also that inequality *within* countries is ignored.

Concept 2 inequality

Concept 2 inequality is similar to Concept 1. Like Concept 1, Concept 2 measures international inequality by relying on the representative income of a country: GDI per capita. Differently from Concept 1, however, Concept 2 takes into consideration the population of countries. In these calculations China's weight is approximately 20 per cent of the world rather than, as in Concept 1, having the same weight as any other country. Consequently, when calculating the inequality of Concept 2, the role of China and India would be very important. To make the difference clear, note that Concept 1 inequality is akin to the UN General Assembly: there is one ambassador for each country and each country is represented by its GDI per capita. In contrast with Concept 1, here we have 6 billion ambassadors (the world's population) and all the ambassadors from, say, China display the mean income of China, all ambassadors from India display the mean income of India and so forth. Hence with Concept 2, each country would be represented in accordance with its population but it would be still represented by ambassadors having *representative* incomes of their nations – not actual incomes of people who live there. Thus Concept 2 also ignores differences in incomes within countries.

Concept 3 inequality

The final type of measurement we will rely on to explore inequality in this chapter is Concept 3 inequality. Concept 3 denotes *world inequality* or *global inequality*. Differently from international inequality, this concept captures inequality between individuals. To use the previous metaphor, we dispense with ambassadors: every individual enters into the calculations with his/her actual income. The only source of data from which we learn about people's incomes is household surveys. Ideally, we should have a world household survey to find out what is world income distribution. But short of that we have to use individual country's household surveys, collate them and derive a world distribution of income across individuals. This further differentiates Concept 3 from the other two Concepts: it relies on an entirely different source of data, income distribution data obtained from household surveys. Thus the data requirements are much more formidable than they are for Concepts 1 and 2 where we need respectively only one variable (GDI per capita) or two (GDI per capita and population). This huge jump in the data requirement makes the move from Concept 2 to Concept 3 even more problematic because of the difference between disposable income from household surveys (our welfare aggregate in Concept 3

Table 2.1 Three concepts of inequality summarized			
	Concept 1: unweighted international inequality	Concept 2: weighted international inequality	Concept 3: global or world inequality
Main source of data	National accounts	National accounts	Household surveys
Unit of observation	Country	Country (weighted by its population)	Individual
Welfare concept	GDI per capita	GDI per capita	Mean per capita disposable income or expenditures
National currency Conversion	Market exchange rate or PPP exchange rate		
Within-country distribution (inequality)	Ignored	Ignored	Included

Source: Milanovic (2005)

calculations) and national accounts data from which we get our GDIs per capita. The largest part of the difference is definitional: household disposable income is after-tax income and it excludes publicly provided health, education and other government services and goods. The latter are, of course, included in Gross Domestic Income. Another part of the discrepancy comes from the undersurvey of rich people and their income sources (mostly property income) in household surveys. These sources are better captured by national accounts simply because rich people are loath to fully reveal their actual income to survey enumerators. These points will be discussed further. Table 2.1 summarizes the three Concepts and their sources of data.

Patterns of Inequality

Let us now see how Concepts 1, 2 and 3 have moved over time in order to explain the changing patterns of inequality. I will start with a historical perspective before discussing the contemporary patterns of inequality. This historical perspective applies primarily to Concepts 1 and 2. We do not know much about how Concept 3 has moved over time simply because we lack the relevant data on household surveys. Since incomes or expenditures from household surveys are not available for a historical period, we shall focus on a briefer period, 1988–98.

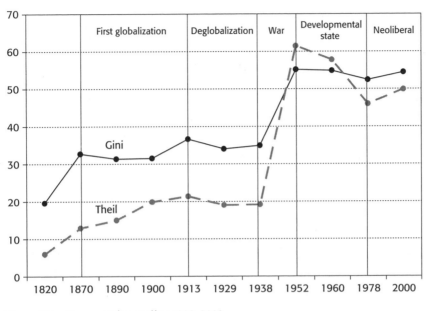

Figure 2.1 Concept 1 inequality, 1820–2000

Source: Calculated from Maddison (2004)

Historical perspective

Figure 2.1 displays the historical movement of Concept 1 inequality.
This figure, based on Maddison (2004) GDI per capita data which are
the only source of long-run historical income statistics, shows that
between 1820 and 1870 international inequality was on the rise. The
increase is present whether measured by the Gini coefficient or Theil
Index.[1] Inequality also ascended during 1870–1913, although it
declined or stabilized during the inter-war period of 'deglobalization',
1913–38. Following this period, we witness a sharp increase in Concept
1 inequality between 1938 and 1952. This is related to the Second
World War and the fact that some of the rich countries (United States,
Australia, New Zealand, Argentina) did very well while most of the rest
of the world lost out. From roughly 1952 to 1978, Concept 1 inequality
remains at the same level as measured by the Gini and declines rather
substantially as measured by the Theil Index. For the less developed
countries, this was the period associated with decolonization and
application of import substitution policies including a strong role of
the state. For the rich world that was the period of unmatched growth
that became known as the 'Golden Age'. But despite the rich world's
fast growth, there was clearly, on average, a catch up of poor and
middle-income countries or income convergence; it proved short-
lived. Starting from around 1978, the beginning of the 'neoliberal

regime', there is a sharp turnaround and Concept 1 inequality rises whether measured by the Gini or Theil.

Figure 2.1 demonstrates that Concept 1 inequality has generally been on an upward trend from 1820 up to today. This finding tells us that differences between mean incomes of countries are much greater today than they were some 200 years ago. It is also true that our sample size has gone up because originally in Maddison's data we had approximately only 35 or 40 countries, but over time the number of countries has increased to 50, 60 or 80. Today we have more than 150 nations in the sample. Thus a *part* of the increase in Concept 1 inequality can be explained by the increase in the sample size (that is, in the number of independent states in the world). But, it is important to emphasize that only a part of the change can be attributed to this factor. If we were to take only the countries for which we have data over the entire period 1820–2000, we would still find that international inequality of this sort has been on the rise.

When we use Concept 2 inequality, we observe a different picture. Here, I use the same data as I did for Concept 1 inequality above, viz. the same GDI per capita data from Maddison (2004) and the same countries, but this time around the data are weighted by population. I will discuss later some pitfalls of the data on China but let us assume here that these data are reliable. Figure 2.2 demonstrates the historical journey of Concept 2 inequality. As this figure shows, during the period from 1850, which is the first year in the figure, to about 1950, which represents a

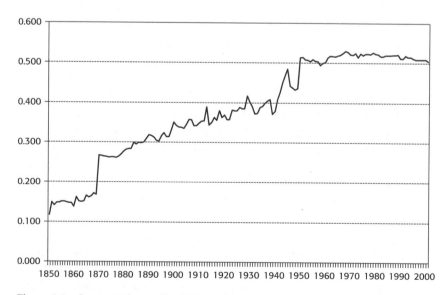

Figure 2.2   Concept 2 inequality (Gini coefficient), 1820–2000

Source: Calculated from Maddison (2004)

peak, there is a clear upward trend. From the mid-1950s to today, Concept 2 inequality remains broadly stable (or just slightly decreasing). This finding is confirmed by Bourguignon and Morrisson (2002).

Contemporary patterns of inequality

Now let us move from this very brief historical sketch to a focus on what inequality is today, analysing the period 1950–2000. To para-phrase a well-known dictator, figure 2.3 illustrates the 'mother of all inequality disputes'. The essence of the dispute is about what happened to inequality roughly between 1950 and 2000.

Figure 2.3 examines inequality during this period using the three Concepts of inequality. As we see from the figure, unweighted inter-national inequality – the Concept 1 inequality – has gone up. Of partic-ular importance to note is that it has been going up over the last 20 years. Moreover, we see that the 'watershed years' 1978–80 – the term coined by Paul Bairoch (1997) – characterized by rising oil prices and real interest rates, the onset of the debt crisis and the beginning of the Thatcher and Reagan rule in Great Britain and the United States, were at the origin of this unmistakable upward trend which has persisted ever since.

Concept 2 inequality charts a very different course. As figure 2.3 shows, Concept 2 inequality has declined over precisely the same time during which Concept 1 inequality rose. Moreover Concept 2 inequal-ity begins its downward trend exactly around 1978–80. The decline is driven by the fact that China has grown very fast ever since 1978 when the responsibility system was introduced in the countryside and communes were dismantled by the Deng Xiaoping regime. China was a very poor country with a huge population, and as people in China have become richer, overall inequality in the world has tended to go down. The role of China is crucial, as it becomes clear when we calcu-late Concept 2 inequality without China: we see that inequality of this sort has been stable or even rising (see the dotted line in figure 2.3). In sum, *inequalities between countries have been rising since around 1978, although population-weighted inequality between countries has been decreas-ing since 1978 thanks to growth in China and more recently in India.*

Let us now look at global inequality, Concept 3. Based on my own calculations, figure 2.3 displays three dots – years 1988, 1993 and 1998 – that capture global inequality. These three dots are based on household survey data. There are some important points to highlight here. To begin with, we cannot really extract similar data for the past because we do not have household surveys for many important parts of the world (China, the Soviet Union, most of Africa) for any years before the early 1980s. As we see in figure 2.3, these three years do not follow a pattern: there is first a strong increase in inequality followed by a

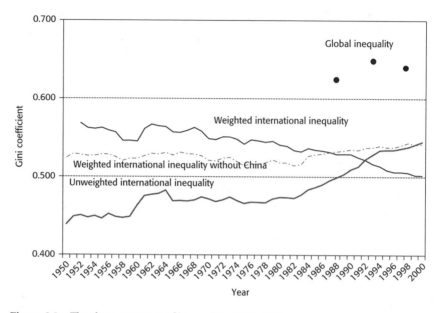

Figure 2.3   The three concepts of inequality, 1950–2000

Source: Calculated using World Bank *WDI* data

more modest decline. The gap between global inequality (the three dots) and weighted international inequality is explained by inequality within nations. We can write it out as,

(1) Global inequality = Concept 2 inequality (or between-country inequality) + within-country inequality

Overall, the three dots inform us that *inequality among people in the world today is extremely high, though its direction of change is unclear*. The Gini Index of inequality between people in the world lies between 62 and 66. A Gini of 62, which is a very high number, is a higher level of inequality than what is found in any individual country: for instance, Brazil's inequality is in the upper 50s level; South Africa is in the low 60s. This level of inequality is perhaps unparalleled in world history. If such extreme inequality existed in smaller communities or in a nation-state, governing authorities would find it too destabilizing to leave it alone, or revolutions or riots might break out. The fact that such extreme levels of inequality exist on the global level perhaps causes us to react against it relatively less severely.

A number of different forces impact upon global inequality, causing a very complicated pattern to emerge. First, fast economic growth in China and India – populous nations that were very poor and are still relatively poor – pushes world inequality down. Second, the relative decline of many poor and middle-income countries has the opposite effect: it contributes to global inequality. Third, higher inequality within large nations, such as the United States, China, India, and Russia, adds to global inequality, pushing the dots in figure 2.3 further upwards from the line that captures Concept 2 inequality. Thus as one force reduces global inequality, the other one or two increase it.

Regionally, the last 20 to 25 years have been characterized by the following basic trends: China and India pulled ahead, Latin America and Eastern Europe – the middle-income countries – declined, and Africa's position became even worse. The rich world (Western Europe, North America and Oceania) grew relatively fast. As for within–nation inequalities, they increased almost everywhere. *We are witnessing the Africanization of poverty*, since most of the African nations are now extremely poor and many of them are actually poorer than they were in 1960. The correlation between being poor and being African is probably stronger than ever in recorded history. Another interesting fact is that, for the first time since the early nineteenth century, all Latin American nations are poorer in per capita terms than the poorest West European country (Portugal).

The complicated way in which different forces impact upon global inequality should encourage us to avoid broad generalizations. The difficulty of saying what happens to global inequality stems, in part, from the fact that it is hard to calculate because it requires access to detailed household survey data from most countries in the world. While there is no dispute that global inequality is extremely high today, there remains a debate on the direction of change in global inequality as well as on the significance and meaning of this putative change. We would also like to draw some sort of causal link between globalization and global inequality. This is exceedingly difficult because globalization affects differently the growth rates of GDIs per capita of poor and rich nations, within-national inequalities in poor and rich countries, and may influence differently the populous and small nations. Sometimes these effects may work in the same direction, for example if greater openness helps accelerate growth of poor countries and reduces within-nation inequalities, and sometimes they may offset each other, for example if openness helps poor countries but widens their internal income distributions.

The Three Concepts Explored Further

Why inequality between countries matters

Before we explore the relationship between the three concepts of inequality and how they are related to globalization, let us briefly address one question that the debate on inequality raises: why does inequality between countries matter? The convergence hypothesis, grounded in growth economics, posits that poor countries should grow faster than rich countries, whether controlling for other factors (so called beta convergence) or even unconditionally (so called sigma convergences). The latter is no different to our Concept 1 inequality which as we have seen, *pace* economic theory, has rapidly increased during the last two decades. Since we expect from economic theory that convergence should take place, the question becomes why it did not. Some authors claim that it did not because some countries were not really 'globalizing' so only those countries that follow 'globalization friendly' policies should be considered and they are, these authors claim, converging (Sachs and Warner 1997; World Bank 2002; Dollar and Kraay 2001). Evidence disproves these claims: economic policies (including those that can be included under the heading of 'globalization-friendly') are much more similar today than they were 20 or 30 years ago.

The pertinent question then becomes why there is a divergence of outcomes while economic policies converge. I believe that the currently available studies do not allow us to come up with a definitive answer to the question. There are several possible explanations however. According to one explanation (Mukand and Rodrik 2002), divergence of outcomes may coexist with convergence of policies if the same set of policies (basically, of the Washington Consensus type) is applied in different institutional settings. Since efficiency of policies is not independent of the environment where they are applied, the same policies will produce inferior outcomes in countries that are institutionally very different from the advanced market economies. According to Mukand and Rodrik, some poor countries would have been better off had they followed a 'heterodox' mix of policies, that is policies not identical to the ones contained in the Washington Consensus package. This is because a heterodox mix might have been more appropriate for their conditions. This is how Mukand and Rodrik explain China's and India's success since neither country followed the dominant paradigm *à la lettre*. Another explanation is that recent technological progress has been characterized by economies of scale. In such a world, diminishing marginal productivity of capital, on which the convergence hypothesis rests, no longer holds. On the contrary, marginal productivity of capital may be greater in more capital-rich countries – which then of course implies divergence.[2]

Beyond its potential implications for the convergence theory, inequality between countries matters for other reasons too. Inequality between nations is important for migration issues, for instance. Concept 1 inequality may matter also if countries represent distinct cultures and modes of life. If we believe that cultures have some intrinsic value in themselves, then we might feel discomforted by the idea that there are huge differences in income or unbridgeable differences of wealth between nations so that the nations that are in decline might over time disappear. However, a social Darwinist view of the world might refute the importance of this argument. The point is that inequality between countries does not only matter in terms of assessing the efficacy of our current set of development policies, it may also have important social repercussions.

How solid is the Concept 2 inequality decline?

In my analysis Concept 2 inequality derives its significance because it is the lower bound to Concept 3 inequality. Concept 3 inequality is critical if we want to know what is happening to the income of individuals in the world, but, as I said before, oftentimes we lack the necessary data to calculate it. Given such difficulties with data, some authors have used a shortcut to Concept 3 inequality by calculating Concept 2, the population-weighted international inequality. They have done so because (a) Concept 2 inequality accounts for a large part of global inequality, and (b) it can be calculated relatively easily with the knowledge of only two data points for each country (GDI per capita and population). Notice that at the extreme, Concept 2 inequality becomes global inequality: to see this, break the countries into finer and finer partitions continuing all the way to a situation where each individual is a country. Then, clearly, Concepts 2 and 3 coincide.

We can move somewhat in that direction (raising as it were the lower bound to global inequality) by breaking large countries into their provinces and rural/urban areas. If after doing this, we find that this new more detailed Concept 2 inequality has been more or less stable over the last two decades, then Concept 3 inequality cannot have gone down. The reason is as follows: we know that the within-component (see equation 1) of global inequality has gone up during the last two decades driven by the almost unanimous increase in within-national inequalities.

So let us see how the previously calculated Concept 2 decline is affected by data modifications and improvements. We can recalculate Concept 2 inequality by doing three things. First, we can use alternative GDI per capita data for China. The data on the Chinese GDP remains subject to intense debate amongst specialists. While most economists agree that the current levels of Chinese GDI are accurate, they disagree about the historical statistics, and in particular about the officially claimed growth rates. The problem with them is that if they are extrapolated all the way back into the past, the 1952 level of China's GDI per capita becomes unreasonably, and even impossibly, low: less than $PPP 300 at 1990 prices. It is very difficult to believe that

Table 2.2 Change in Concept 2 inequality between 1985 and 2000 using different data sources and finer partitions (in Gini points)			
	World Bank data	World Bank data except Maddison for China	Maddison data
Whole countries	−3.3	−1.9	−1.1
Populous countries[a] divided in states or provinces (the rest unchanged)	−3.8	−2.3	−1.5
Adding rural–urban divide for China	−3.3	n/a	−1.0

[a] 'Populous countries' are China, India, United States, Indonesia and Brazil.

Source: Calculated from Maddison (2004) and World Bank *WDI*

China, which indeed was poor, was below the subsistence level (on average). Thus Maddison's 2004 data, based on his detailed study of long-run Chinese growth (Maddison 1998), display lower growth rates than the official Chinese sources.[3] If China was less poor in the 1950s, 1960s, and so on then its catch up with the rich world was less, and the decrease in Concept 2 inequality was less too. If we recalculate Concept 2 using all the same World Bank data as before, except for China for which we use Maddison's GDI numbers, the decline of Concept 2 inequality which was 3.3 Gini points previously becomes only 1.9 Gini points (see table 2.2 and figure 2.4). This shows the extreme sensitivity of Concept 2 and global inequality calculations to the assumptions about Chinese growth.

Second, we can assess the firmness of the data on Concept 2 inequality by breaking five most populous countries (China, India, United States, Indonesia, and Brazil) into their provinces/states. In addition, we know that for both China and India there are serious and apparently growing rural–urban disparities. By taking an aggregate number for China, we fail to show the inequality which exists between rural and urban areas or between poor and rich provinces. So we can further break each Chinese province into rural and urban parts, using of course for each province mean rural and mean urban income. What we do thereby is to vastly improve the precision of our estimates: rather than using one GDI per capita number for China, we now use either 28 numbers (means for each province) or even 56 numbers (28 provinces times two – for rural and for urban). The same is done for the other four countries: for example, instead of one value for the United States, we have fifty.

Third, we can broaden our coverage of countries. World Bank data have a more restricted country coverage because a number of war-torn or 'excluded' countries like the Congo, Sudan, Cuba, North Korea, Afghanistan and Somalia are not part of the database. This omission,

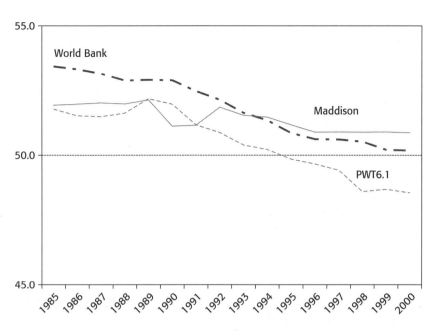

Figure 2.4 Concept 2 inequality recalculated using three different GDI databases

Source: Calculated from Maddison (2004), World Bank *WDI* and Penn World Table 6.1

however, is not random: these are mostly poor countries and their inclusion raises Concept 2 inequality and may also slow down its downward slide (since these countries have tended to fall further behind the rich world, thus adding to inequality). Maddison data do include all these countries: for example, in 2000, Maddison data include 160 countries while the World Bank data include only 138 countries.

Figure 2.4 demonstrates the sensitivity of Concept 2 inequality to different data sources as well as the remarkable importance of China in these calculations. If we use Maddison's data, we find – between 1985 and 2000 – only a minimal decrease in Concept 2 inequality of 1.1 Gini points (see table 2.2). This is less than a third of the decrease as calculated using World Bank numbers. Finally, if we break the five most populous countries into their provinces/states and use the rural–urban divide for China, Maddison's data yield a decrease of only 1 Gini point. This finding suggests that Concept 2 numbers are not as firm as we originally might have thought. Another important implication is that the likelihood that Concept 3 inequality decreased over the 1985–2000 period is also significantly less; if Concept 2 inequality – which is the main driving force behind a possible decrease in global inequality – went down by only 1 rather than by 3.3 Gini points, it is quite possible, even likely, that the increase in within-national inequalities offset this decline, and that global inequality remained about the same.

This last point is illustrated in table 2.3. It displays the within-component of global inequality. It increased between 1988 and 1998 by 0.8 Gini points, about as much as Concept 2 inequality, according to Maddison's data, has gone down.

There also remains a technical issue, to which I alluded above. There is a discrepancy between the movements in national accounts and movements in household survey data, making comparisons of results using the two sources difficult. In some calculations of global inequality which are not based directly on household surveys, the authors (e.g., Bhalla 2002 and Sala-i-Martin 2002) mix GDI per capita data from national accounts and some fragmentary (quintile) distributions from household surveys. Thus they apply to a distribution not of its own mean but a mean derived from another source (national accounts). As explained before, GDI is by definition greater than household disposable income. In addition, the difference is magnified because of inadequate coverage of property incomes by household surveys. Call this total difference between GDI per capita and mean household per capita income d, consisting of d_1, the definitional difference, and d_2, the difference due to the survey of inadequate coverage. Both d_1 and d_2 are composed of income sources that are predominantly received by the rich. Then assigning d across the board to everybody (as these authors do) artificially boosts incomes of the poor and reduces global inequality. These calculations, despite their pretence, are merely thinly disguised Concept 2 inequality calculations.[4]

India has become somewhat of a cause célèbre in this respect because there the discrepancy between national accounts and household surveys has been particularly pronounced in the last ten years. GDI per capita has been growing faster than the household survey mean. The use of GDI per capita and distribution shares derived from surveys therefore produces lower poverty rates than the 'normal' procedure (i.e., the use of both distributions and means from surveys). However, even in this instance, Picketty and Banerji (2005) show that 20 to 40 per cent of the discrepancy can be explained by the under-reporting of high incomes. In short, we need to be very wary of a blind application of national accounts data to household surveys. The

Table 2.3 The within-component of global inequality (in Gini points)	
Year	Gini Index
1988	13.7
1993	14.5
1998	14.5

Source: Milanovic (2005)

approach is simply inconsistent because it mixes up two different aggregates and ignores their differences.

Inequality between World Citizens Today

Having explored the relationship between different concepts of inequality, we can revisit the 'true world inequality' – the Concept 3 inequality and where it stands today. As emphasized before, we find extreme inequalities today. Earlier in the chapter I indicated that the world inequality today varies between 62 and 66 Gini points and emphasized how such levels of inequality surpass the disparities seen in some very unequal countries, such as Brazil and South Africa. Table 2.4 shows the evolution of global inequality in three different years (recall our three dots in figure 2.3 above). Global inequality calculated using current exchange rates (displayed in column 3) is even greater: its Gini is probably the highest ever recorded, around 80.

The ratios displayed in table 2.5 below show the extreme levels of contemporary inequalities. These ratios help us understand the significance of a Gini of 62–66. If we look at incomes expressed in international dollars received by the various fractiles of the distribution, we

Table 2.4 Global inequality, distribution of persons by $PPP and dollar incomes per capita

	Gini Index	
	International dollars ($PPP)	US dollars
1988	61.9 (1.8)	77.3 (1.3)
1993	65.2 (1.8)	80.1 (1.2)
1998	64.2 (1.9)	79.5 (1.4)

Gini standard errors are given between brackets.

Source: Milanovic (2005)

Table 2.5 Share of total global income received by various fractiles of global distribution

	Top	Bottom	Ratio top-to-bottom
In $PPP			
5%	33%	0.2%	165–1
10%	50%	0.7%	70–1
In current US dollars			
5%	45%	0.15%	300–1
10%	67.5%	0.45%	150–1

Source: Milanovic (2005)

find that the top 5 per cent of highest earners in the world receive one-third of the world income, whereas the bottom 5 per cent receive only 0.2 per cent. Consequently, the ratio of the top 5 per cent to the bottom 5 per cent is 165 to 1. Differently, the top 10 per cent of people in the world get around one-half of world income, leaving the remaining 90 per cent of the world's population the other half of the global income. If we do the same calculations in US dollars, the ratio of the top 5 per cent to the bottom per cent becomes 300 to 1.

Key determinants of global inequality summarized

In discussing the three concepts of inequality, this chapter has already touched upon the contradictory movements which influence global inequality today. Here, I expand upon these discussions before offering policy recommendations. In order to understand inequality today, we need to focus on the interaction between: (a) the rich countries of the West; (b) urban incomes in China and India; and (c) rural incomes in these two countries. It is necessary for us to separate China and India into urban and rural categories because the urban–rural income gap in both countries, and indeed in most Asian nations such as Indonesia and Thailand, is large and has been growing rapidly. Thus if mean incomes in urban China and India increase fast enough, they will move closer to mean incomes of the rich countries in the West. That would be good news for world equality. However, if urban incomes in China and India increase very fast but people in rural China and India fall behind, then we have an offsetting effect, namely, rising differences between these two parts (urban and rural) that add to global inequality. This is particularly so because we are talking about massive numbers of people: 800 million rural dwellers versus almost 500 million urban in China, and 750 million rural versus 300 million urban in India. The crucial thing for global inequality is, then, how these three 'components', (a) to (c), evolve.

Position of people from different countries in the global income distribution

We need also to compare the distributions of different countries. This is, as we shall argue below, especially pertinent when making policy recommendations. We do this in figure 2.5 which plots the position of each 5 per cent (ventile) of different countries' distributions in the global income distribution. Consider the line for France. We calculate the mean income (in international dollars) of each French ventile from the lowest (first) to the highest – arrayed on the horizontal axis – and then find their positions in global income distribution. The bottom ventile of the population in France represents people with the lowest

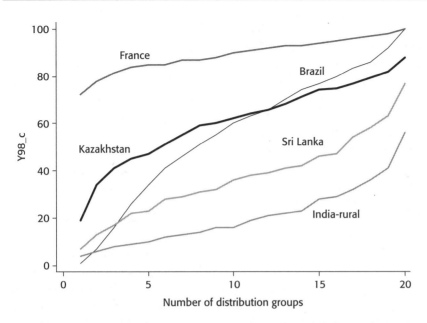

Figure 2.5 The position of different countries' ventiles in global income distribution

Source: Calculated from World Income Distribution (WID) data, at http://econ.worldbank.org/projects/inequality

incomes in France. In terms of world distribution of income, they are placed around the 72nd percentile of the world. This statistic tells us that the poorest Frenchmen are actually richer than 72 per cent of people in the world. The top 5 per cent of people in France (and also in the rest of Western Europe and the United States; not shown here) are in the top percentile of the world. Let us now look at the distribution (by ventiles) in rural India (bottom line in figure 2.5). Even the richest 5 per cent of people in rural India are poorer than the poorest 5 per cent of people in France. These findings have the following policy significance. If there is aid from a richer to a poorer country, when income distributions do not overlap at all it is very difficult *not* to transfer from a richer person to a poorer person. In other words, the chance of a regressive transfer is very small. If one argues in favour of some transfer of income from the rich to the poor then these are relatively easy situations since the danger of a mistransfer (regressive transfer) is almost nil. One could tax a Frenchman around the median of income distribution and distribute aid to rural India randomly: there would be no danger of a regressive transfer.

In making transfers from rich to poor countries, we can use results from the figures, for example figure 2.5, as our guidance (obviously, the position of each country can be charted): for instance, the distribution of Kazakhstan can be used as a proxy for transition countries.

In figure 2.5, the Brazilian distribution presents a very interesting case. Brazil's distribution essentially mimics the world (world distribution would have been a straight line). Brazil approximates the world because the poorest people in Brazil are poorer than almost everybody else and the rich people in Brazil are as rich as rich Western Europeans and Americans. This is a crucial piece of information because, if we envisage a transfer from France to Brazil, we run the risk of making a regressive transfer unless appropriate targeting is made. In other words, there are countries for which the likelihood of conducting a regressive transfer is not negligible: for instance, it could well be that somebody who is in the bottom decile or quintile in France subsidises the income of someone who is richer than himself in Brazil. The perception that aid is misguided in the sense that the middle class in rich countries transfers a portion of its income to the rich people in poor countries is responsible for a great deal of resentment against aid. While only at times accurate, this perception contributes to the aid fatigue. The key lesson to take from figure 2.5 is that income distribution of the recipient country must be taken into account when decisions on aid are made: given an equally poor country and lack of knowledge regarding targeting of transfers a country with more equal distribution should be preferred.

The Future of Global Inequality

Where is global inequality heading? Lucas (1998) and Firebaugh (2003) argue that we are likely to experience 'inequality transition' and that global inequality has peaked so that we can actually expect a decline. This will happen because the effects of the industrial and technological revolutions will spread gradually across the globe evening out incomes. The repercussions of the industrial revolution, which originated in England and later encompassed Western Europe before broadening to Northern America and elsewhere, are today felt in China and India. Lucas and Firebaugh essentially argue that because Concept 2 inequality drove global inequality since the Industrial Revolution and since this type of inequality has been on the decline for the last 30 years,[5] then Concept 3 inequality should follow the same trajectory.

I find the Lucas and Firebaugh argumentation problematic for several reasons. First, as already discussed, policy convergence has not led to income convergence and the 20 years of recent history demonstrate this point. Second, the authors present a static view of technological progress. There have been many technological revolutions since the Industrial Revolution, most recently the computer revolution. Thus we might have poor countries catching up in some areas while rich countries carry on with further technological innovations in others and the gap between the two increases rather than narrows. Third, the expectation Lucas and Firebaugh set out depends on the decline in Concept 2 inequality. Yet as I have suggested, the downward slide in Concept 2 inequality hinges on one set of numbers for one country, China. These numbers themselves can be questioned, and more importantly the future evolution of the Chinese economy (particularly since the country still needs – one would expect – to democratize) remains a matter of speculation, not a certainty.

Although we have gained some understanding of inequality today, we have not yet addressed the most important question: does global inequality matter?

Does Global Inequality Matter?

Some commentators put forward that global inequality really does not matter because it is too abstract an idea and the world lacks a government, an entity that should, in principle, be 'in charge' of inequality. It even lacks a 'global polity' that would, through political pressure or persuasion, raise the issues and effect change. But the situation in which we find ourselves today is not much different from the situation in which people found themselves prior to the creation of nation-states. As long as there were disparate groups of individuals who hardly interacted at all, living in small hamlets and villages, there was no concept of a nation. Without this mental concept, inequality does not matter because there are only very few people (those from the village) to be compared against. It is only once a mental concept of what constitutes a nation is born (or created), and there is a government that governs that nation, that people may begin to compare themselves to others from the same nation. Similarly, as the world becomes more globalized, the concept of one world will become much more acceptable. As we increase our awareness of the globe as a whole, poverty and inequality elsewhere will affect many more of us than they do today. In this regard, global inequality matters, not the least because the globalization process itself increases people's awareness of each other and highlights income differences.

So much for the change in mutual awareness and creation of a global polity. But one could still argue that inequality does not matter because people are only interested in their own welfare and not in the welfare of those who are better off.

So what is the correct utility function then? Asked in another way, are we interested only in our own consumption or income, or does relative consumption/income matter too? Two different quotes capture the opposing answers to this question. On the one hand, Anne Krueger (2002) remarks that: 'Poor people are desperate enough to improve their material conditions in absolute terms rather than to march up the income distribution. Hence it seems far better to focus on impoverishment than on inequality.' Krueger claims the only thing which matters is one's own income and incomes of others are immaterial. The implication here, drawn explicitly by Feldstein (1999), is that people who take into account other people's incomes are full of envy and their preferences should not concern us. On the other hand, we have a quote from Simon Kuznets (1965) that advocates a position that opposes Krueger's. He contends that 'one could argue that the reduction of physical misery associated with low income and consumption levels . . . permit[s] an increase rather than a diminution of political tensions.' Kuznets goes on to explain that these 'political tensions' stem from 'the *political misery* of the poor, the tension created by the observation of the much greater wealth of other communities'. Long before the days of the current globalization, Kuznets captured that people are social animals. Although we are concerned about our absolute income first because we have essential needs, such as food, clothing and shelter, that have to be satisfied, we are also concerned about our own income compared to that of others. Recent empirical studies confirm this concern with one's relative position as soon as the essential needs are satisfied (see Graham and Felton 2005; Frank 2005). Whether we believe that this concern with other people's income is grounded in the desire for fairness or in envy, the key and the only relevant point is that we are not indifferent to other people's incomes. This is where globalization comes in. If, as hypothesized, globalization increases awareness of what other people are receiving, then to a person living in a poor country, the income with which he or she would normally be satisfied may no longer seem enough. The very process of globalization might influence our perception and our satisfaction with a given level of income. This is a crucial point: as the process of globalization enfolds how much will it influence our perception of our own position in it? If it does, maintaining large inter-country income differences becomes more and more difficult. But in the face of greater mutual interaction between people and declining travel costs, the rich world will have to become a fortress in order to keep the poor people out; but this is almost impossible. So, what else can be done?

What Can We Do about Global Inequality?

There exists a litany of literature on the remedies for global inequality, but I would like to make one more radical proposal. Some of the usual recommendations to alleviate global inequality include changing the rules of the international trading system to benefit the poor. The removal of agricultural subsidies in rich countries is one such change. Like some other authors in this volume, I also believe that changing the WTO rules and ensuring the decision-making at the global level is more democratic, not least transforming the current voting rights in the IMF and the World Bank, would be very important. We can also think about special programs for Africa (for instance on combating AIDS).

My own, perhaps more radical, proposal to reduce global inequality is to establish 'global transfers', a concept akin to a 'global safety net'. If we really think of the world as a whole, we have to start thinking about an arrangement that would constitute a very modest *global safety net*. But if we do so, we also need some rules for the functioning of this safety net. I envision the first rule of this global safety net to be the 'Progressivity 1 Condition': transfers should flow from a rich country to a poor country. This is not a controversial point, as obviously transfers already flow from rich to poor nations. Second, we should also require that transfers at the global level satisfy the same conditions that within-national transfers are supposed to satisfy at the national level, that is that they should be 'globally progressive'. In other words, we need to ensure the transfers go from a richer person (taxpayer) to a poorer person (beneficiary). It is not desirable, for instance, for a middle-class Frenchman to make a transfer to somebody who is very rich in South Africa or Brazil. This is where national income distributions and the data displayed in figure 2.5 become relevant.

The third condition that should govern global transfers is to preserve 'national progressivities'. Progressive transfers at the global level should not worsen national distributions. Taxation should not only be 'globally progressive' but also be sensitive to 'national progressivities'. To illustrate this point examine figure 2.6 below.

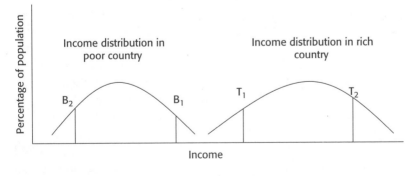

T = tax payer B = aid beneficiary.

Figure 2.6   Globally progressive transfers

In this figure we have T (tax payer) and B (aid beneficiary) across the two distributions, with the rich country (obviously) on the right and the poor country on the left. Now a transfer from T_1 to B_1 does satisfy the axiom of 'global progressivity' because the person in the rich country is better off than the beneficiary B. Yet such a transfer would also make national distributions in *both* countries worse simply because the tax would be borne by somebody who is relatively poor in the United Kingdom or France and benefits would be received by a person who is relatively well off in an African nation. Globally progressive transfer is compatible with making both national distributions (of the participant countries) more unequal. This is not desirable. We would like to ensure that we tax rich people in rich countries in favour of poor people in poor countries because only then can we hope to improve the distributions within-nations. This would probably also help reduce the opprobrium in which aid is currently held in some quarters. All in all, paying attention to 'national progressivities' requires that tax payers from the rich world that finance global transfers should indeed be rich even within their own countries, and that the beneficiaries should be poor even within their own (poor) countries – a transfer should flow from T_2 to B_2.

These three principles of global transfers – 'progressivity 1', 'global progressivity', and 'national progressivities' – need to be coupled with a supranational taxation authority which would collect taxes and distribute aid. The first component of this proposal (taxation) is easy to understand, as we have already had a number of writers argue for a Tobin tax – a global tax assessed on some particularly income elastic commodities or activities. The tax would be paid by the globally (and nationally) rich. The second part of the 'equation' concerns the allocation of thus collected money, that is disbursement of aid. We have already explained the key principles which should govern it, but if we are thinking about 'global tax' we must also accept 'global aid', that is aid that flows directly to the poor individuals in poor countries without their government's intermediation. If some sovereignty is conceded by the rich countries to the new global safety net agency (due to the vesting of taxing rights in the agency), then some sovereignty must be conceded by the poor countries as well. Rather than their governments being recipients of aid, aid would go directly to citizens. The global safety net should introduce a relationship between the global authority and individuals in poor countries or poor people wherever they are.

In other words, we would like to eliminate the filter of state-to-state relationship because we know that this filter has not been very successful. This change in approach to handling global inequality is necessitated by the lessons of the past. I have already outlined the need to adopt a global approach to global problems. In addition, we know that development approaches done in the fifties and the sixties have not been successful. We also know that structural adjustment has failed to deliver. We thus need direct transfer of purchasing power; we need to give money to people who are unemployed or people who are very poor, handicapped, sick and generally disenfranchised. Such transfers of money already take place in rich countries. We simply need to apply this on a global level. This idea dawned on me more than a decade ago when I observed the situation in Russia and the plight of Russian pensioners. Both the ethical and pragmatic approach to dealing with the problem of pensioners would have been to earmark money for pensions instead of lending to the Russian government and letting corruption suck it away. An international organization, like the one we have in mind here, could have simply used the existing infrastructure of the Russian state, pension rolls, and distributed cash grants to some 20 million Russian pensioners. And citizens would have fondly remembered receiving cash aid from the international community rather than blaming that same international community for transferring funds to corrupt leaders. The same principles could be applied today to give cash grants to (say) mothers of all kids under a certain age in a state in Nigeria or to all landless peasants in a district in India.

The approach I advocate here is based on four simple principles:

1 *symmetry*: global agency limits sovereignty of both rich and poor nation-states;
2 *grants*: transfers are pure grants but they are not charity;
3 *cash*: money is disbursed to individuals in cash; and
4 *categorical targeting*: instead of trying to implement fine-grained targeting, cash grants should be disbursed to vulnerable categories of people.

Notes

This essay is based on the talk given at the occasion of the Ralph Miliband Memorial Lecture delivered at the London School of Economics in February 2005. I am extremely grateful to Ayse Kaya for kindly transcribing the lecture; without her help this essay would not have been produced. The views in the essay are the author's own and should not be attributed to the World Bank and its affiliated organizations.

1   Both Gini and Theil are commonly used measures of inequality. The Gini coefficient ranges from 0 (all recipients have the same income) to 1 (or 100 as expressed in percentages) when only one recipient takes the entire income. The Theil Index of entropy begins at 0 (perfect equality) but does not have an upper bound. Obviously, the greater the value of each index the greater the inequality. However, Gini is more sensitive to what is happening around the mode of the distribution and Theil is more sensitive to the extremes.

2   A very common example mentioned is that a computer scientist working in isolation in a poor country will be less productive than if he worked in Silicon valley.
3   The latter are basically also reproduced by the World Bank.
4   For a critique, see Milanovic (2002).
5   Although, as we have just seen, this is dubious too.

References

Bairoch, Paul 1997. *Victoires et déboires: Histoire économique et sociale du monde du XVIe siècle à nos jours*, vol. 2. Paris: Folio Histoire Gallimard.

Banerji, Abhijit and Piketty, Thomas 2005. 'Top Indian Incomes, 1956–2000.' *World Bank Economic Review*, 19 (1): 1–20.

Bhalla, Surjit 2002. *Imagine There's No Country*. Washington, DC: Institute for International Economics.

Bourguignon, François and Morrisson, Christian 2002. 'The Size Distribution of Income Among World Citizens, 1820–1990.' *American Economic Review*, September: 727–44.

Dollar, David and Kraay, Aart 2001. 'Trade, Growth, and Poverty.' Policy Research Worrking Paper, no. 2615. Washington DC: World Bank.

Feldstein, Martin 1999. 'Reducing Poverty not Inequality.' *Public Interest*, Fall 1999.

Firebaugh, Glenn 2003. *The New Geography of Global Income Inequality*. Cambridge, Mass.: Harvard University Press.

Frank, Robert H. 2005. 'Positional Externalities Cause Large and Preventable Welfare Losses.' *American Economic Review*, Papers and Proceedings 95 (2): 137–51.

Graham, Carol and Felton, Andrew 2005. 'Does Inequality Matter to Individual Welfare? An Exploration Based on Happiness Surveys From Latin America.' Center on Social and Economic Dynamics Working Paper, no. 38. Washington, DC: Brookings Institution.

Krueger, Anne O. 2002. 'Supporting globalization.' Remarks at the 2002 Eisenhower National Security Conference on 'National Security for the 21st Century: Anticipating Challenges, Seizing Opportunities, Building Capabilities', 26 September 2002. At www.imf.org/external/np/speeches/2002/092602a.htm.

Kuznets, Simon 1965. *Economic Growth and Structure: Selected Essays*. New Delhi: Oxford & IBH Publishing Company.

Lucas, Robert 1998. 'The Industrial Revolution: Past and Future.' Mimeo: University of Chicago.

Maddison, Angus 1998. *Chinese Economic Performance in the Long Run*. Paris: OECD, Development Centre.

Maddison, Angus 2004. 'World population, GDP and GDP per capita, 1–2000 AD.' At www.ggdc.net/maddison/.

Milanovic, Branko 2002. 'The Ricardian Vice: Why Sala-i-Martin's Calculations of World Income Inequality are Wrong.' At SSRN: http://ssrn.com/abstract= 403020.

Milanovic, Branko 2005. *Worlds Apart: Global and International Inequality 1950–2000*. Princeton, NJ: Princeton University Press.

Mukand, Sharun and Rodrik, Dani 2002. 'In Search of the Holy Grail: Policy

Convergence, Experimentation, and Economic Performance.' At http://
ksghome.harvard.edu/~drodrik/papers.html.

Sachs, Jeffrey D. and Warner, Andrew M. 1997. 'Fundamental Sources of Long-
Run Growth.' *American Economic Review*, Papers and Proceedings 87 (2), May
1997: 184–8.

Sala-i-Martin, Xavier 2002. 'The Disturbing "Rise" of Global Income Inequality.'
NBER Working Paper, no. 8904, April. At www.nber.org/papers/w8904.

World Bank 2002. *Globalization, Growth and Poverty: Building an Inclusive World
Economy*. Policy Research Report. Washington, DC and New York: World Bank
and Oxford University Press.

3

The Unequalled and Unequal Twentieth Century

Bob Sutcliffe

THE Ralph Miliband lectures from which this chapter is derived were concerned with the overlap between four things: the rush of obituaries of the recently deceased twentieth century; the appearance of an original set of economic statistics allowing a more revealing retrospect of the international economy than had ever been available before; my interest in theoretical questions concerning international power, imperialism and hegemony as well as in the interpretation and measurement of inequality; and a more recent enthusiasm for the visual presentation of economic information, especially about inequality. That was too much for four lectures and much too much for this chapter, which will, therefore, concentrate narrowly on the measurement aspects of world inequality. But this seemingly detailed question has a lot to do with the historical verdict on the late departed century.

It is striking that two recent books, both very relevant to some of the questions I am looking at here, bear the titles: *The Long Twentieth Century* (by Giovanni Arrighi) and *The Age of Extremes: The Short Twentieth Century* (by Eric Hobsbawm). Both of them argue that there is an identifiable historical story which can be called the 'Twentieth Century' – one which lasts somewhat longer and somewhat shorter than 100 years respectively. There is certainly some relation between both of their (very different) concepts of the century and the data and arguments expounded here. Lack of space obliges me to leave it for readers to discover.

My direct concern here is to assess the flood of claims and counter claims which have been made about the course of equality and inequality between 1900 and 2000. I am not arguing that in relation to inequality there is some self-contained story which lasts exactly these 100 years. What happened to inequality during the course of these years is decomposable into many different stories (either in different places or different periods); some of them began before 1900 and some are continuing after 2000. One reason to focus on this arbitrary period of 100 years is that historical quantitative economic research has recently produced large amounts of data which tell us something new about inequality. Of course, the further you go back the less data there is. But there are a growing number of comparisons and trends which can be traced back decades, and in some cases as much as a century.

Amartya Sen has emphasized the importance of asking 'Inequality of what?' when examining inequalities (see Sen 1996). We could be interested in inequality of income, welfare, health, education, power and so on. An equally crucial question is 'Inequality between whom?' We could be interested in inequality between nations, regions, genders, ethnic groups, social classes, individuals and so on. For the most part I will be discussing inequality of income between countries and households, partly because that is one area where there has been a great flowering of historical data and partly because seemingly major authorities disagree very fundamentally about the correct position to take.

Interpreting Data on Inequality

I am going to use some of the simplest and commonest measures of inequality: first, the standard deviation and coefficient of variation (C of V) of a set of figures; second, the Gini coefficient (an integral measure of inequality, summarizing the data of a whole population and varying from 0 which signifies complete equality to 1 which signifies maximum inequality); and, third, the ratio of incomes received by the rich to those received by the poor (usually the richest and poorest 20 or 10 per cent of the population). Even these simple measures may give confusing results and we should beware of drawing erroneous conclusions from them. A very simple example will reveal some reasons for caution. Imagine that there are five people (or equal size groups) in a population and in year 0 all have the same annual income (1 ducat each). The country now embarks on a process of rapid growth which involves the whole population moving in the space of five years from a low income (1 ducat) to a high income (5 ducats); each year another fifth move from low to high income so that in year 1 one person has 5 ducats, in year 2 two people have 5 ducats, and so on until year 5 when everyone has 5 ducats a year. What happens to inequality during these five years? It goes from complete equality in year 0 to complete equality again in year 5. In the intervening years there are various degrees of inequality. Measured by the Gini coefficient and by the 20/20 ratio (the ratio of incomes received by the richest 20 per cent to the poorest 20 per cent), they are shown in table 3.1.

Table 3.1 Measuring inequality						
Year	0	1	2	3	4	5
Gini coefficient	0	0.36	0.37	0.28	0.15	0
20/20 ratio	1	5	5	5	5	1

The first thing we see from these figures is that the Gini coefficient rises and then falls again. On a graph it traces an inverted-U shape. This is an instance of the famous Kuznets curve, named after a pioneer of historical studies of inequality, Simon Kuznets. As one of my teachers back in the mid-twentieth century, he argued that an economy developing from general poverty to general wealth would show this kind of movement (associated in particular with the movement of the population from low productivity agriculture to high productivity industry, services and eventually high productivity agriculture as well). If this is really what happens, and if it happens quickly, then temporarily growing inequality may not be a very serious evil, especially if nobody becomes absolutely worse off in the process. Needless to say, actual processes of inequality are much more complex. Almost invariably defenders of the economic system will argue, when faced with evidence of a growth in inequality, that it is another example of the Kuznets curve, a concept which, quite reasonable in itself, is a frequently misused tool by apologists for inequality.

A second thing which we see from the example displayed in table 3.1 is that, according to the Gini coefficient, inequality is much greater in years 1 and 2 than in year 4, whereas according to the rich to poor ratio inequality is the same in both those years. Evaluating poverty by the relation of the extremes often gives very different results from an integral measure like the Gini coefficient. Which is more accurate? It is something for readers to discuss: in year 1 all are poor except the richest 20 per cent; in year 4 all are rich except the poorest 20 per cent. Which of those two situations is the more unequal? Is a society more equal if it lets its rich have a lot, or if it lets its poor have a little? I would argue the latter, on the grounds that in year 4, if the society redistributed its income, everyone would be relatively well off so that the poor remain so even in the presence of general wealth. This is more than a notional question since many countries have moved in the twentieth century from a situation like year 2 to one more like year 4. As a result their Gini coefficient has fallen and they are said to be more equal. At the same time, at the beginning of the twenty-first century the more unequal countries tend to be those where a very small elite receives a large proportion of the national income and most people are poor. They have much higher Gini coefficients than richer countries which have a minority of poor people. Most people are content to accept that the latter are less unequal than the former, but in my opinion it is very debatable.

Concepts of Inequality

Just about all questions studied by social science are reducible to questions of inequality. If all nations had equal power, if all individuals had equal income, or the same length of life, or the same status, then social science would be largely redundant. The varieties of inequalities are extremely numerous and my intention is to whet your appetite for studying inequality by concentrating on two kinds of inequality during the twentieth century – first, the inequality of the power and wealth of nations, which is the central kind of inequality considered in theories of imperialism and international relations, and to some extent in economic development. Second, inequality in the distribution of income among the human inhabitants of the world – a something which is closely connected with the first kind of inequality but which is also connected with questions of the relative power of classes and with justice and equity. This division of the subject has been suggested by two sets of data which have appeared relatively recently.

The first is the latest expanded edition of estimates of population, national income (to be exact Gross Domestic Product or GDP), and thus of national income per head by Angus Maddison (now published on a CD by the OECD) for all the countries of the world since 1950, and for many of them from a much earlier date (Maddison 2003). These estimates use a way of measuring national income which permits comparisons to be made simultaneously over time and space. Imagine that we are in a world with three countries and each of them publishes annual figures for their income per head since 1950. We place them in three columns. What comparisons can we make either vertically or horizontally? In other words, what can we conclude about a single country between different dates, or between different countries at a single date? To begin with, we can make no valid comparisons. To compare values for one country over time we have to adjust its figures to eliminate the effects of price changes, in the modern world usually inflation. We have to separate out the part of the year-to-year change in national income per head which is due to changing prices so that we leave only the part which is due to real change. The process of making figures comparable over time, price adjustment, is now almost universal, though even now the media are forever trumpeting the fact that some economic variable has reached record levels, when they are really only talking about its current monetary value. But in general price adjustment is well understood and very widely used. Maddison's historical estimates are, of course, adjusted for price changes so they allow us to make real (as opposed to monetary) comparisons over time (see the Bibliographical Note).

So our three columns are now comparable vertically between different dates for each country. But we cannot compare horizontally since the columns are respectively in ducats, yuan and dirhams. So we must convert them all into a common currency. The most common way of doing this is to convert all countries to US dollars using the current exchange rate. Until recently there was not much of an alternative. Now there is and it is called purchasing power parity (PPP). For many reasons the exchange rate between two currencies does not reflect their relative purchasing power; hence the conversion of national income from one to the other may distort very considerably the relative real value income. Tourists have always known about this since they see that in some countries things seem to be very cheap compared with home and in others it is the opposite. Finally economists, too, have accepted that and have launched various projects to produce exchange rates which really reflect PPP, eliminating the faulty data given by exchange rates. This is almost exactly the same kind of adjustment over space which inflation adjustment does over time (see the Bibliographical Note). If we do it to our three columns of figures then we can now make valid comparisons both vertically and horizontally and even diagonally. We can get more or less coherent answers not only to questions such as whether the national income per head in A is higher than five years ago, or whether it is higher than it is in B, but even if it is higher than it was in C 20 years ago. All the figures I am going to quote will have been processed using the PPP methodology. It is only if we have consistent estimates over time and space that we can say anything at all about inequality in the world as a whole.

Changing Inequality between Continents

A continent is as arbitrary a unit of space as a century is of time. Nonetheless modern economic development – industrialization, technical progress and an increase in productivity – has tended to be concentrated by continents. If we sum or average the value of production of continents then we see some version of world inequality. The next two diagrams show the total value of production for the world at the start, in the middle and at the end of the century and its division between continents.

The left-hand chart in figure 3.1 emphasizes the huge rise in the total amount of economic production during the century measured as the value of the gross product, especially during its second half. This is

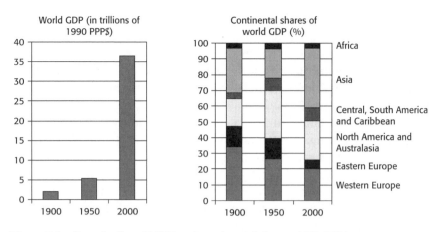

Figure 3.1   Growth of world GDP and continental shares, 1900–2000

Source: Data from Maddison (2003)

one of the facts most used by enthusiasts for the twentieth century to confirm its unequalled character. Despite its deep occasional crises, it was certainly, according to all evidence, the century of fastest economic growth in human history. It was also the century in which the population grew most rapidly, multiplying by four. Admirers of the twentieth century point to this as another instance of the century's success. The larger number of humans resulted not from higher birth rates but from better survival rates. So there were more mouths to feed, but a lot more goods and services per person: population grew by a multiple of 3.9, output by a multiple of 18.5, which means that output and income per person in 2000 were 4.8 times their level in 1900.

If those figures are an important element of the case for the defence of the century, so their obverse is part of the case for the prosecution. According to some ecological critics, such an enormous increase in the volume of production and trade has placed an almost fatal burden upon the earth's capacity, robbing irreplaceable raw materials and polluting the atmosphere to the point where dangerous changes in climate are unavoidable. And the population growth is a negative event in the view of modern Malthusians. Partisans of economic growth tend to assume that it has some kind of relationship with human welfare. Increasingly, however, those who have tried to measure human happiness and fulfilment directly have found that the relationship is a weak one. Growth, they say, has on average not made people happier. Finally, more productive technology has been used not only for unequalled production but also unequalled destruction. These contrary considerations do not on the whole worry the century's defenders. There is, however, one piece of evidence that is not only widely used as a stick with which to beat the twentieth century but that has also been acknowledged as a serious flaw even by the century's admirers. This evidence points to the distribution of income, or the degree of inequality. The rest of this paper looks at what the evidence says about this aspect of the twentieth century and draws some conclusions.

The right-hand chart in figure 3.1 shows that twentieth century economic growth has been extremely unequally distributed between continents. Africa's share was lower at the end of the century than at the beginning, and was very low across time. The continents that contain the 'developed' countries increased their share in the first half of the twentieth century but then lost part of it in the second half. Europe lost far more than the USA, Canada and Australasia. During the first half century the continents which contain the 'developing countries' were losing share; in the second half they, in particular Asia, gained. These differences are important in relation to geopolitics but their connection with human welfare is unknown unless we know at least the sizes of the populations. That is why we need to look at production not in total but per person. This is done in figure 3.2 below, again by continents. The changes of the first half century are summarized but those after 1950 are shown as an annual series.

It has been very common in the twentieth century and indeed in previous centuries to see the world as a dualistic whole consisting of the West and the non-West, the imperialist nations and the oppressed/colonized nations, advanced and backward, developed and underdeveloped/developing, and most recently and, now probably most commonly, the North and the South. This modern dualism is an outcome of modern economic growth. Five centuries ago the economic levels of different areas of the world were quite similar: subsistence and short life expectancy for the great majority was the rule everywhere. Then some areas of the world started a fairly rapid technological and economic advance. One form of the idea of dualism emphasizes the advancement of these areas which opened a gap with the rest that is still to be bridged. The emphasis is on why some areas/countries advanced more quickly than others. Dualism is therefore seen as being relatively benign, corresponding to the top of the inverted U of the Kuznets curve, which was previously discussed. Early writings in post-World War II development economics stressed that this dualism contained an opportunity to catch up due to the presence of abundant labour, low costs and the ability to 'jump' to the latest levels of technology.

Yet another version of dualism gained ascendancy in development thinking during the 1960s: dualism as continuous polarization. In this malign version, the advance of the few is gained at the expense of the

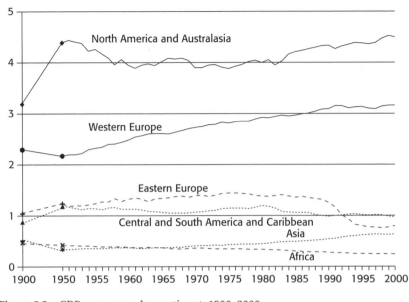

Figure 3.2   GDP per person, by continent, 1900–2000

Source: Data from Maddison (2003)

many. This perception was partly the outcome of Marxist and nation-alist theories of imperialism. At the same time, though, it was also a central feature of ideas, which have become known as dependency or world-systems theory. Dependency and similar theories have been harshly criticized by orthodox economics and in recent years by heterodox ones as well. But the data summarized in figure 3.2 nonetheless suggests that there is a considerable amount of truth in the idea that twentieth century economic growth has been profoundly polarizing. In 1900 the GDP per person of North America and Australasia was 8 times that of Africa; by 1950 the multiple had risen to 10.4 and by 2000 to 18.5. Judging by this criterion, which surely helps us infer something about inequality, the twentieth century has generated a much greater degree of inequality between the two ends of the dualistic world economy. In figure 3.2 the gap between the lines, measuring the ratio of each continent to the world average, has widened even more rapidly in the last two decades. The six lines in the diagram, however, disguise the fact that they refer to populations of very different sizes. To bring in population in some ways makes the situation worse since Africa's population in the twentieth century has risen much faster (over 7 times) than that of the higher income conti-nents. However, 60 per cent of the world's population are inhabitants of Asia and the diagram shows that in the last 35 years the GDP per head of Asia rose in relation to the world average. This fact is much

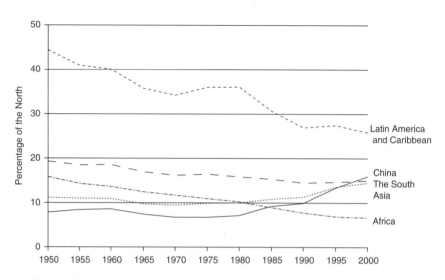

The North = USA, Canada, Australia, New Zealand, Western Europe and Japan; the South = all the rest except for Eastern Europe and the former USSR. Asia includes China, which is also shown separately. Eastern Europe and the former USSR do not appear in the graph.

Figure 3.3   GDP per person, as a percentage of the North, 1950–2000

Source: Author's calculations based on data in Maddison (2003)

more significant than it looks in this diagram and I will address its consequences later. Meanwhile, however, Africa, Latin America and Eastern Europe were on the wrong end of world economic polarization for virtually the whole century.

Figure 3.3 looks at the same data as figure 3.2 in another way. It shows the average incomes of the continents as a share of the North as a whole. Since 1950 the average income of the South has fallen from 19.3 per cent to less than 15 per cent of that of the North. The decline for Africa is from 15.8 to 6.6 per cent and for Latin America from 44.4 to 25.8 per cent. The Asian percentage also fell up to about 1975, after which it started rising (China even more so). These changes have occurred in an epoch of development planning, aid, NGOs, specialized development agencies of the UN, and billions of words about the urgency of eliminating poverty and fostering development. Nonetheless, it is a picture of relentless divergence between North and South, reversed in Asia only in the closing years of the century.

Changing Inequality of Countries

Data by continents show something, but the units are much too large to allow any detailed conclusions about inequality. At a lower level of aggregation we can look at countries. This in fact is the lowest level of

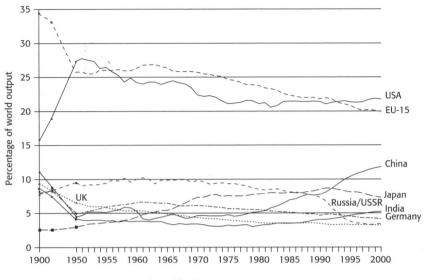

Figure 3.4　National shares of world GDP, 1900–2000

Source: Author's calculations based on data in Maddison (2003)

disaggregation reached by many datasets, including that of Maddison, as well as some other PPP indicators. This means that we can look at the overall economic size of nations (their total GDP) and the GDP per head but we cannot perceive differences between groups within the nations. This national level of aggregation, however, does have its uses. It seems likely, for example, that the relative power of countries is strongly affected by the total amount of what they produce. It is one of the ways in which the relative power of the USA and its potential rivals has been measured during the twentieth century. To keep things simple I will graph the country GDP as a share of the world's GDP for the five economically largest countries at the beginning of the twentieth century, together with any that joined the top five club during the century, while also adding for comparison a line showing the total for the 15 EU members in 2000 (see figure 3.4).

It is easy to make out in figure 3.4 the prodigious increase in the economic weight of the USA during the first half of the century and then its relatively slow decline until 1980 after which, in comparison with the European countries, it gained ground again. Most of the writing about the decline of US hegemony around 1980 assumed that the inheritor of any lost US power would be Europe or Japan. Certainly, if the criterion is the overall size of the economy then that looks very wrong in retrospect. The relative size of production of both the EU and Japan declined noticeably in the last years of the decade. But that is not to say that foreseeing the decline of US hegemony was itself wrong. For its remarkable success in retaining its share of the world economy it has in many ways paid a large price, which is partly reflected by the debt it has postponed to the future.

Moreover, a serious potential rival has appeared. Astronauts say that one of the only human-made features of the earth visible from outer space is the Great Wall of China. Equally, in figure 3.4, one of the few things visible from a distance is appropriately the extraordinary resurgence of the Chinese economy. In 1900 China was the world's second largest economy, the USA already being the largest. Its 11 per cent of the world's GDP fell in the first half of the century to a mere 4.5 per cent and in 1950 it was the fourth largest economy. This post-revolutionary level was not exceeded by much during the next 15 years when the economy hit a new nadir of only 4 per cent of the world total in the catastrophic aftermath of the inappropriately named Great Leap Forward. The real leap forward only occurred after the beginning of the introduction of a capitalist economy from 1978 onwards. In the next two decades Chinese GDP rose from 4 to nearly 12 per cent of that of the world, a rate of growth never equalled over such a period by the already industrialized economies. If figure 3.3 were to be projected forwards, assuming relative rates of growth of the last 20 years continued, the Chinese GDP would exceed that of the USA in the year 2010 or 2011. This will surprise many people, accustomed to reading in the press that China is still only the world's fifth largest economy. That error results from converting national figures using exchange rates and not PPP. It is a good illustration of how PPP transforms the economic picture of the world.

Neither total production nor income per head of a country alone decide its economic and military power, but in combination with each other they play a large part in determining its potential power. Neither a very small country with a very high income per head, nor a very large country with a very low income per head is likely to have much international power. But it is not really the level of either of these two variables which decides relative power, but the direction in which they are moving. In 1900, China's GDP was two-thirds that of the USA (figure 3.4), and its income per head was about 12 per cent of the USA's (figure 3.5). In 2000, perhaps surprisingly, both percentages were just about the same. The difference is that then the USA was a rapidly rising economic power and China a stagnant or declining one whereas now the roles are to a great extent reversed.

Figures 3.4 and 3.5 taken together provide a good illustration of changing national power during the twentieth century. They show that at the start of the century when British hegemony was rapidly waning, the UK's GDP per head was still higher than any other country, including the USA but the total size of its GDP was less than that of the USA and not very much higher than that of Germany. Small

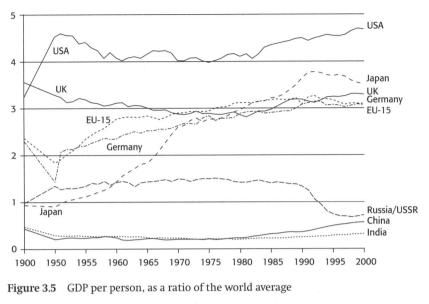

Figure 3.5 GDP per person, as a ratio of the world average

Source: Author's calculations based on data in Maddison (2003)

wonder that it could no longer pretend to rule the waves, let alone the world, although it could still rule India whose GDP was nearly the size of the British but whose living standard was very much lower. Of course, power does not come from economics alone, but also from political attitudes and alliances. The attitudes of the USSR under Stalinist rule allowed that country to contest US power in some ways during the Cold War, even though its total GDP was less than half that of the USA and less than one quarter of the USA plus the military alliance which it dominated, NATO.

The most striking of all facts to emerge from these historic estimates of GDP is the change during the century in the relative position of the USA. Virtually throughout the century it had both the highest total level of GDP and the highest GDP per person. While this had also been the case for the UK in the nineteenth century, it was much more a *primus inter pares* than the USA during the heyday of its power. The enormous strengthening of US economic primacy between 1900 and 1950 is amply clear from figures 3.4 and 3.5, but in fact the most significant period in this expansion of relative wealth took place during and immediately after World War II. Since, unlike other partici-pants it suffered little physical damage, social disintegration or demographic catastrophe, the USA's power at the end of the war was unchallengeable. Its ruling class used the opportunity to reshape the world which it was to dominate, albeit with Soviet competition, for 30 years. Its hegemony, however, became increasingly vulnerable, partly because of growing economic competition from the very countries whose rebirth it had assisted after 1945. As Soviet power looked more insecure, the then US allies felt more confident in confronting their hegemon, especially on economic questions, though none of this led to anything close to serious political conflict. After the 1970s, however, numerous writers started to write of a crisis of US hegemony. But, if its hitherto allies were becoming more recalcitrant, its hitherto prime enemy, the USSR, was rapidly losing power and political coherence and eventually shattered due both to internal and external pressures. The virtual economic disappearance of Russia after the fall of communist rule is again shown with great clarity in figures 3.5 and 3.6.

The economic decline of its old enemy and the relative stagnation of its major allies, Western Europe and Japan, meant that the decline in the USA's share of world production, continuous from 1950 to 1980, came to an end, as the USA seemed in some respects to acquire a new wind. But several things were happening from the early 1980s onwards which meant that, although the USA maintained its economic lead, its hegemony had qualitatively mutated since the Cold War epoch. First, one reason for the continued rapid growth of the total size of the US economy was an acceleration of immigration. The US economy partly expanded because its population expanded more than that of Western Europe's or Japan's. And this process of expansion led to an increase in the country's cultural diversity, another factor which may influence national power. Second, the US economy fell deeper and deeper into debt, both internationally and during most of the period also internally. The hegemony of the UK and the first phase of US hegemony after 1950 emanated partly from the fact that those countries were at the time the world's largest creditors. Since 1984 the USA has moved further and further into debt and is now in absolute terms by far the world's largest debtor. A hegemonic power which is a debtor is a novelty in the modern international economy and its consequences are not yet clear. The third change after 1980 is the astoundingly fast economic growth of China, greatly exceeding that of the USA. It is no longer fanciful to foresee that, if the USA is to have a serious rival for world hegemony in the foreseeable future, the only serious candidate for the job is China. And while US hegemony was magnified after 1950 by its alliances with other rich powers, those same powers are now in the process of experimenting with a closer relationship to China. They see the way the world economy is moving, and they are increasingly unwilling to follow the rules of the relationship which the US government seeks to impose. The USA too, however, finds itself economically increasingly enmeshed with China. China now provides a very significant share of the lending which the USA needs to cover its massive twin deficits – balance of payments and government budget. Like the UK in the early part of the century, the doddering hegemon of today is falling ever deeper into debt to its most likely challenger and perhaps successor.

Changing Inequality of Households and People

So far, I have looked at international inequality in the twentieth century by comparing national totals and national averages of economic variables. There is another way in which we can look at exactly the same figures – by calculating a single measure of inequality for the world. Perhaps the simplest of such measures is the ratio of richest to the poorest countries or people. This measurement is obtained by taking the 10 richest and poorest countries in the world and calculating their average income and the result of this calculation is captured by the line labelled '10/10 countries' in figure 3.6. These countries are not necessarily the same from one year to the next, and there is no indication of their population, so this is a very crude indicator of world inequality. Nevertheless, it does give an idea of the range of incomes which exist. It is also possibly very influential in forming popular ideas about inequality, since people compare what they see of the wealth of the richest countries and the poverty of the poorest. This

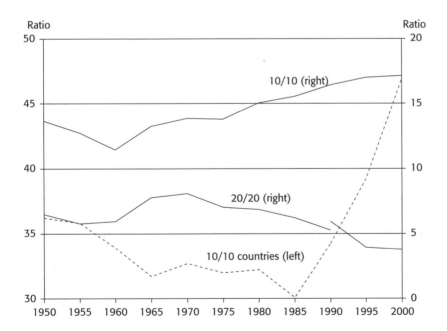

For an explanation of the break in the 20/20 line see the note to figure 3.7.

Figure 3.6　Measures of world inequality 1950–2000 ratios of extremes

Source: Author's calculations from data in Maddison (2003)

ratio fell from 1950 to about 1980 since when it has risen at lightning speed, from about 30 to about 45.

The other two lines in figure 3.6 are more, though still only partly, indicative of the relative wealth of *people* rather than *countries*. These lines were produced by making a list of countries according to their national income per person and cumulatively adding the total income of countries starting at the top until reaching 10 (or 20) per cent of the world's population. The same method is repeated starting at the bottom and the ratio of the two totals is calculated. This would be the ratio of the richest to the poorest 10 (or 20) per cent of the world's population if everyone received the average income of the country in which they lived. In the absence of figures for inequality within countries, this calculation is the best that we can do and it does help us make important inferences about inequality. The two lines in figure 3.6 show that both ratios fell from 1950 to 1960 (less inequality), rose in the decade to 1970 (more inequality) and then clearly diverged after 1970. If this result can be confirmed it shows that there was declining inequality between the top and bottom 20 per cent of the population but rising inequality between the smaller extremes, the top and bottom 10 per cent, a result which suggests that the very rich were doing inordinately well or the very poor were doing inordinately badly, or both. I will substantiate this important conclusion below.

Figure 3.7 uses the same data to produce more complex measures of world inequality, but as with the ratios in figure 3.6, there is no data on internal inequality, which still amounts to assuming that within each country everyone receives the same income. Yet, in contrast to the calculations which are the basis of figure 3.6, in figure 3.7 *all* countries are included *not just* the richest and poorest, in order to produce integral measures of inequality. Two such measures are shown here: (a) the coefficient of variation (C of V) (the standard deviation divided by the average), both unweighted (line 1) and weighted by population (line 2); (b) the Gini coefficient, unweighted (line 3), weighted (line 4) and weighted excluding China (line 5). Looking at measures unweighted by population, when trying to capture inequality, makes little, if any, sense, if at all. Unweighted measures assume in effect that all countries have an equal population – which would mean China has the same weight as Luxembourg! In this regard, unweighted measures are not helpful. But, they are included here (lines 1 and 3), since they are sometimes uncritically presented as measures of inequality. Thus, it may be useful for the reader to see what a difference population weighting makes. So lines 1 and 3 should be glanced at and then forgotten. Line 2, however, represents probably the commonest of all measures of the degree of inequality in a set of data, the C of V. This statistic shows the world becoming slightly more equal between 1950 and 1960, but thereafter becoming

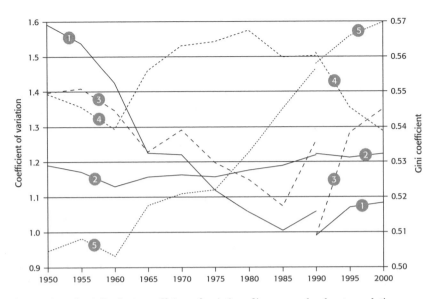

The meaning of each line is: 1 – coefficient of variation of income per head, not population weighted; 2 – the same, population weighted; 3 – Gini coefficient, unweighted; 4 – Gini coefficient weighted; 5 – Gini coefficient weighted excluding China. Lines 1 and 2 refer to the left hand axis and lines 3, 4 and 5 to the right-hand one. There is a break in the series in 1990 because from that time the individual countries of the former USSR and former Yugoslavia are included separately.

Figure 3.7   Measures of world inequality 1950–2000: integral measures

Source: Author's calculations based on data in Maddison (2003)

more or less continuously more unequal up to 1990 and then remaining more or less unchanged. The other measure used here, the Gini coefficient, follows more or less the same direction of change as the C of V until 1980, when it diverges markedly and shows a clear reduction in inequality. The comparison between lines 4 and 5 shows one of the main reasons for this: the subtraction of China from the calculation makes the Gini coefficient for the rest of the world continue its sharply upward path after 1980. That was the year when China began its current period of breakneck industrialization and economic growth.

For the second half of the twentieth century, for which we have comparable national data of national income and population, these results suggest some tentative conclusions. The extremes of distribution between countries have clearly widened. More integral measures also suggest that inequality increased up to 1980. After that it depends on the measure used. The Gini coefficient suggests a reduction in inequality while the C of V suggests that it has increased a little. It is not surprising that China is the country which affects this result the most. It is the world's most populous country and for more than 20 years it has been near the very top of the international growth league. Even so the results remain limited due to the fact that the data still comes in country-sized chunks. A deeper understanding of the question means searching for more disaggregated data.

Ideally, an estimate of the degree of income inequality among the world's human population requires income data for every individual. That, however, is a luxury which just does not exist. In the first place the data almost never comes in smaller units than the family. So intra-family/household income distribution (often an important source of inequality, especially on the basis of gender and age) cannot be studied by this kind of method, although there are sample studies of various kinds about intra-household distribution. Even in the countries for which good distribution data exist they are seldom at the level of the individual household, but come in larger chunks. While many empirical studies of inequality have been done in most countries, they usually tend to be one of a kind and do not have the regularity, consistency and comparability which (to some extent) figures for income and population have. Hence it is difficult to put them all in the same dataset and draw conclusions from them. Also, good studies of distribution are relatively recent. Only for a very few are there data which go back a half century, let alone a century. Given these limitations, we have no choice but to rely on the data we have available.

Here, let us briefly discuss some studies, which calculate inter- and intra-country inequality. Bourguignon and Morrisson (2002), for instance, attempt to calculate the evolution of the global Gini coefficient in the long run. These authors conclude that global, like inter-country, inequality increases more or less continuously during the whole twentieth century, and that the inter-country component increases faster than the intra-country component. Only in the final years covered by their study (from 1980 to 1992) did the level stop rising. Most people agree with their conclusion for the century as a whole, as some of the verdicts referred to at the start of this essay make clear, but there is considerable disagreement about the period since 1980. This is, however, exactly the period in which more, if not yet enough, figures relevant to resolving this issue exist.

The most convenient available set of data on *intra-country income distribution* is published by the World Bank (2005) which compares, for 127 countries (with over 90 per cent of world population), the shares of the national income or consumption enjoyed by each tenth of a country's population, from richest to poorest. Using this we can calculate the income per head not merely of each country but of each tenth/fifth of the population of each country. That still, of course, means that the data comes in large chunks. For instance, one tenth of the population of China is 120 million people, who are all assumed to have the same income. This set of data, however, allows us to measure the *overall level of inequality* in the world in a much more detailed way than that shown in figures 3.6 and 3.7. But there are still not many annual series of data concerning inequality since it is surveyed in detail in most countries only every few years. I have taken the latest estimates of inequality from the World Bank's *World Development Indicators* and have combined them with the figures for national income in purchasing power parity in the latest available year (2003) to produce the results shown in the last column of table 3.2. The first three columns in table 3.2 (years 1980, 1990, 2000) were calculated in a similar way using earlier intra-country distribution estimates (Deininger and Squire 1996) together with Maddison's income figures.

Table 3.2 displays important conclusions, although these results are not completely conclusive and nor are they immune to challenge by other numbers. The first line of table 3.2 measures the Gini coefficient for 167 countries with internal distribution included, which I refer to as global inequality, distinguishing it from inter-country inequality. My estimates show the Gini coefficient falling – that is, less inequality – during the last two decades of the century. While several other studies produce a similar result (for instance, Firebaugh 2003; Sala-i-Martin 2002b), it is by no means an indisputable result. Another study, using what is in principle a more satisfactory methodology and more disaggregated distribution data, finds an increase in the Gini coefficient during a sub-period (1988–93) (Milanovic 2002). In any case, in my calculations the coefficient for 2000 was 0.62, a figure very similar to many other calculations. This is markedly higher than the figure of 0.54 for inter-country distribution (line 4 in figure 3.7). That global inequality is greater than inter-country inequality is not surprising, but it is not inevitable. Whether or not including internal distribution will alter the overall level of distribution depends on the details of the data. If income distribution is unequal in the countries with highest and lowest incomes per head, we will experience relatively greater

Table 3.2 Global Gini coefficients and percentile ratios, 1980–2003				
Date of data	1980	1990	2000	2003[a]
Gini coefficient	0.66	0.65	0.62	0.63
50/50 ratio	13.62	10.21	8.83	8.60
20/20 ratio	45.73	33.85	29.49	31.96
10/10 ratio	78.86	64.21	57.41	64.41
5/5 ratio	120.75	101.02	116.41	130.46
1/1 ratio	216.17	275.73	414.57	564.27

[a] The last column is not strictly comparable with the previous ones but following the earlier methodology would produce very similar results.

Sources: For 1980 to 2000, see Sutcliffe (2003) for an explanation of the method. For 2003, author's calculations based on data from World Bank (2005)

global inequality compared with international inequality. Even though it remains true that the global Gini coefficient is greater than the inter-country Gini coefficient, as virtually all studies on inequality agree, inter-country rather than intra-country inequality is the greatest contributor to inequality as a whole.

What do these figures really say about the degree of world inequality? There are a number of ways in which we can try to answer this question. One possibility is to compare them with the equivalent figures for individual countries. First, the Gini coefficient of the world is 0.63 (see row 1 of table 3.2). This is about the same as its most unequal component countries. Only Namibia (0.707) and Lesotho (0.632) have higher figures. Countries which are emblematic of inequality such as South Africa and Brazil (both with a Gini of 0.59) are not as unequal as the world as a whole. The world's ratio between the top and bottom 10 per cent of the population is almost exactly the same as South Africa's; there are seven countries, including Brazil, which are higher. As far as the 20 per cent ratio is concerned the situation is similar: there are seven countries, including Brazil and South Africa which have a more unequal ratio than the world as a whole.

In the remainder of table 3.2, based on the same figures as row 1, we see the ratios of extremes of the population from the ratio of the richest half to the poorest half (the 'Robin Hood ratio') to the ratio of the richest to poorest 1 per cent. The global ratios of extremes, however, do not all behave in the same way as the Gini coefficient. The 50/50 ratio has fallen in line with the Gini; the 20/20 ratio fell up to 2000 but then rose again; the 10/10 ratio did the same but the more recent rise has been more marked. The 5/5 ratio has risen notably since 1990. Strikingly, the ratio of the income of the richest 1 per cent to the poorest 1 per cent of the world's population has risen continuously and very sharply indeed during the whole period.

These figures do indeed suggest that there is more than one story unfolding. While the fast growth of some Asian countries has the effect of lowering inequality on some measures, explosive increase is taking place in the incomes of the rich in developed countries compared to those of the very poor. In this calculation the top 1 per cent of the world's population is composed of the richest 10 per cent of the following countries: USA, Hong Kong, Switzerland, Singapore, Ireland, Austria, Germany, Belgium, Luxembourg, France, Netherlands, Italy, UK, Norway, Canada, Australia and Denmark; and the poorest 1 per cent are composed of the poorest 40 per cent in Sierra Leone, the poorest 30 per cent in Malawi, the poorest 20 per cent in Burundi, Central African Republic, Guinea-Bissau, Madagascar, Niger, Nigeria, Tanzania and Zambia, and the poorest 10 per cent in Burkina Faso, Honduras, Kenya, Lesotho, Mali and Yemen.[1]

As far as the rich are concerned, it seems that the smaller the extreme which is studied the greater is the disproportionate growth of income. Paul Krugman (2002) has drawn attention to the 'tectonic shifts that have taken place in the distribution of income in [the USA]'. He quotes studies which show that out of the major income gains of the top 10 per cent of US taxpayers in the last 30 years, most of them were really gains of the top 1 per cent; and 60 per cent of their gains went in turn to the top 0.1 per cent. Such a small number of people receive enough income to have an appreciable effect on the level of global inequality. Another way of seeing the dimension of this inequality is by comparison: while the ratio of national income per head of the richest to the poorest country is 104 to 1 (Luxembourg to Sierra Leone), and the ratio of average white to black income in South Africa is 12.5 to 1, and the ratio of the richest to the poorest 10 per cent of the population of the world's most unequal country (Namibia) is 79 to 1, the ratio of the average salary of CEOs of large US corporations to that of an average US worker is 245 to 1. The exploding riches of this small class gives them the means to exercise vast influence on the policies of the US and other governments, which themselves have a major impact on the world's inequalities. For instance, the cause of US borrowing from China and other countries is that its tax revenues are insufficient to pay for its military spending due to the policy of tax cutting to benefit the ultra-rich. So the two stories, that of the inequalities of national power and the conflicts over hegemony and that of the personal distribution of income and the conflict of classes, are intimately related to each other.

A Century of Unequalled Inequality

As they end, centuries, decades and other arbitrary units of time generate irresistible temptations for commentators to write epitaphs. The world's rulers in 2000 generally look back at 1900 and judge that the century went their way, was even a triumph for liberal democratic capitalism. Various dragons had been slain and the world's economy had never been so productive. This, of course, ignores the fact that it was a century of gigantic crises and appalling destruction. But one economic feature of the twentieth century moved in a direction so contrary to the conventional optimistic story that even positive judgements have felt obliged to acknowledge it. This feature was inequality. This chapter provides a rough guide to the maze of facts and methods which have been and can be used to measure international and inter-class inequality in aggregate and to tell briefly the story, or rather the stories, about what happened to it over the century.

The evidence demonstrates that on some measures economic inequality grew throughout the last century. On others there was a slight and questioned alleviation of inequality in its closing years but projections of present trends suggest that will be reversed. This stain on the record of the unequalled century was an embarrassing one for those who have taken a heroic view of it. They have confronted the problem using three approaches: *inequality denial*, which leads them to ignore or criticize measures which do not show an improvement; *inequality displacement*, which leads them to emphasize the importance of other variables like life expectancy for which inequality has declined or to shift the debate away from inequality towards the elimination of absolute poverty; and *inequality embellishment*, which means that they argue that the growth in inequality is part of a benign process of economic growth which will bring benefits to all and which will in time rectify itself.

None of these tactics works very well. In any case it seems strange that the inequality produces such defensive responses. It is not as if egalitarianism is part of today's ruling ideology. Quite the contrary, in fact. Politics and policies, especially in the countries competing for hegemony, the USA and China in particular, are strongly anti-egalitarian. In a perverse sense, however, the defensiveness is welcome. It is a sign that those who defend and benefit from the present unequal world economic and political system are afraid – afraid that today's many struggles against particular economic injustices will sooner or later come together as a more unified and determined struggle against economic injustice in general.

Note

1   Afghanistan and Ethiopia would surely have been represented here but there are no data for those countries.

Bibliographical Note and References

The following references contain the bibliographical details of works referred to in the text, along with some other writings which have had some influence on this essay and were cited in the lectures on which the essay is based.

On inequality
Callinicos, Alex 2000. *Inequality*. Cambridge: Polity Press.
Rawls, John 1999 [1971]. *A Theory of Justice*. Oxford: Oxford University Press.
Sen, Amartya K. 1996. *Inequality Re-examined*. New York and Cambridge, Mass.: Russell Sage Foundation and Harvard University.

On the twentieth century
Anderson, Perry 2002. 'Confronting Defeat.' *London Review of Books*, 17 October 2002 (commentary on Hobsbawm).

Arrighi, Giovanni 1994. *The Long Twentieth Century: Money, Power, and the Origins of Our Times*. London: Verso.

Arrighi, Giovanni 2005. 'Hegemony Unravelling.' *New Left Review*, 32, (March/April).

Boltho, Andrea and Toniolo, Gianni 1999. 'The Assessment: The Twentieth Century – Achievements, Failures, Lessons.' *Oxford Review of Economic Policy*, 15 (4).

Emmott, Bill 2004. *20:21 Vision: The Lessons of the 20th Century for the 21st*. London: Penguin Books.

Hobsbawm, Eric 1994. *The Age of Extremes: The Short Twentieth Century 1914–1991*. London: Penguin Books.

Recent studies of changes in world income distribution

Bourguignon, François and Morrisson, Christian 2002. 'Inequality Among World Citizens: 1820–1992.' *American Economic Review*, September: 727–44.

Firebaugh, Glenn 2003. *The New Geography of Global Income Inequality*. Cambridge, Mass. and London: Harvard University Press.

Melchior, Arne 2001. 'Global Income Inequality: Beliefs, Facts and Unresolved Issues.' *World Economics*, 2 (3), July–September.

Melchior, Arne, Telle, Kjetil and Wiig, Henrik 2000. 'Globalisation and Inequality: World Income Distribution and Living Standards, 1960–1998.' Studies on Foreign Policy Issues, Report 6B. Royal Norwegian Ministry of Foreign Affairs.

Melchior, Arne and Telle, Kjetil 2001. 'Global Income Distribution 1965–98: Convergence and Marginalisation.' *Forum for Development Studies*, 28 (1).

Milanovic, Branko 2002. 'True World Income Distribution, 1988 and 1993: First Calculation Based on Household Surveys Alone.' *Economic Journal*, 112 (476), January.

Milanovic, Branko 2005. *Worlds Apart: Measuring International and Global Inequality*. Princeton, NJ and Oxford: Princeton University Press.

Pritchett, Lant 1995. 'Divergence, Big Time.' Policy Research Working Paper, no. 1522, Washington, DC: World Bank.

Sala-i-Martin, Xavier 2002a. 'The Disturbing "Rise" of Global Income Inequality.' NBER Working Paper, no. 8904. At www.nber.org/papers/w8904.

Sala-i-Martin, Xavier 2002b. 'The World Distribution of Income (estimated from individual country distributions).' NBER Working Paper, no. 8933. At www.nber.org/papers/w8933.

Sutcliffe, Bob 2003. 'A more or less unequal world?' *Indicators: The Journal of Social Health*, Summer.

Sutcliffe, Bob 2004. 'Globalization and Inequality.' *Oxford Review of Economic Policy*, 20 (1), Spring.

Sources of PPP data on incomes and other variables

The following three sources provide in principle much of the same data. Maddison's go back the furthest and fill in all the blanks with estimates. The Penn World Table 6.1 begins for most countries in 1960; it contains more macro-economic variables than Maddison. The World Bank's PPP figures for national product begin in 1975.

Heston, Alan, Summers, Robert and Aten, Bettina 2002. *Penn World Table Version 6.1*. Philadelphia: University of Pennsylvania, Center for International Comparisons (CICUP).

Maddison, Angus 2003. *The World Economy: Historical Statistics.* Paris: OECD, Development Centre Studies.

World Bank 2005. *World Development Indicators 2005.* Washington, DC: World Bank.

Sources of data on intra-country income distribution

Deininger, Klaus and Squire, Lyn 1996. 'A New Data Set Measuring Income Inequality.' World Bank. At http://econ.worldbank.org.

Luxembourg Income Study. At www.lisproject.org.

World Bank 2005. *World Development Indicators 2005.* Washington, DC: World Bank

World Income Inequality Database. At www.wider.unu.edu/wiid/wiid.htm.

On the incomes of the very rich

Atkinson, Anthony B. 2005. 'Top Incomes in the UK over the 20th Century.' *Journal of the Royal Statistical Society: Series A (Statistics in Society)*, 168 (2), March.

Forbes Magazine 2005. 'The World's Billionaires.' At www.forbes.com/billionaires/.

Krugman, Paul 2002. 'For Richer.' *New York Times Magazine*, 20 October.

Merrill Lynch and CapGemini 2005. *World Wealth Report 2005.* At www.ml.com/media/48237.pdf.

Piketty, Thomas and Saez, Emmanuel 2003. 'Income Inequality in the United States, 1913–1998.' *Quarterly Journal of Economics*, CXVIII (1), February.

On the inequality of variables other than income

Becker, Gary S., Philipson, Tomas J. and Soares, Rodrigo R. 2003. 'The Quantity and Quality of Life and the Evolution of World Inequality.' NBER Working Paper, no. 9765. At www.nber.org/papers/w9765.

Crafts, Nicholas 2000. 'Globalization and Growth in the Twentieth Century.' IMF Working Paper, WP/00/44. Washington, DC: IMF. At www.imf.org/external/pubs/ft/wp/2000/wp0044.pdf.

Fogel, Robert William 2004. *The Escape from Hunger and Premature Death 1700–2100.* Cambridge: Cambridge University Press.

UNDP. *Human Development Report*, annual since 1990.

4

Globalization, Poverty and Inequality since 1980

David Dollar

THERE is an odd disconnect between debates about globalization in developed economies and developing economies. Among intellectuals in developed areas one often hears the claim that global economic integration is leading to rising global inequality – that is, that integration benefits rich people proportionally more than poor people. In the extreme claims poor people are actually made out to be worse off absolutely. In developing economies, though, intellectuals and policymakers often view globalization as providing good opportunities for their countries and people. To be sure, they are not happy with the current state of globalization. But the point of these critiques is that integration – through foreign trade, foreign investment, and immigration – is basically a good thing for poor countries and that rich countries could do a lot more to facilitate integration, that is, make it freer. The claims from anti-globalization intellectuals in rich countries, however, lead inescapably to the conclusion that integration is bad for poor countries and that therefore trade and other flows should be more restricted.

The first goal of this chapter is to document what is known about trends in global inequality and poverty over the long term and during the recent wave of globalization that began around 1980. Global inequality is used to mean different things in different discussions – distribution among all the citizens of the world, distribution within countries, distribution among countries, distribution among wage earners – all of which are used here. A second goal of this chapter is to relate these trends to globalization. The first section briefly discusses the growing integration of developing economies with industrialized countries and with each other, starting around 1980. The opening up of large developing countries, such as China and India, is arguably the most distinctive feature of this wave of globalization. The second section, the heart of the argument, presents evidence in support of five trends in inequality and poverty since 1980:

• Growth rates in poor countries have accelerated and are higher than growth rates in rich countries for the first time in modern history.

- The number of extremely poor people (those living on less than $1 a day) in the world has declined significantly – by 375 million people – for the first time in history, though the number living on less than $2 a day has increased.
- Global inequality has declined modestly, reversing a 200-year trend towards higher inequality.
- Within-country inequality is generally not growing.
- Wage inequality is rising worldwide. This may seem to contradict the fourth trend, but it does not because there is no simple link between wage inequality and household income inequality.

The third section then tries to draw a link between increased integration and accelerated growth and poverty reduction. Individual cases, cross-country statistical analysis, and micro-evidence from firms all suggest that opening to trade and direct investment has been a good strategy for such countries as China, India, Mexico, Uganda, and Vietnam. The fourth section looks at how developing economies have a lot to do to develop in general and to make effective use of integration as part of their development strategy. Rich countries could do a lot more with foreign aid to help with that work: for example, access to markets in rich countries is important. Many protections remain in OECD markets from the goods and people of developing economies, and globalization would work much better for poor people if developing areas had more access to those markets.

Growing Integration between Developed and Developing Economies

Global economic integration has been going on for a long time. In that sense, globalization is nothing new. What is new in this most recent wave of globalization is the way developing countries are integrating with rich countries. As in previous waves of integration, this change is driven partly by technological advances in transport and communications and partly by deliberate policy choices.

Earlier waves of globalization

From 1820 to 1870 the world had already seen a fivefold increase in the ratio of trade to gross domestic product (GDP) (table 4.1). Integration increased further from 1870 to 1914, spurred by the development of steam shipping and by an Anglo-French trade agreement. In this period the world reached levels of economic integration comparable in many ways to those of today. The volume of trade relative to world

	Capital flows	Trade flows	Transport and communications costs (constant US$)		
Year	Foreign assets/ world GDP (%)	Trade/GDP (%)	Sea freight (average ocean freight and port charges per ton)	Air transport (average revenue per passenger mile)	Telephone call (average price for a 3 minute call between New York and London)
1820	–	2	–	–	–
1870	6.9	10	–	–	–
1890	–	12	–	–	–
1900	18.6	–	–	–	–
1914	17.5	18	–	–	–
1920	–	–	95	–	–
1930	8.4	18	60	0.68	245
1940	–	–	63	0.46	189
1945	4.9	–	–	–	–
1950	–	14	34	0.30	53
1960	6.4	16	27	0.24	46
1970	–	22.4–20	27	0.16	32
1980	17.7	–	24	0.10	5
1990	–	26	29	0.11	3
1995	56.8	–	–	–	–

Table 4.1 Measures of global integration

– not available.

Source: Crafts (2000) for capital flows; Maddison (1995) and Crafts (2000) for trade flows; World Bank (2002) for transport and communications costs

income nearly doubled from 10 per cent in 1870 to 18 per cent on the eve of World War I. There were also large capital flows to rapidly developing parts of the Americas, and the ownership of foreign assets (mostly Europeans owning assets in other countries) more than doubled in this period, from 7 per cent of world income to 18 per cent. Probably the most distinctive feature of this era of globalization was mass migration. Nearly 10 per cent of the world's population permanently relocated in this period (Williamson 2004). Much of this migration was from poor parts of Europe to the Americas. But there was also considerable migration from China and India (much of it forced migration in India). While global indicators showed considerable integration in 1870–1914, this was also the heyday of colonialism, and most of the world's people were greatly restricted in their opportunities to benefit from the expanding commerce.

Global integration took a big step backward during the two world wars and the Great Depression. Some discussions of globalization today assume it was inevitable, but this dark period is a powerful reminder that policies can halt and reverse integration. By the end of this dark era both trade and foreign asset ownership were back close to their levels of 1870 – the protectionist period undid 50 years of integration. The era of free migration was also at an end, as virtually all countries imposed restrictions on immigration.

From the end of World War II to about 1980, industrialized countries restored much of the integration that had existed among them. They negotiated a series of mutual trade liberalizations under the auspices of the General Agreement on Tariffs and Trade (GATT). But liberalization of capital flows proceeded more slowly, and not until 1980 did the level of ownership of foreign assets return to its 1914 level. Over this period there was also modest liberalization of immigration in many industrialized countries, especially the United States. In this postwar period of globalization, many developing economies chose to sit on the sidelines. Most developing areas in Asia, Africa and Latin America followed import-substituting industrialization strategies, keeping their levels of import protection far higher than in industrialized countries to encourage domestic production of manufactures and usually restricting foreign investment by multinational firms to encourage the growth of domestic firms. While limiting direct investment, several developing economies turned to the expanding international bank borrowing sector in the 1970s and took on significant amounts of foreign debt.

Recent wave of globalization

The most recent wave of globalization started in 1978 with the initiation of China's economic reform and opening to the outside world, which roughly coincides with the second oil shock, which contributed to external debt crises throughout Latin America and in other developing economies. In a growing number of countries in Latin America, South Asia and Sub-Saharan Africa political and intellectual leaders began to fundamentally rethink development strategies. The distinctive part of this latest wave of globalization is that the majority of developing economies (in terms of population) shifted from an inward-focused strategy to a more outward-oriented one.

This altered strategy can be seen in the huge increases in trade integration of developing areas over the past two decades. China's ratio of trade to national income has more than doubled, and countries such as Mexico, Bangladesh, Thailand and India have seen large increases as well (figure 4.1). But several developing economies trade less of their income than two decades ago, a fact that will be discussed later. The change has been not only in the amount, but also in the nature of what is traded. Twenty years ago, nearly 80 per cent of developing country merchandise exports were primary products: the stereotype of poor countries exporting tin or bananas had a large element of truth. The

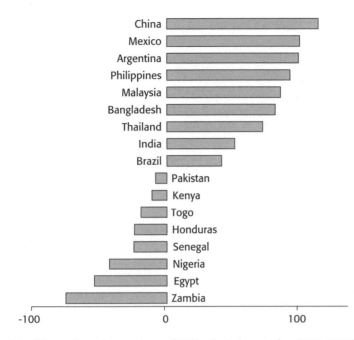

Figure 4.1   Change in trade as a share of GDP, selected countries, 1977–1997 (%)

Source: World Bank (2002)

big increase in merchandise exports in the past two decades, however, has been of manufactured products, so that 80 per cent of today's merchandise exports from developing countries are manufactures (figure 4.2). Garments from Bangladesh, CD players from China, refrigerators from Mexico, and computer peripherals from Thailand – these are the modern face of developing economy exports. Service exports from developing areas have also increased enormously – both traditional services, such as tourism, and modern ones, such as software from Bangalore, India.

Manufactured exports from developing economies are often part of multinational production networks. Nike contracts with firms in Vietnam to make shoes; the 'world car' is a reality, with parts produced in different locations. So part of the answer to why integration has taken off must lie with technological advances that make integrated production feasible (see table 4.1 for evidence of the dramatic declines in the cost of air transport and international communications). But part of the answer also lies in policy choices of developing economies. China and India had almost totally closed economies, so their increased integration would not have been possible without steps to gradually liberalize trade and direct foreign investment.

Some measure of this policy trend can be seen in average import tariff rates for developing economies. Since 1980 average tariffs have

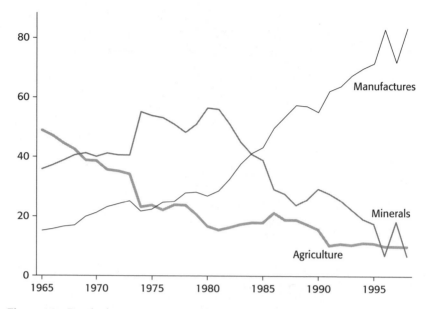

Figure 4.2 Developing country exports by sector, 1965–1999 (% of total)

Source: World Bank (2002)

declined sharply in South Asia, Latin America and the Caribbean, and East Asia and Pacific, whereas in Africa and the Middle East there has been much less tariff cutting (figure 4.3). These reported average tariffs, however, capture only a small amount of what is happening with trade policy. Often the most pernicious impediments are non-tariff barriers: quotas, licensing schemes, restrictions on purchasing foreign exchange for imports, and the like. China started to reduce these non-tariff impediments in 1979, which led to a dramatic surge in trade (figure 4.4). In 1978 external trade was monopolized by a single government ministry.[1] Specific measures adopted in China included allowing a growing number of firms, including private ones, to trade directly and opening a foreign exchange market to facilitate this trade.

Another major impediment to trade in many developing areas is inefficient ports and customs administration. For example, it is much more expensive to ship a container of textiles from a Mombasa (Kenya) port to the East Coast of the United States than from Asian ports such as Mumbai, Shanghai, Bangkok, or Kaohsiung, Taiwan (China), even though Mombasa is closer (Clark et al. 2004). The extra cost, equivalent to an 8 per cent export tax, is due to inefficiencies and corruption in the port. Long customs delays often act as import and export taxes. Developing economies that have become more integrated with the world economy have reasonably well-functioning ports and customs, and their improvement has often been a deliberate policy target. Several countries, including Kenya, trade less of their income today

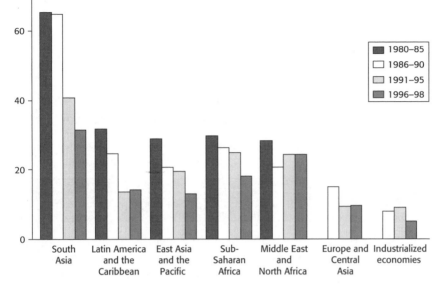

Figure 4.3 Average unweighted tariff rates, by region, 1980–1998 (%)

Source: World Bank (2002)

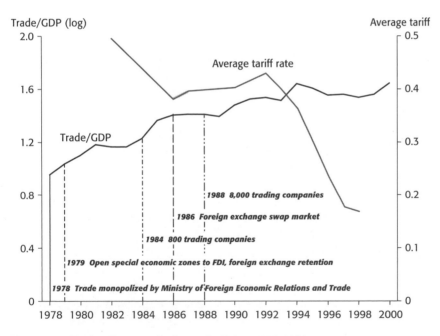

Figure 4.4 Trade reforms and volumes in China, 1978–2000

Source: Dollar and Kraay (2003)

than 20 years ago; surely this is partly the result of restrictive trade policies, defined broadly to include inefficient ports and customs.

Thus, one key development in this current wave of globalization is a dramatic change in the way many developing countries relate to the global economy. Developing economies as a whole are a major exporter of manufactures and services – many of which compete directly with products made in industrialized countries. The nature of trade and competition between rich and poor countries has fundamentally changed.

Accelerated Growth and Poverty Reduction in Developing Economies

Some of the debate about globalization concerns its effects on poor countries and poor people, including several sweeping statements that assert that global economic integration is increasing poverty and inequality in the world. But the reality is far more complex – and to some extent runs exactly counter to what is being claimed by anti-globalists. Thus, this section focuses on the trends in global poverty and inequality, and the following section links them to global integration. The trends of the last 20 years highlighted here are:

- Growth rates of developing economies have accelerated and are higher than those of industrialized countries.
- The number of extremely poor people (those living on less than $1 a day) has declined for the first time in history, though the number of people living on less than $2 a day has increased.
- Measures of global inequality (such as the global Gini coefficient) have declined modestly, reversing a long historical trend towards greater inequality.
- Within-country inequality in general is not growing, though it has risen in several populous countries (China, India, the United States).
- Wage inequality in general has been rising (meaning larger wage increases for skilled workers than for unskilled workers).

The fifth trend may seem to run counter to the fourth trend; why it does not will be explained here. The fifth trend is important for explaining some of the anxiety about globalization in industrialized countries.

Growth rates in developing economies have accelerated

Reasonably good data on economic growth since 1960 for about 100 countries that account for the vast majority of world population are

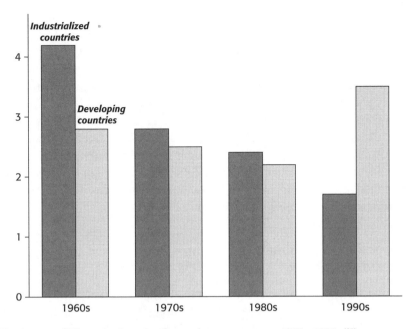

Figure 4.5   GDP per capita growth rate, by country type, 1960s–1990s (%)

Source: Center for International Comparisons (2004)

summarized in the Penn World Tables (Center for International Comparisons 2004). Aggregating data on growth rates for industrialized countries and developing economies for which there are data since 1960 shows that in general growth rates have declined in rich countries while accelerating in developing countries (figure 4.5). In particular, in the 1960s growth of OECD countries was about twice as fast as that of developing areas. Per capita growth rates in rich countries have gradually declined from about 4 per cent in the 1960s to 1.7 per cent in the 1990s – close to the long-term historical trend rate of the OECD countries. The rapid growth in the 1960s was still to some extent a rebound from the destruction of World War II as well as a pay-off to economic integration among rich countries.

In the 1960s and early 1970s, the growth rate of developing economies was well below that of rich countries, a paradox whose origin has been long debated. The slower growth of less developed economies was a paradox because neoclassical growth theory suggested that other things being equal poor countries should grow faster. This pattern finally emerged in the 1990s, with per capita growth in developing countries of about 3.5 per cent – more than twice the rate of rich countries.

This high aggregate growth depends heavily on several large countries that were among the poorest in the world in 1980 but that have grown well since then. Ignoring differences in population and averaging growth rates in poor countries over 1980–2000 result in an average growth of about zero for poor countries. China, India and several small countries, particularly in Africa, are among the poorest quintile of countries in 1980. Ignoring population, the average growth of Chad and China is about zero, and the average growth of India and Togo is about zero. Accounting for differences in population, though, the average growth of poor countries has been very good in the past 20 years. China obviously carries a large weight in any calculation of the growth of poor countries in 1980, but it is not the only poor country that did well: Bangladesh, India and Vietnam also grew faster than rich countries in the same period. Several African economies, notably Uganda, also had accelerated growth.

The number of extremely poor people has declined by 375 million globally

The most important point in this section is that poverty reduction in low-income countries is very closely related to the GDP growth rate. The accelerated growth of low-income countries has led to unprecedented poverty reduction. By poverty I mean subsisting below some absolute threshold. Most poverty analyses are carried out with countries' own poverty lines, which are set in country context and naturally differ. China, for example, uses a poverty line defined in constant Chinese yuan. The poverty line is deemed the minimum amount necessary to subsist. In practice, estimates of the number of poor in a country such as China come from household surveys carried out by a statistical bureau. These surveys aim to measure what households actually consume. Most extremely poor people in the world are peasants, and they subsist to a large extent on their own agricultural output. To look only at their money income would not be very relevant, because the extremely poor have only limited involvement in the money economy. Thus measures ask households what they actually consume and attach a value to their consumption based on the prices of different commodities. So a poverty line is meant to capture a certain real level of consumption. Estimating the extent of poverty is obviously subject to error, but in many countries the measures are good enough to pick up large trends. In discussing poverty it is important to be clear on the poverty line being used. In global discussions international poverty lines of either $1 a day or $2 a day, calculated at purchasing power parity, are used. For discussions of global poverty a common line should be applied to all countries.

Chen and Ravallion (2004) used household survey data to estimate the number of poor people worldwide based on the $1 a day and $2 a day poverty lines back to 1981. They found that the incidence of

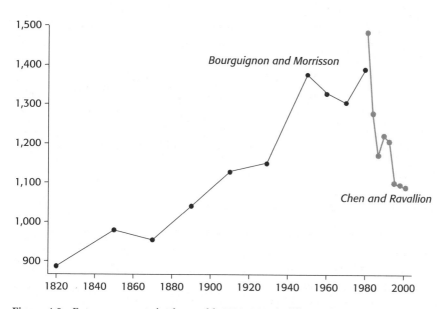

Figure 4.6 Extreme poverty in the world, 1820–2001 (millions of people living on less than $1 a day)

Sources: Bourguignon and Morrisson (2002); Chen and Ravallion (2004)

extreme poverty (consuming less than $1 a day) was basically cut in half in 20 years, from 40.4 per cent of the population in developing economies in 1981 to 21.1 per cent in 2001. It is interesting that the decline in $2 a day poverty incidence was not as great, from 66.7 per cent to 52.9 per cent, over the same period.

Poverty incidence has been gradually declining throughout modern history, but in general population growth has outstripped the decline in incidence so that the total number of poor people has actually risen. Even in 1960–80, a reasonably prosperous period for developing economies, the number of extremely poor people continued to rise (figure 4.6).[2] Most striking in the past 20 years is that the number of extremely poor people declined by 375 million, while at the same time world population rose by 1.6 billion. But the decline was not steady: in 1987–93 the number of extremely poor people rose, as growth slowed in China and India underwent an economic crisis. After 1993 growth and poverty reduction accelerated in both countries.

The 1981–2001 decline in the number of extremely poor people is unprecedented in human history. At the same time many of those who rose above the very low $1 a day threshold are still living on less than $2 a day. The number of people living on less than $2 a day increased between 1981 and 2001 by nearly 300 million. About half the world's population still lives on less than $2 a day, and it will take several more decades of sustained growth to bring this figure down significantly.

Although the overall decline in extreme poverty is positive news, performance has varied by region. South Asia, and East Asia and Pacific grew well and reduced poverty, but Sub-Saharan Africa had negative growth between 1981 and 2001 and a rise in poverty: the number of extremely poor people there increased from 164 million (41.6 per cent of the population) to 316 million (46.9 per cent of the population). Two-thirds of extremely poor people still live in Asia, but if strong growth there continues, global poverty will be increasingly concentrated in Africa.

Global inequality has declined modestly

Global inequality is casually used to mean several things, but the most sensible definition is the same as for a country: line up all the people in the world from the poorest to the richest and calculate a measure of inequality among their incomes. There are several measures, of which the Gini coefficient is the best known. Bhalla (2002) estimates that the global Gini coefficient declined from 0.67 in 1980 to 0.64 in 2000 after rising from 0.64 in 1960. Sala-i-Martin (2002) likewise finds that all the standard measures of inequality show a decline in global inequality since 1980. Both Bhalla and Sala-i-Martin combine national accounts data on income or consumption with survey-based data on distribution. Deaton (2004) discusses the problems of using national accounts data for studying poverty and inequality, noting among other things that the growth rates in national accounts data for China and India are arguably overestimated. This bias would tend to exaggerate the decline in global inequality over the past 25 years. Hence, there is a fair degree of uncertainty about the magnitude of the estimated decline in global inequality.[3]

For historical perspective, Bourguignon and Morrisson (2002) calculate the global Gini coefficient back to 1820. Although confidence in these early estimates is not high, they illustrate an important point: global inequality has been on the rise throughout modern economic history. Bourguignon and Morrisson estimate that the global Gini coefficient rose from 0.50 in 1820 to about 0.65 around 1980 (figure 4.7). Sala-i-Martin (2002) estimates that it has since declined to 0.61.

Other measures of inequality such as mean log deviation show a similar trend, rising until about 1980 and then declining modestly after (figure 4.8). Roughly speaking, the mean log deviation is the percentage difference between average income in the world and the income of a randomly chosen individual who represents a typical person. Average per capita income in the world today is around $5,000, but the typical person lives on 20 per cent of that, or $1,000. The advantage of the mean log deviation is that it can be decomposed into

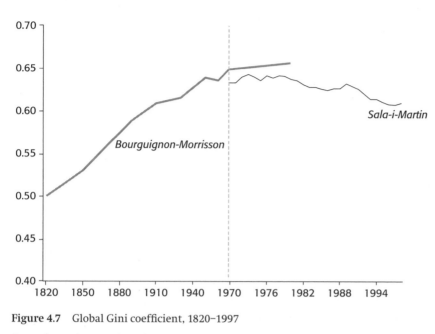

Figure 4.7   Global Gini coefficient, 1820–1997

Sources: Bourguignon and Morrisson (2002); Sala-i-Martin (2002)

inequality between countries (differences in per capita income across countries) and inequality within countries. This decomposition shows that most inequality in the world can be attributed to inequality among countries. Global inequality rose from 1820 to 1980, primarily because already relatively rich countries (those in Europe and North America) grew faster than poor ones. As noted in the discussion of the first trend, that pattern of growth was reversed starting around 1980, and the faster growth in such poor countries as Bangladesh, China, India and Vietnam accounts for the modest decline in global inequality since then.[4] (Slow growth in Africa tended to increase inequality, faster growth in low-income Asia tended to reduce it, and Asia's growth modestly outweighed Africa's.)

Thinking about the different experiences of Africa and Asia, as in the last section, helps give a clearer picture of what is likely to happen in the future. Rapid growth in Asia has been a force for greater global equality because that is where the majority of the world's extremely poor people lived in 1980 – and they benefited from growth. But if the same growth trends persist, they will not continue to be a force for equality. Sala-i-Martin (2002) projects future global inequality if the growth rates of 1980–98 persist: global inequality will continue to decline until about 2015, after which global inequality will rise sharply (see figure 4.8). A large share of the world's poor people still lives in India and other Asian countries, so that continued rapid growth there will be equalizing for another decade or so; increasingly

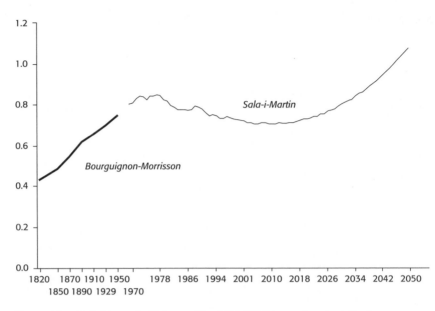

Figure 4.8   Global household inequality, 1820–2050 (mean log deviation)

Sources: Bourguignon and Morrisson (2002); Sala-i-Martin (2002)

poverty will be concentrated in Africa; so that if slow growth persists there, global inequality will eventually rise again.

Within-country inequality is in general not growing

The previous analysis shows that inequality within countries has a relatively small role in measures of global income inequality. But people care about trends in inequality in their own societies (arguably more than they care about global inequality and poverty). So a different question is what is happening to income inequality within countries. One common claim about globalization is that it leads to greater inequality within countries and thus fosters social and political polarization.

To assess this claim Dollar and Kraay (2002) collected income distribution data from more than 100 countries, in some cases going back decades. They found no general trend towards higher or lower inequality within countries. Focusing on the share of income going to the bottom quintile, another common measure of inequality, they found increases in inequality for some countries (for example, China and the United States) in the 1980s and 1990s and decreases for others. They also tried to use measures of integration to explain the changes in inequality that have occurred, but none of the changes were related to any of the measures. For example, countries in which trade integration increased showed rises in inequality in some cases and declines in others (figure 4.9). They found the same results for other measures,

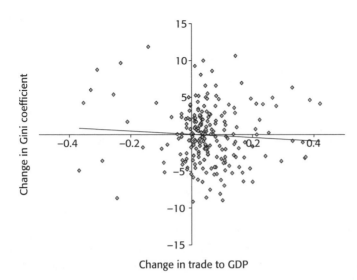

Figure 4.9   Correlation between change in Gini coefficient and change in trade as a share of GDP

Source: Dollar and Kraay (2002)

such as tariff rates and capital controls. Particularly in low-income countries, much of the import protection benefited relatively rich and powerful groups, so that integration with the global market went hand in hand with declines in income inequality. It is widely recognized that income distribution data have a lot of measurement error, which makes it difficult to identify systematic relationships, but given the available data, there is no robust evidence that integration is systematically related to higher inequality within countries.

There are two important caveats to this conclusion. First, inequality has risen in several very populous countries, notably China, India and the United States. This means that a majority of citizens of the world live in countries in which inequality is rising. Second, the picture of inequality is not so favourable for rich countries in the past decade. The Luxembourg Income Study, using comparable, high-quality income distribution data for most rich countries, finds no obvious trends in inequality through the mid- to late 1980s. Over the past decade, though, inequality has increased in most rich countries. Because low-skilled workers in these countries now compete more with workers in developing economies, global economic integration can create pressure for higher inequality in rich countries while having effects in poor countries that often go the other way. The good news from the Luxembourg Income Study is that 'domestic policies and institutions still have large effects on the level and trend of inequality within rich and middle-income nations, even in a globalizing world. . . . Globalization does not force any single outcome on any country' (Smeeding 2002, p. 179). In other words, some rich countries have maintained stable income distributions in this era of globalization through their social and economic policies (on taxes, education, welfare, and the like).

Wage inequality is rising worldwide

Much of the concern about globalization in rich countries relates to workers, wages, and other labour issues. The most comprehensive examination of globalization and wages used International Labour Organization (ILO) data from the past two decades (Freeman et al. 2001). These data look across countries at what is happening to wages for very specific occupations (for example, bricklayer, primary schoolteacher, nurse, autoworker). The study found that wages have generally been rising fastest in more globalized developing economies, followed by rich countries, and then less globalized developing economies (figure 4.10). More globalized developing economies are the top third of developing economies in terms of increased trade integration over the past 20 years (Dollar and Kraay 2004). Less globalized developing economies are the remaining developing economies. The fastest wage growth is occurring in developing economies that are actively increasing their integration with the global economy.

Although the general rise in wages is good news, the detailed findings from Freeman et al. (2001) are more complex and indicate that certain types of workers benefit more than others. First, increased trade is related to a decline in the gender wage gap. More trade appears to lead to a more competitive labour market in which groups that have been traditionally discriminated against – women, for example – fare especially well (Oostendorp 2002). Second, the gains from increased trade appear to be larger for skilled workers. This finding is consistent with other work showing a worldwide trend towards greater wage inequality – that is, a larger gap between pay for educated workers and pay for less educated and unskilled workers. Galbraith and Liu (2001), for example, find a worldwide trend towards greater wage inequality among industries. Wages in skill-intensive industries, such as aircraft production, have been going up faster than wages in low-skill industries, such as garments.

If wage inequality is going up worldwide, how can income inequality not be rising in most countries? There are several reasons. First, in the typical developing economy wage earners make up a small share of the population. Even unskilled wage workers are a relatively elite group. Take Vietnam, for example, a low-income country with a survey of the same representative sample of households early in liberalization (1993) and five years later. The majority of households in the

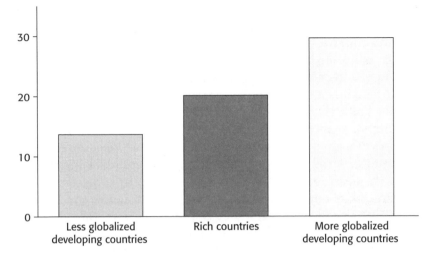

Figure 4.10   Wage growth by country type, 1980s–1990s (%)

Source: Freeman et al. (2001)

country (and thus in the sample) are peasants. The household data show that the price of the main agricultural output (rice) went up dramatically while the price of the main purchased input (fertilizer) actually went down. Both movements are related directly to globalization because over the survey period Vietnam became a major exporter of rice (raising its price) and a major importer of fertilizer from cheaper producers (lowering its price). Poor families faced a much bigger wedge between rice's input price and output price, and their real income went up dramatically (Benjamin and Brandt 2002). So, one of the most important forces acting on income distribution in this low-income country had nothing to do with wages.

Several rural households also sent a family member to a nearby city to work in a factory for the first time. In 1989 the typical wage in Vietnamese currency was the equivalent of $9 a month. Today, factory workers making contract shoes for US brands often make $50 a month or more. So the wage for a relatively unskilled worker has gone up nearly fivefold. But wages for some skilled occupations, for example, computer programmers and English interpreters, may have gone up ten times or more (Glewwe et al. 2004). Thus, a careful study of wage inequality is likely to show rising inequality. But how wage inequality translates into household inequality is very complex. For a surplus worker from a large rural household who obtains a newly created job in a shoe factory, earnings increase from $0 to $50 a month. If many new wage jobs are created, and if they typically pay much more than people earn in the rural or informal sectors, a country can have rising wage inequality but stable or even declining income inequality. (The

Gini coefficient for household income inequality in Vietnam actually declined between 1993 and 1998, according to Glewwe 2004b.)

In rich countries most household income comes from wages, but household income inequality and wage inequality do not have to move in the same direction. If there are changes in the way that people partner and combine into households, household inequality can rise even if wage inequality stays the same. Another point about wage inequality and household income inequality relevant to rich countries is that measures of wage inequality are often made before taxes are taken out of earnings. If the country has a strongly progressive income tax, inequality measures from household data (which are often made after taxes are taken out of earnings) do not have to follow pre-tax wage inequality. Tax policy can offset some of the trends in the labour market.

Finally, households can respond to increased wage inequality by investing more in their children's education. A higher economic return to education is not a bad thing, as long as there is equal access to education for all. Vietnam saw a tremendous increase in the secondary school enrolment rate in the 1990s – from 32 per cent in 1990–1 to 56 per cent in 1997–8 (Glewwe 2004a). This increase partly reflects society's and the government's investment in schools (supported by aid donors) and partly reflects households' decisions. If little or no return to education is perceived (that is, no jobs at the end of the road), it is much harder to convince families in poor countries to send their children to school. Where children have decent access to education, a higher skill premium stimulates a shift of the labour force from low-skill to higher-skill occupations.

It should also be noted that there has been a large decline in child labour in Vietnam since the country started integrating with the global market. There is ample evidence that child labor is driven primarily by poverty and educational opportunities. Child labour is more prevalent in poor households, but between 1993 and 1998 it declined for all income groups (figure 4.11). The change resulted from the fact that everyone was richer than they were five years earlier and from the expansion of schooling opportunities.

From this discussion of wage trends, it is easy to see why some labour unions in rich countries are concerned about integration with developing economies. It is difficult to prove that integration is increasing wage inequality, but it seems likely that integration is one factor. Concerning the immigration side of integration, Borjas et al. (1997) estimate that flows of unskilled labour into the United States have reduced wages for unskilled labour by 5 per cent from where they otherwise would be. Immigrants who find new jobs earn much more than they did before (ten times as much, according to World Bank 2002), but their competition reduces the wages of US

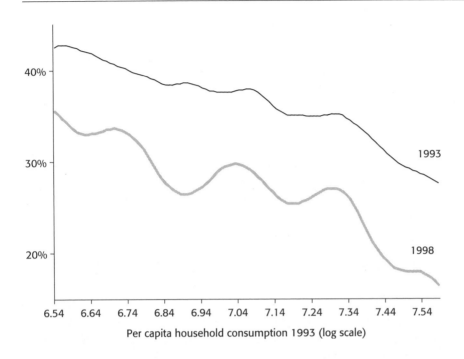

Figure 4.11   Child labour and household consumption levels in Vietnam, 1993 and 1998

Source: Edmonds (2001)

workers already doing such jobs. Similarly, imports of garments and footwear from countries such as Bangladesh and Vietnam create jobs for workers that pay far more than other opportunities in those countries but put pressure on unskilled wages in rich countries.

Thus overall the era of globalization has seen an unprecedented reduction of extreme poverty and a modest decline in global inequality. But it has put real pressure on less skilled workers in rich countries – a key reason why the growing integration is controversial in industrialized countries.

Is There a Link between Integration and Poverty Reduction?

To keep track of the wide range of explanations that are offered for persistent poverty in developing nations, it helps to keep two extreme views in mind. The first is based on an object gap: Nations are poor because they lack valuable objects like factories, roads, and raw materials. The second view invokes an idea gap: Nations are poor because their citizens do not have access to the ideas that are used in industrial nations to generate economic value . . .

> Each gap imparts a distinctive thrust to the analysis of development policy. The notion of an object gap highlights saving and accumulation. The notion of an idea gap directs attention to the patterns of inter-action and communication between a developing country and the rest of the world. (Romer 1993)

Developing economies have become more integrated with the global economy in the past two decades, and growth and poverty reduction have accelerated. A natural question is whether there is a link between the two. In other words, could countries such as Bangladesh, China, India and Vietnam have grown as rapidly if they had remained as closed to foreign trade and investment as they were in 1980? This cannot be answered with scientific certainty, but several different types of evidence can be brought to bear on it.

It is useful to begin with what to expect from economic theory. As the quote from Romer suggests, traditional growth theory focuses on accumulation and the 'object gap' between poor countries and rich ones. If increasing the number of factories and workplaces is the only important action, it does not matter whether the environment is closed or dominated by the state. This model was followed in the extreme by China and the Soviet Union, and to a lesser extent by most developing economies, which followed import-substituting industrial-ization strategies throughout the 1960s and 1970s. The disappointing results from this approach led to new thinking by policymakers in developing areas and economists studying growth. Romer was one of the pioneers of the new growth theory that emphasized how innov-ation occurs and is spread and the role of technological advances in improving the standard of living. Different aspects of integration – sending students abroad to study, connecting to the internet, allowing foreign firms to open plants, purchasing the latest equipment and components – can help overcome the 'idea gap' that separates poor countries from rich countries.

What is the evidence on integration spurring growth? Some of the most compelling evidence comes from case studies that show how this process can work in particular countries. Among the countries that were very poor in 1980, China, India, Uganda and Vietnam provide an interesting range of examples.

China

China's initial reforms in the late 1970s focused on the agricultural sector and emphasized strengthening property rights, liberalizing prices and creating internal markets. Liberalizing foreign trade and investment was also part of the initial reform programme and played an increasingly important role in growth as the 1980s proceeded (see figure 4.4 above). The role of international links is described in a case study by Eckaus (1997, pp. 415–37):

> China's foreign trade began to expand rapidly as the turmoil created by the Cultural Revolution dissipated and new leaders came to power. Though it was not done without controversy, the argument that opening of the economy to foreign trade was necessary to obtain new capital equipment and new technology was made official policy. . . . Most obviously, enterprises created by foreign investors have been exempt from the foreign trade planning and control mechanisms. In addition, substantial amounts of other types of trade, particularly the trade of the township and village enterprises and private firms, have been relatively free. The expansion of China's participation in international trade since the beginning of the reform movement in 1978, has been one of the most remarkable features of its remarkable transformation.

India

It is well known that India pursued an inward-oriented strategy into the 1980s with disappointing results in growth and poverty reduction. Bhagwati (1992, p. 48) crisply states the main problems and failures of the strategy:

> I would divide them into three major groups: extensive bureaucratic controls over production, investment and trade; inward-looking trade and foreign investment policies; and a substantial public sector, going well beyond the conventional confines of public utilities and infrastructure.

Under this policy regime India's growth in the 1960s (1.4 per cent a year) and 1970s (−0.3 per cent) was disappointing. During the 1980s India's economic performance improved, but this surge was fuelled by deficit spending and borrowing from abroad that was unsustainable. In fact, the spending spree led to a fiscal and balance of payments crisis that brought a new, reform government to power in 1991. Srinivasan (1996, p. 245) describes the key reform measures and their results:

> In July 1991, the government announced a series of far reaching reforms. These included an initial devaluation of the rupee and subsequent market determination of its exchange rate, abolition of import licensing with the important exceptions that the restrictions on imports of manufactured consumer goods and on foreign trade in agriculture remained in place, convertibility (with some notable exceptions) of the rupee on the current account; reduction in the number of tariff lines as well as tariff rates; reduction in excise duties on a number of commodities; some limited reforms of direct taxes; abolition of industrial licensing except for investment in a few industries for locational reasons or for environmental considerations, relaxation of

restrictions on large industrial houses under the Monopolies and Restrictive Trade Practices (MRTP) Act; easing of entry requirements (including equity participation) for direct foreign investment; and allowing private investment in some industries hitherto reserved for public sector investment.

In general, India has seen good results from its reform program, with per capita income growth above 4 per cent a year in the 1990s. Growth and poverty reduction have been particularly strong in states that have made the most progress liberalizing the regulatory framework and providing a good environment for delivery of infrastructure services (Goswami et al. 2002).

Uganda

Uganda has been one of the most successful reformers in Africa during this recent wave of globalization, and its experience has interesting parallels with Vietnam's. It, too, was a country that was quite isolated economically and politically in the early 1980s. The role of trade reform in its larger reform context is described in Collier and Reinikka (2001, pp. 30–9):

> Trade liberalization has been central to Uganda's structural reform program. . . . In 1986 the NRM government inherited a trade regime that included extensive non-tariff barriers, biased government purchasing, and high export taxes, coupled with considerable smuggling. The non-tariff barriers have gradually been removed since the introduction in 1991 of automatic licensing under an import certification scheme. Similarly, central government purchasing was reformed and is now subject to open tendering without a preference for domestic firms over imports. . . . The average real GDP growth rate was 6.3 percent per year during the entire recovery period (1986–99) and 6.9 percent in the 1990s. The liberalization of trade has had a marked effect on export performance. In the 1990s export volumes grew (at constant prices) at an annualized rate of 15 percent, and import volumes grew at 13 percent. The value of non-coffee exports increased fivefold between 1992 and 1999.

Vietnam

The same collection that contains Eckaus's (1997) study of China also has a case study of Vietnam, analysing how the country went from being one of the poorest countries in the 1980s to being one of the fastest growing economies in the 1990s (Dollar and Ljunggren 1997, pp. 452–5):

> That Vietnam was able to grow throughout its adjustment period can be attributed to the fact that the economy was being increasingly opened to the international market. As part of its overall effort to

stabilize the economy, the government unified its various controlled exchange rates in 1989 and devalued the unified rate to the level prevailing in the parallel market. This was tantamount to a 73 percent *real* devaluation; combined with relaxed administrative procedures for imports and exports, this sharply increased the profitability of exporting.

This . . . policy produced strong incentives for export throughout most of the 1989–94 period. During these years real export growth averaged more than 25 percent per annum, and exports were a leading sector spurring the expansion of the economy. Rice exports were a major part of this success in 1989; and in 1993–94 there was a wide range of exports on the rise, including processed primary products (e.g., rubber, cashews, and coffee), labor-intensive manufactures, and tourist services. . . . In response to stabilization, strengthened property rights, and greater openness to foreign trade, domestic savings increased by twenty percentage points of GDP, from negative levels in the mid-1980s to 16 percent of GDP in 1992.

Are these individual country findings generalizable?

These cases provide persuasive evidence that openness to foreign trade and investment – coupled with complementary reforms – can lead to faster growth in developing economies. But individual cases always beg the question, how general are these results? Does the typical developing economy that liberalizes foreign trade and investment get good results? Cross-country statistical analysis is useful for looking at the general patterns in the data. Cross-country studies generally find a correlation between trade and growth. To relate this to the discussion in the first section, some developing economies have had large increases in trade integration (measured as the ratio of trade to national income), and others have had small increases or even declines. In general, the countries that had large increases also had accelerations in growth. The group of developing economy globalizers identified by Dollar and Kraay (2004) had population-weighted per capita growth of 5 per cent in the 1990s, compared with 2 per cent in rich countries and −1 per cent for other developing countries (figure 4.12). This relationship between trade and growth persists after controlling for reverse causality from growth to trade and for changes in other institutions and policies (Dollar and Kraay 2003).

A third type of evidence about integration and growth comes from firm-level studies and relates to the quotation from Romer at the beginning of this section. Developing economies often have large productivity dispersion across firms making similar things: high-productivity and low-productivity firms coexist, and in small markets there is often insufficient competition to spur innovation. A consistent finding of firm-level studies is that openness leads to lower productivity dispersion

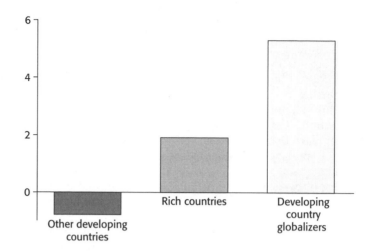

Figure 4.12   Per capita GDP growth rates, by country type, 1990s (%, based on GDP in PPP terms)

Source: Dollar and Kraay (2004)

(Haddad 1993; Haddad and Harrison 1993; Harrison 1994). High-cost producers exit the market as prices fall; if these firms were less productive or were experiencing falling productivity, their exits represent productivity improvements for the industry. Although the destruction and creation of new firms is a normal part of a well-functioning economy, attention is simply too often paid to the destruction of firms – which misses half the picture. The increase in exits is only part of the adjustment – granted, it is the first and most painful part – but if there are no significant barriers to entry, there are also new entrants. The exits are often front loaded, but the net gains over time can be substantial.

Wacziarg (1998) uses 11 episodes of trade liberalization in the 1980s to examine competition and entry. Using data on the number of establishments in each sector, he calculates that entry rates were 20 per cent higher in countries that liberalized than in countries that did not. This estimate may reflect other policies that accompanied trade liberalization, such as privatization and deregulation, so this is likely to be an upper bound of the impact of trade liberalization. However, it is a sizeable effect and indicates that there is plenty of potential for new firms to respond to the new incentives. The evidence also indicates that exit rates may be significant, but entry rates are usually of a comparable magnitude. Plant-level data from Chile, Colombia and Morocco, spanning several years in the 1980s when these countries initiated trade reforms, indicate that exit rates range from 6 per cent to 11 per cent a year and entry rates from 6 per cent to 13 per cent. Over time the cumulative turnover is quite impressive, with a quarter to a third of firms having turned over in four years (Roberts and Tybout 1996).

The higher turnover of firms is an important source of the dynamic benefit of openness. In general, dying firms have falling productivity and new firms tend to increase their productivity over time (Aw et al. 2000; Liu and Tybout 1996; Roberts and Tybout 1996). Aw et al. (2000) find that in Taiwan (China) within a five-year period the replacement of low-productivity firms with new, higher-productivity entrants accounted for half or more of the technological advances in many Taiwanese industries.

Although these studies shed some light on why open economies are more innovative and dynamic, they also show why integration is controversial. There will be more dislocation in an open, dynamic economy – with some firms closing and others starting up. If workers have good social protection and opportunities to develop new skills, everyone can benefit; without these policies there can be some big losers.

Surveys of the literature on openness and growth generally find the totality of the evidence persuasive. Winters (2004, p. F4), for example, concludes: 'While there are serious methodological challenges and disagreements about the strength of the evidence, the most plausible conclusion is that liberalisation generally induces a temporary (but possibly long-lived) increase in growth. A major component of this is an increase in productivity.' Similarly, economic historians Lindert and Williamson (2001, pp. 29–30) sum up the different pieces of evidence linking integration to growth: 'The doubts that one can retain about each individual study threaten to block our view of the overall forest of evidence. Even though no one study can establish that openness to trade has unambiguously helped the representative Third World economy, the preponderance of evidence supports this conclusion.' They go on to note the 'empty set' of 'countries that chose to be less open to trade and factor flows in the 1990s than in the 1960s and rose in the global living-standard ranks at the same time. As far as we can tell, there are no anti-global victories to report for the postwar Third World. We infer that this is because freer trade stimulates growth in Third World economies today, regardless of its effects before 1940.'

Making Globalization Work Better for Poor People

So far, the most recent wave of globalization starting around 1980 has been associated with more rapid growth and poverty reduction in developing economies and with a modest decline in global inequality. These empirical findings from a wide range of studies help explain what otherwise might appear paradoxical: opinion surveys reveal that globalization is more popular in poor countries than in rich ones. In particular, the Pew Research Center for the People and the Press (2003) surveyed 38,000 people in 44 countries in all developing regions. In general, there was a positive view of growing economic integration worldwide. But what was striking in the survey was that views of globalization were distinctly more positive in low-income countries than in rich ones.

Although most people expressed the view that growing global trade and business ties are good for their country, only 28 per cent of people in the United States and Western Europe thought that such integration was 'very good'. By contrast, the share who thought integration was very good was 64 per cent in Uganda and 56 per cent in Vietnam. These countries stood out as particularly pro-globalization, but respondents from developing economies in Asia (37 per cent) and Sub-Saharan Africa (56 per cent) were also far more likely to find integration 'very good' than respondents from rich countries. Conversely, a significant minority (27 per cent) in rich countries thought that 'globalization has a bad effect' on their country, compared with a negligible number of households in developing economies in Asia (9 per cent) or Sub-Saharan Africa (10 per cent).

Developing economies also had a more positive view of the institutions of globalization. Some 75 per cent of households in Sub-Saharan Africa thought that multinational corporations had a positive influence on their country, compared with only 54 per cent in rich countries. Views of the effect of the International Monetary Fund, the World Bank, and the World Trade Organization (WTO) were nearly as positive in Africa (72 per cent of households said these organizations had a positive effect on their country). By contrast, only 28 per cent of households in Africa thought that anti-globalization protestors had a positive effect on their country. Views of the protestors were more positive in the United States and Western Europe (35 per cent said the protestors had a positive effect on their country).

Although global economic integration has the potential to spur further growth and poverty reduction, whether this potential is realized depends on the policies of developing economies and the policies of industrialized countries. True integration requires not just trade liberalization but also wide-ranging reforms of institutions and policies, as the cases of China and India illustrate so clearly. Many of the countries that are not participating very much in globalization have serious problems with the overall investment climate, for example, Kenya, Myanmar, Nigeria and Pakistan. Some of these countries also have restrictive policies towards trade. But even if they liberalize trade, not much is likely to happen without other measures. It is not easy to predict the reform paths of these countries. (Consider the relative successes cited here: China, India, Uganda, Vietnam. In each case their reform was a startling surprise.) As long as there are locations with weak institutions and policies, people living there are going to fall further behind the rest of the world in terms of living standards.

Building a coalition for reform in these locations is not easy, and what outsiders can do to help is limited. But one thing that industrialized countries can do is make it easy for developing areas that do choose to open up to join the club of trading nations. Unfortunately, in recent years rich countries have made it harder for poor countries to do so. The General Agreement on Tariffs and Trade was originally built around agreements concerning trade practices. Now, however, a certain degree of institutional harmonization is required to join the WTO, for example, on policies towards intellectual property rights. The proposal to regulate labour standards and environmental standards through WTO sanctions would take this requirement for institutional harmonization much further. Developing economies see the proposal to regulate their labour and environmental standards through WTO sanctions as a new protectionist tool that rich countries can wield against them.

Globalization will proceed more smoothly if industrialized countries make it easy for developing economies to have access to their markets. Reciprocal trade liberalizations have worked well throughout the postwar period. There still are significant protections in OECD countries against agricultural and labour-intensive products that are important to developing economies. It would help substantially to reduce these protections. At the same time, developing economies would benefit from opening their own markets further. They have a lot to gain from more trade in services. Also, 70 per cent of the tariff barriers that developing areas face are from other developing economies. So there is much potential to expand trade among developing areas, if trade restrictions are further eased. But the trend to use trade agreements to impose an institutional model from OECD countries on developing economies makes it more difficult to reach trade agreements that benefit poor countries. The current Doha round of WTO negotiations is taking up these issues of market access, but it remains to be seen whether rich countries are willing to significantly reduce their trade barriers in agriculture and labour-intensive manufactures.

Another reason to be pessimistic about further integration of poor economies and rich ones is geography. There is no inherent reason why coastal China should be poor – or southern India, or Vietnam, or northern Mexico. These locations were historically held back by misguided policies, and with policy reform they can grow very rapidly and take their natural place in the world income distribution. However, the same reforms are not going to have the same effect in Chad and Mali. Some countries have poor geography in the sense that they are far from markets and have inherently high transport costs. Other locations face challenging health and agricultural problems. So, it would be naive to think that trade and investment can alleviate poverty in all locations. Much more could be done with foreign aid targeted to developing medicines for malaria, HIV/AIDS, and other health problems in poor areas and to building infrastructure and institutions in these locations. The promises of greater aid from Europe and the United States at the Monterrey Conference were encouraging, but it remains to be seen if these promises will be fulfilled.

So integration of poor economies with rich ones has provided many opportunities for poor people to improve their lives. Examples of the beneficiaries of globalization can be found among Chinese factory workers, Mexican migrants, Ugandan farmers and Vietnamese peasants. Lots of non-poor people in developing and industrialized economies alike also benefit, of course. But much of the current debate about globalization seems to ignore the fact that it has provided many poor people in developing economies with unprecedented opportunities. After all the rhetoric about globalization is stripped away, many of the practical policy questions come down to whether rich countries are going to make it easy or difficult for poor communities that want to integrate with the world economy. The world's poor people have a large stake in how rich countries answer these questions.

Notes

This chapter first appeared as an article in *World Bank Research Observer*, vol. 20, 2005, pp. 1–31. It is reprinted here with permission from OUP Journals.

1   The phrase *free trade* refers to a situation in which trade is not monopolized by the government, but rather is permitted to private firms and citizens as well – so China began to shift to a policy of free trade in 1979.
2   It is difficult to obtain survey-based estimates of poverty before 1980. Bourguignon and Morrisson (2002) combine what survey data are available with national accounts data to provide rough estimates of poverty since 1820. The broad trend is clear: the number of poor people in the world kept rising until about 1980.
3   Bhalla (2002) and Sala-i-Martin (2002) also estimate very large reductions in global poverty based on the national accounts data, but Deaton (2004) makes a convincing case that the survey-based estimates from Chen and Ravallion (2004) are a more reliable indicator of changes in global poverty.
4   Milanovic (2002) estimates an increase in the global Gini coefficient for the short period between 1988 and 1993. How can this be reconciled with the Bhalla (2002) and Sala-i-Martin (2002) findings? Global inequality has declined

over the past two decades primarily because poor people in China and India have seen increases in their incomes relative to incomes of rich people (that is, OECD populations). As noted, 1988–93 was the one period in the past 20 years that was not good for poor people in China and India. India had a serious crisis and recession, and rural income growth in China was temporarily slowed.

References

Aw, B. Y., Chung, S. and Roberts, M. J. 2000. 'Productivity and the Decision to Export: Micro Evidence from Taiwan and South Korea.' *World Bank Economic Review*, 14 (1): 65–90.

Benjamin, D. and Brandt, L. 2002. 'Agriculture and Income Distribution in Rural Vietnam under Economic Reforms: A Tale of Two Regions.' William Davidson Institute Working Paper, no. 519. Available at SSRN: http//ssrn.com/abstract= 373603.

Bhagwati, J. 1992. *India's Economy: The Shackled Giant*. Oxford: Clarendon Press.

Bhalla, S. 2002. *Imagine There's No Country: Poverty, Inequality, and Growth in the Era of Globalization*. Washington, DC: Institute for International Economics.

Borjas, G. J., Freeman, R. B. and Katz, L. F. 1997. 'How Much Do Immigration and Trade Affect Labor Market Outcomes?' *Brookings Papers on Economic Activity*, 1: 1–90.

Bourguignon, F. and Morrisson, C. 2002. 'Inequality Among World Citizens: 1820–1992.' *American Economic Review*, 92 (4): 727–44.

Center for International Comparisons 2004. *Penn World Tables*. Philadelphia: University of Pennsylvania.

Chen, S., and Ravallion, M. 2004. 'How Have the World's Poorest Fared since the Early 1980s?' Policy Research Working Paper, no. 3341. Washington, DC: World Bank.

Clark, X., Dollar, D. and Micco, A. 2004. 'Port Efficiency, Maritime Transport Costs, and Bilateral Trade.' *Journal of Development Economics*, 75 (2): 417–50.

Collier, P. and Reinikka, R. 2001. 'Reconstruction and Liberalization: An Overview.' In *Uganda's Recovery: The Role of Farms, Firms, and Government*. Washington, DC: World Bank, Regional and Sectoral Studies.

Crafts, N. 2000. 'Globalization and Growth in the Twentieth Century.' Working Paper 00/44. Washington, DC: International Monetary Fund.

Deaton, A. 2004. 'Measuring Poverty in a Growing World (or Measuring Growth in a Poor World).' Princeton, NJ: Princeton University, Woodrow Wilson School of Public and International Affairs.

Dollar, D. and Kraay, A. 2002. 'Growth is Good for the Poor.' *Journal of Economic Growth*, 7 (3): 195–225.

Dollar, D. and Kraay, A. 2003. 'Institutions, Trade, and Growth.' *Journal of Monetary Economics*, 50 (1): 133–62.

Dollar, D. and Kraay, A. 2004. 'Trade, Growth, and Poverty.' *Economic Journal*, 114 (493): F22–F49.

Dollar, D. and Ljunggren, B. 1997. 'Going Global: Vietnam.' In Padma Desai (ed.), *Going Global: Transition from Plan to Market in the World Economy*. Cambridge, Mass.: MIT Press.

Eckaus, R. 1997. 'Going Global: China.' In Padma Desai (ed.), *Going Global:*

Transition from Plan to Market in the World Economy. Cambridge, Mass.: MIT Press.

Edmonds, E. 2001. 'Will Child Labor Decline with Improvements in Living Standards?' Working Paper 01-9. Hanover, NH: Dartmouth College, Department of Economics.

Freeman, R., Oostendorp, R. and Rama, M. 2001. 'Globalization and Wages.' Washington, DC: World Bank.

Galbraith, J. and Liu, L. 2001. 'Measuring the Evolution of Inequality in the Global Economy.' In James Galbraith and Maureen Berner (eds), *Inequality and Industrial Change: A Global View.* New York: Cambridge University Press.

Glewwe, P. 2004a. 'An Investigation of the Determinants of School Progress and Academic Achievement in Vietnam.' In David Dollar, Paul Glewwe and Nisha Agrawal (eds), *Economic Growth, Poverty, and Household Welfare in Vietnam.* Washington, DC: World Bank.

Glewwe, P. 2004b. 'An Overview of Economic Growth and Household Welfare in Vietnam in the 1990s.' In Paul Glewwe, Nisha Agrawal and David Dollar (eds), *Economic Growth, Poverty, and Household Welfare in Vietnam.* Washington, DC: World Bank.

Glewwe, P., Agrawal, N. and Dollar, D. (eds) 2004. *Economic Growth, Poverty, and Household Welfare in Vietnam.* Washington, DC: World Bank.

Goswami, O., Arun, A. K., Gantakolla, S. et al. 2002. 'Competitiveness of Indian Manufacturing: Results from a Firm-Level Survey.' Research report by Confederation of Indian Industry and World Bank, Washington, DC.

Haddad, M. 1993. 'The Link between Trade Liberalization and Multi-Factor Productivity: The Case of Morocco.' Discussion Paper, no. 4. Washington, DC: World Bank.

Haddad, M. and Harrison, A. 1993. 'Are There Spillovers from Direct Foreign Investment? Evidence from Panel Data for Morocco.' *Journal of Development Economics*, 42 (1): 51–74.

Harrison, A. 1994. 'Productivity, Imperfect Competition, and Trade Reform.' *Journal of International Economics*, 36 (1–2): 53–73.

Lindert, P. and Williamson, J. 2001. 'Does Globalization Make the World More Unequal?' NBER Working Paper, no. 8228. Cambridge, Mass: National Bureau of Economic Research.

Liu, L. and Tybout, J. 1996. 'Productivity Growth in Chile and Columbia: The Role of Entry, Exit, and Learning.' In M. Roberts and J. Tybout (eds), *Industrial Evolution in Developing Countries.* Oxford: Oxford University Press.

Maddison, A. 1995. *Monitoring the World Economy 1820–1992.* Paris: OECD, Development Centre Studies.

Mazur, J. 2000. 'Labor's New Internationalism.' *Foreign Affairs*, 79 (1): 79–93.

Milanovic, B. 2002. 'True World Income Distribution, 1988 and 1993: First Calculation Based on Household Surveys Alone.' *Economic Journal*, 112 (476): 51–92.

Oostendorp, R. 2002. 'Does Globalization Reduce the Gender Wage Gap?' Amsterdam: Free University, Economic and Social Institute.

Pew Research Center for the People and the Press 2003. *Views of a Changing World: June 2003.* Second Major Report of the Pew Global Attitudes Project. Washington, DC.

Roberts, M. and Tybout, J. 1996. *Industrial Evolution in Developing Countries: Micro*

Patterns of Turnover, Productivity and Market Structure. New York: Oxford University Press.

Romer, P. 1993. 'Idea Gaps and Object Gaps in Economic Development.' *Journal of Monetary Economics*, 32 (3): 543–73.

Sala-i-Martin, X. 2002. 'The Disturbing "Rise" of Global Income Inequality.' New York: Columbia University.

Smeeding, T. M. 2002. 'Globalization, Inequality and the Rich Countries of the G-20: Updated Results from the Luxembourg Income Study (LIS) and Other Places.' Prepared for the G-20 Meeting, Globalization, Living Standards and Inequality: Recent Progress and Continuing Challenges, 26–8 May, Sydney, Australia.

Srinivasan, T. N. 1996. 'Indian Economic Reforms: Background, Rationale, Achievements, and Future Prospects.' New Haven, Conn.: Yale University, Department of Economics.

Wacziarg, R. 1998. 'Measuring Dynamic Gains from Trade.' Policy Research Working Paper, no. 2001. Washington, DC: World Bank.

Williamson, J. G. 2004. *The Political Economy of World Mass Migration*. Washington, DC: American Enterprise Institute Press.

Winters, L. A. 2004. 'Trade Liberalisation and Economic Performance: An Overview.' *Economic Journal*, 114 (493): F4–F21.

World Bank. 2002. *Globalization, Growth, and Poverty: Building an Inclusive World Economy*. Policy Research Report. Washington DC and New York: World Bank and Oxford University Press.

5

Should We Worry about Income Inequality?

Robert H. Wade

T‍HE liberal approach to economic policy, which has dominated policy thinking in developed and developing countries for the past 25 years, claims that income inequality is not something to worry about. 'Don't mind the gap' is its motto. Until the 1970s micro-economists even claimed that distribution and efficiency should be considered quite separately; and avowed that the economist should 'stick to his last' and recommend policies which increase efficiency regardless of the distributive effects, provided that the gainers could *potentially* compensate the losers. That separation has more recently been questioned by academic economists, but it retains its potency in wider liberal circles.[1] And liberals (in the European, not American sense) still emphasize that inequality is, first, an inevitable consequence of private property rights, and second, a necessary condition for effort, risk taking and entrepreneurship, and thereby for efficiency, innovation, competitiveness and panache. Reduce inequality through, for example, progressive taxation and a shift from private goods to public goods and you reduce innovation and growth – and make everyone worse off. Liberals therefore tend to dismiss questions about the growing gap between rich and poor as 'the politics of envy'. Public policy, they say, should not worry about income inequality as long as it results from 'fair' market processes, including fair access to opportunities to earn income; and as long as it does not reach the point where popular resentment of great gaps threatens the liberal order.

What matters is not income inequality as such but inequality of *opportunities* for earning income. Public policy should try to 'even up' opportunities, so that one's country of birth, or class, or gender counts for less in determining one's wealth, health and privileges. Free markets are in general good for evening up opportunities, so free markets and equity are complements. On the other hand, inequalities of income not due to 'pre-determined' characteristics are presumed to be the result of differences in effort and talent or just plain luck, and here the moral case for more equality falls away.

The exception is at the bottom. Just about everyone agrees that reducing extreme poverty should be a high priority for international and national action. Jeffrey Sachs' *The End of Poverty* (2005) shows that only very small amounts of additional resources – amounting to only a few US dollars or so per year per person in the West – could make a dramatic cut in the number of people in the world living on less than $1 or $2 a day. And just about everyone can agree that reducing inequality in life expectancy should be a high priority, for there is something compellingly unjust about a world in which one quarter of the world's population living in low-income countries (excluding China and India) has a life expectancy at birth of around 55 years and the one sixth of the world's population living in high-income countries has more than 20 years longer. But reducing *income* inequality not due to predetermined characteristics is apparently another story.

As applied to developing countries, the liberal policy reform agenda is known as the 'Washington Consensus' – a set of mainly microeconomic policy reforms to do with making markets work better ('getting the prices right'), including strengthening property rights, liberalizing domestic markets, privatizing state-owned enterprises and opening the economy to free trade and investment. The Consensus was augmented in the 1990s by reforms of certain institutions ('getting the institutions right'), especially to make the judiciary more rule bound, the civil service less corrupt and the government more responsive and accountable; plus more emphasis on state responsibility for the supply of certain public goods, including primary health and education ('social sectors').[2] In the context of middle-income countries, the Augmented Washington Consensus supports a strong push towards the 'financialization' of the economy: stock markets are to be the institutional pivot of the economy, company performance is to be judged primarily by return on capital, corporate law should facilitate hostile takeovers, pension systems should move from the principle of taxation-financed 'defined benefit' towards individual 'defined contribution' retirement accounts invested in stock-market portfolios, and collective bargaining and other labour market 'rigidities' should be removed.[3] These reforms raise the share of capital income relative to labour income, which is regarded as a good thing; a higher share for capital income makes for more investment and so for more employment.

The Augmented Washington Consensus leaves the economic core of the Washington Consensus untouched, focused on microeconomic market liberalization, free trade and privatization. This agenda has come to be accepted as so universally valid that the word 'reform' is used exclusively for policy changes in this direction. Other changes (higher protection as part of an industrial strategy, for example) are described as 'deviant', not as 'reform'.

To quote Martin Wolf of the *Financial Times*, 'What the successful countries all share is a move towards the market economy, one in which private property rights, free enterprise and competition increasingly took the place of state ownership, planning and protection. They chose, however haltingly, the path of economic liberalization and international integration. This is the heart of the matter. All else is commentary' (Wolf 2004, pp. 143–4).

The consensus is forged in the echo chamber of the Washington-based organizations, including the World Bank, the IMF, the US Treasury,[4] USAID and assorted think tanks; amplified through transatlantic components including the *Financial Times*, the *Economist*, the UK Treasury; and bandwagoned into finance and development ministries in many developing countries.

In this 'climate of opinion' arguments and evidence consistent with liberalism are accepted at face value, with little critical scrutiny. Protracted recession in Japan? Obviously due to labour market rigidities, excessive regulation of industry, and high non-performing loans (NPLs) in the banking system. Chronic unemployment in Germany? Must be due to labour market rigidities. Is executive pay in the United States too high in relation to average pay? No, because optimal-contracting theory shows how high pay helps to align the interests of managers with those of the owners, overcoming the 'principal-agent problem' that bedevils the relationship between shareholders and managers. If trade liberalization worsens the current account deficit of developing countries it must be because governments are blocking the natural adjustment of the exchange rate, which would ensure that an increase in imports due to trade liberalization is offset by an increase in exports. Governments should get out of the way.

Alternative hypotheses are given much less attention. Chronic unemployment in Germany may be due to 'excessively contractionary macroeconomic policy'. In Japan, 'excessive regulation of industry' and 'high NPLs' should be confronted with the argument that high tech, telecoms and other growth industries are not obstructed by regulation, that regulation in old economy industries is needed to prevent hidden underemployment becoming overt unemployment, and that insufficient bank lending is due less to NPLs than to macroeconomically induced unwillingness to borrow. In the US, 'present levels of executive pay are justified by optimal-contracting theory' should be weighed against 'executives inflate their pay beyond any contribution to efficiency and dividends thanks to their power to influence the board members who set their pay.' And in developing countries, the trade deficit may worsen after trade liberalization – and national income may shrink in the absence of aid or other capital inflows – because supply and demand inelasticities for exports make them unresponsive to exchange rate changes.

Inside the World Bank, the researcher who finds empirical evidence that confirms standard liberal prescriptions can send his paper off to the editorial office of the *Economist* with the approval only of his head of division, whereas the one who finds evidence not consistent with standard liberal prescriptions has to send the paper through rounds of 'internal reviews'. Should it survive, approval for outside release has to come from much higher up the hierarchy and may be delayed by months or even years. The signal to researchers is clear: you get ahead by going along, and you go along by finding just enough evidence to justify liberal conclusions. The criterion is 'Can I believe this (a liberal conclusion)?', not 'Must I believe this?'

This is faith-based social science. It smacks of the spirit of the George W. Bush White House, as articulated by a person identified by *New York Times* journalist Ron Suskind as 'a senior advisor to Bush'. The advisor told Suskind that people like him (Suskind) were 'in what we call the reality-based community', which he defined as people who 'believe that solutions emerge from your judicious study of discernible reality'. The advisor continued, 'That's not the way the world really works anymore. We're an empire now, and when we act, we create our own reality. And while you're studying that reality – judiciously, as you will – we'll act again, creating other new realities, which you can study too, and that's how things will sort out' (Suskind 2004).

I shall assess the liberal claims using reality-based methods. First, I examine the argument that a liberal policy regime is good for economic growth and development, good for poverty reduction and good for keeping a lid on income inequality. Here I treat inequality as a 'dependent' variable. If the liberal argument holds up, there is not much of a case for public policy measures targeted at lowering inequality per se, for inequality will be contained by 'the market' provided we stick to the liberal agenda. Second, I examine the evidence on the impacts of income inequality on other variables, treating inequality as an 'independent' variable. If inequality has no significant bad effects on other variables, there is again not much of a case for public policy measures designed to reduce inequality. Third, I examine the liberal theory of capitalist politics and economics, and consider how adequately it deals with what we observe as central tendencies in the role of advanced capitalist states.

The Liberal Argument on Growth, Poverty and Inequality

Let us distinguish two periods: the first is the era of 'managed capitalism', including 'Rhine capitalism', 'Japanese capitalism' and 'import-substituting industrialization' in developing countries, and ran from roughly 1960 to 1979; the second is the era of 'globalization' and 'liberal' policies worldwide, from 1980 to the present. If the liberal argument about the benefits of a liberal policy regime is true, we expect an improvement in world economic growth between the first and second periods. We also expect a fall in the number of poor people in the world, or at least a fall in the proportion of poor. Thirdly, we expect a fall in income inequality between countries and between the world's individuals or households.[5]

These expectations are well confirmed by the evidence, say the liberal champions. For example, the World Bank said in 2002, 'The number of people subsisting on less than $1 per day rose steadily for nearly two centuries, but in the past 20 years it has . . . fallen by as much as 200 million, even as the world's population has risen by about 1.6 billion' (World Bank 2002). Since the number of people in extreme poverty is moving in the right direction – and also the other big outcomes, including economic growth and income inequality – we can conclude that the world system in its current liberal configuration meets a 'fairness' test. Martin Wolf makes the causality clear: 'economic integration, where successful, has reduced poverty and global inequality, not increased it. The tragedy is that there has been too little successful economic integration, not too much' (Wolf 2001).

The liberal argument carries prophetic clout: provided we hold steady to the central thrust towards free markets, private property and lower taxes, extreme poverty will be eliminated, income gaps between countries will 'level up', and income gaps within countries will also level up as the poor become better off. The proviso is important. National governments and GEMS (global economic multilaterals, including the World Bank, IMF, WTO) must press ahead with the liberal-globalization or Washington Consensus agenda, against the forces of special interests and anti-Enlightenment NGOs. As Wolf puts it,

> The failure of our world is not that there is too much globalization, but that there is too little. *The potential for greater economic integration has barely been tapped.* We need more global markets, not fewer, if we want to raise the living standards of the poor of the world. Social democrats, classical liberals and democratic conservatives should unite to preserve and improve the liberal global economy against *the enemies mustering both outside and inside the gates.* (2004, p. 4, emphasis added)

Elsewhere Wolf reaches even further, accusing the 'anti-globalists' of preaching 'the big lie', a phrase usually reserved for a favourite Nazi propaganda technique.

In liberal eyes, Sub-Saharan Africa is a special case which has not shared in the general lifting of boats. Special efforts are needed to supplement the liberal-globalization agenda with more aid, debt forgiveness and public health interventions.

Trends and Causes

Growth

Has the worldwide shift towards free markets in the past 25 years been associated with an increase in the rate of world economic growth? No. We have seen a dramatic growth slowdown in both developed and developing countries.

Between 1960–78, the era of managed capitalism, and 1979–2000, the era of globalization, the world economic growth rate per capita fell by almost half, from 2.7 per cent to 1.5 per cent (Milanovic 2005).[6] Indeed, in every decade since 1960 the average world GDP per capita growth rate fell. For OECD countries the median fell from 3.5 per cent in 1965–79 to 1.8 per cent in 1980–98; and for developing countries it fell from 2.4 per cent to 0.0! (Easterly 2001)[7] Many more countries experienced negative growth in the second period than in the first, and longer, deeper and more frequent recessions.

In the case of Latin America, real per capita income grew by 80 per cent in the 19 years from 1960 to 1979, during the era of 'bad' import-substituting industrialization; in the 24 years from 1980 to 2004, during the era of 'good' liberal policies, real per capita income grew by just 12 per cent. For the past 25 years Latin America has had trouble staying on the right side of zero growth; between 1980 and 2002 average per capita GDP growth in Latin America (in 1995 US dollars) averaged just 0.2 per cent. Indeed, all regions except (non-Japan) Asia had a slowdown in growth rates between the era of managed capitalism and the era of globalization. Liberal champions tend to ignore these awkward facts. Wolf, for instance, presents a table (8.1) that shows the growth slowdown in all regions except Asia, but makes no comment on its implications (Wolf 2004, table 8.1).

Poverty

Has the number of people living in extreme poverty (less than PPP$1 per day) fallen substantially in the past 25 years, reversing the long-term trend? Taking World Bank numbers at face value, the answer is 'Yes, the number fell from 1.5 billion in 1981 to 1.1 billion in 2001, or from 33 per cent of the world population to 18 per cent.' But the fall depends entirely on China. Remove China and the number rises between 1981 and 2001 (Chen and Ravallion 2004). Use the slightly more generous PPP$2 a day as the international poverty line and the total number of people in poverty *increased* from 2.4 billion in 1981 to 2.7 billion in 2001. However, this increase in numbers still amounted to a fall in the proportion of world population living on less than PPP$2 per day, from 53 per cent to 44 per cent, which is a remarkable achievement.

These are two big qualifications to the standard liberal claim about poverty trends, taking the World Bank's figures at face value. A third qualification is that the World Bank poverty numbers are of very uncertain reliability, but the World Bank virtually never acknowledges the wide margins of error.[8] And it is quite likely – though this is a weaker conclusion than the one about margins of error – that they bias the poverty headcount downwards. The international extreme or absolute poverty line of $1 per day is rather arbitrary, not closely related to the consumption or expenditure or income needed to avoid extreme poverty, not closely related to calorific or demographic characteristics. We have no way of knowing what proportion of food-clothing-shelter needs the World Bank's international poverty line captures. But we can be fairly sure that if the World Bank had used a 'basic needs' poverty line rather than its present artificial one the number of absolute poor would rise, because the national poverty lines equivalent to a global basic needs poverty line would rise (perhaps by 30–40 per cent). A 30–40 per cent increase in a basic-needs-based international poverty line would increase the world total of people in extreme poverty by at least 30–40 per cent. A recent study for Latin America by the UN's Economic Commission for Latin America shows that national extreme poverty rates, using poverty lines based on calorific and demographic characteristics, are commonly more than *twice* as high as those based on the World Bank's $1 a day line (Economic Commission for Latin America 2001, p. 51; see also Reddy and Pogge 2003). The $2-a-day line is based on nothing more than a doubling of the extreme poverty line. What could be a more arbitrary standard?

Inequality

Income inequality between countries or 'international income inequality' (using per capita income measured in PPP$, population weights, and the Gini coefficient), increased through the 1960s and 1970s and then started to fall in the 1980s and continued to fall thereafter. This seems to confirm the liberal argument.

Except that, as with the fall in the world extreme poverty headcount, the result depends entirely on China. If China is excluded, inequality between countries – even by this measure, the one most favourable for the liberal argument – increased after 1980. One cannot then say that world income distribution has become more equal thanks to a general process called globalization or economic integration or liberalization. Increased equality between population-weighted country incomes is the result of one – massive – case, not a general trend.

Moreover, other plausible measures show a clear trend towards rising inequality. For example, the income of the top ninetieth percentile over that of the bottom tenth percentile, and regional per capita income over the OECD average, both show increasing gaps. The average income per head of the South (in PPP$) has fallen as a percentage of the North ever since 1950, with a levelling off in the 1990s. Latin America's percentage has fallen precipitously since 1980; also Sub-Saharan Africa's, Eastern Europe's and Central Asia's. East Asia is the exception: its percentage has risen since 1980, driven mainly by China (see figure 5.1). Also, inequality has clearly increased – using the Gini coefficient or other average over the whole distribution, and population weights – if national incomes are commensurated at market exchange rates. Economists tend to say that incomes should always be converted at the PPP exchange rate, which reduces the magnitude of inequality (see table 5.1); but this ignores the point that incomes at market exchange rates are a better measure of the ability of one nation to purchase goods and services produced elsewhere, and that PPP conversions are subject to huge margins of error (Korzeniewicz et al. 2004).

When data on income distribution between countries is combined with data on distribution within countries we get 'global income distribution', or the distribution between all the world's individuals or households. Here the big story is that 50–60 per cent of world economic growth over the 1990s – more than half the increase in world income or consumption – accrued to individuals living on more than PPP$10,000 a year, most of them in the top half of the rich countries' income distribution; that is, to roughly 8 per cent of the world's population. Most of the other half accrued to the burgeoning middle class of China, living on around PPP$3,000–5,000 a year. The Indian middle class, by contrast, benefited very little in terms of its share of world economic growth. Hardly any of the additional world consumption accrued to people – wherever they lived – on less than about $1,000 a year.

The top few percentiles of the income distribution in the high-income states have benefited from a sharp swing in income distribution from labour income to capital income. For the OECD countries as a group, the share of labour remuneration in business revenue hovered around 70 per cent for decades after the Second World War, increased to around 72 per cent by 1980, and then – with Reagan and Thatcher forcing the rollback – fell steadily to about 64 per cent today. On the other hand, the share of profits went up by 8 percentage points between 1980 and 2003, a very satisfactory result for shareholders (Bennhold 2005). In the US the share of household income accruing to the top 0.01 per cent of households fell from roughly 3 per cent in 1929 to 0.5 per cent by the early 1970s, flattened out,

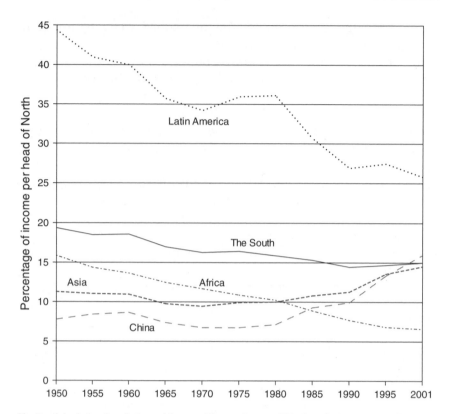

The South includes the whole world except Western Europe, USA, Canada, Japan, Australia, New Zealand. It includes Eastern Europe. (If Eastern Europe and the Former Soviet Union are excluded, the line for the South remains much the same, except that it is a couple of percentage points less in 1950, falls less after that and rises to about the same as shown.) Asia includes everywhere east of Turkey, except Russia and Japan; specifically, it includes China. The separate line for China shows China's influence on the Asia line.

The figures are weighted in the sense that they are calculated as total GDP/total population of the South (or other group) as a percentage of total GDP/total population of the North.

The South goes down to begin with because all its elements go down. Asia starts rising in 1980 but the rest continue to go down, so the South as a whole levels off. Then in the 1990s Asia starts pulling the South average up slightly, though all its other components continue to go down, some of them (Eastern Europe, USSR and Africa) faster than ever. With India now in the growth club and the Russia/Eastern Europe area growing again the South line will probably rise noticeably in 2000 to 2005. I thank Bob Sutcliffe for discussions.

Figure 5.1   Income per head as percentage of North

Sources: Sutcliffe (2004), Maddison (2003)

then – with globalization – shot back up to reach 3 per cent by the early 2000s (Dumenil and Levy 2004). A very satisfactory result for the top 0.01 per cent. Most of the increase in US income inequality cannot be attributed to a rising skill premium (the 'automatic' result of rising supply shortages); most of it results from the institutions that structure markets, which are concentrating a rising share of

Table 5.1 The poverty pyramid below the European Union		
Region/country	**Relative average income at market exchange rates**	**Relative average income at PPP$**
EU 15	100	100
8 new member states	22	46
Turkey	10	24
Russia	8	29
Ukraine, Belarus, Moldova	3	20
Caucasus	3	12
Central Asia	3	14
Magreb	6	17
Middle East[a]	12	28
Sub-Saharan Africa	2	7

[a] Middle East includes Iran, Saudi Arabia, Yemen (others no data).

Source: World Bank (2003)

profits and value-added in the hands of the owners of capital and the topmost corporate executives.

One other point: our normal measures of inequality are misleading because they measure only relative income, not absolute income gaps. Take two countries: A with per capita income of $10,000, and B with per capita income of $1,000. Their relative income is 10:1 and the absolute gap is $9,000. If A's per capita income doubles to $20,000 the degree of income inequality remains constant provided B's increases to $2,000. In which case we conclude that income inequality has *not* become more unequal. But the absolute gap widens from $9,000 to $18,000. No one questions that world absolute income gaps have been increasing fast – as between, for example, the average income of the top 20 per cent of world income recipients and that of the bottom 20 per cent, and also between the top 20 per cent and the intermediate 60 per cent. If, as is likely, people respond not only to relative income trends but also to trends in absolute gaps – those at the lower end feel more marginalized as absolute gaps increase even if relative incomes become more equal – our answer to the question, 'What is happening to income inequality?' should not be blind to absolute gaps.

In short, plausible measures suggest that (relative) income inequality on a world scale has not fallen. Other measures which do indicate a fall get this result thanks to one case, China. In any case, single index numbers like the Gini coefficient are misleading, because they obscure where in the distribution changes are taking place, or who is getting richer and who is not. Evidence on the distribution of the benefits of world economic growth over the 1990s suggests that the growth has accrued largely to the richer half of the population of the high-income countries and to the emerging middle class of China.[9] Absolute income gaps between North America, Europe and Japan, on the one hand, and most of the rest of the world, on the other, have been widening fast.

All this is bad news for the argument that the worldwide shift towards liberal policies over the past quarter century has generated higher economic growth, lower poverty and lower world income inequality. Quite a lot of evidence suggests that the opposite is closer to the truth. Without China, the impact of globalization and liberalization on poverty and income distribution would look dismal. But China has got richer with a form of state-led capitalism very different from that enjoined by the liberal argument. Its big falls in poverty had little to do with China's integration into the world economy; they occurred in response to the decollectivization of agriculture in the 1980s and again in response to the increase in government procurement prices for foodgrains in the 1990s (though of course China's fast growth was enabled to continue by rapid trade expansion). So if we are concerned to see better performance on poverty and inequality on a world scale, we should not place high confidence in the liberal policy agenda as a powerful engine of growth.

The liberal argument focuses on good and bad *policies*. But one can plausibly argue that geography and 'institutions' count for relatively more – with the implication that large parts of the world not blessed with good geography and good institutions are unlikely to come close to, say, 50 per cent of the average income of the North in the next century. One recent study finds that simply the age of states is a good predictor of recent growth performance.

> In recent decades, 'old countries' – countries that gave rise to early states, kingdoms, and empires and those that maintained forms of political organization above the tribal level for large parts of the last two millennia – have been recording more rapid economic growth, on average, than have 'new countries'. This result is remarkably robust, standing up in multivariate regressions for both world samples and samples including developing countries only. (Chanda and Putterman 2005, p. 88)

The Impacts of Income Inequality

We can present a moral case that the magnitude of inequalities in the world today is simply 'unacceptable', especially in light of the rather small cost to the rest of the world's population of substantially raising up the bottom tail of the distribution (eliminating extreme poverty). The size of the gaps is suggested in table 5.1, which shows the income pyramid beneath the European Union in its 'near abroad', with regional per capita income expressed both in market exchange rates and in PPP$. What about the instrumental case, that inequality of income outcomes should be reduced – nationally and internationally – because of their effect on other things?

The liberal argument stresses the desirable incentive effects of inequality, and the necessary trade-off between downwards redistribution and competitiveness. The counterargument is that the desirable effects of inequality on incentives and competitiveness apply only at moderate, Scandinavian-type levels of inequality. Above this, as in the United States over the past 20 years and still more at Brazil-type levels, these effects are likely to be swamped by social costs. Inequality above a moderate level tends to go with an undersupply of 'collective goods' that the owners and managers of capital need from the state, including personal security, skill formation, research and development (R&D), and wage growth in line with productivity growth. And it creates a kind of society that even crusty conservatives hate to live in, unpleasant and unsafe, coarsened by envy and distrust.

National inequality

Does a higher initial level of income inequality cause slower subsequent growth? The cross-sectional evidence gives no robust answer. Too much 'noise'. Even if we found a strong relationship between higher inequality and slower subsequent growth the causality is questionable: the effect on growth might be due to whatever caused the inequality to be high rather than the inequality itself. On the other hand, most economists do not now accept the once conventional belief that they should consider 'efficiency' and 'distribution' separately and base policy recommendations on efficiency impacts alone provided the gainers from an efficiency-enhancing policy change could potentially compensate the losers and still be gainers. Economists today would more likely accept that today's inequality can drive tomorrow's allocation inefficiency through both market and political chains of causation.

The effects of income inequality on other variables are clearer. There is fairly good evidence that higher income inequality within countries goes with: (1) higher poverty and specifically, a lower contribution of economic growth to poverty reduction (lower 'growth elasticity of poverty reduction'); (2) higher unemployment; (3) higher crime; (4) lower average health; (5) weaker property rights; (6) more skewed access to public services and state rule-setting fora, and lower standards of public services; and (7) slower transitions to democratic regimes, and more fragile democracies. (Some of this evidence is gathered together in the World Bank's *World Development Report 2006* and in UNDP's *Human Development Report 2005*).

Correlation is not causation, of course, and the causation in all these cases is probably two-way. But it is plausible that a strong causality does run from income inequality to the other variables.[10] In the case of crime, for example, we expect that higher inequality would raise the returns to crime (the rich have more to steal) and lower the opportunity cost of crime (the poor have fewer alternative livelihoods). And we do find that in the US, cities with higher levels of income inequality also have higher rates of crime. In South Africa one study concluded that 'policymakers would do well to worry about the distribution of income – both within and between racial groups – when devising strategies for economic growth, as the welfare benefits from growth may be attenuated by decreased safety if such growth is accompanied by increased inequality' (Demombynes and Ozler 2005, p. 287). Another study across many countries found that higher income inequality is associated with higher homicide rates and robbery rates, holding several other variables constant (Fajnzylber et al. 2005).

The link between inequality and crime comes partly through the inability of unskilled men in high inequality societies to play traditional male economic and social roles, including a plausible contribution to family income. But higher crime and violence are only the tip of a distribution of social relationships skewed towards the aggressive end of the spectrum, with low average levels of trust and social capital. American states with more equal income distribution, like New Hampshire, also have more social trust.

There is good evidence that income inequality is bad for your health (see the book by Richard Wilkinson, *The Impact of Inequality: How to Make Sick Societies Healthier*, 2005). The level of average health of a population rises with its average income and falls with higher income inequality; so higher income inequality is associated with lower average health, holding average income constant. Life expectancy in rich countries correlates closely with income inequality. Greece has an average income about half that of the US, but its income distribution is more equal and its life expectancy is higher.

The evidence also suggests that other, non-income inequalities may be as or more important for health outcomes; notably, power inequalities and relative deprivation. People who perceive themselves to be lower in the social hierarchy tend to die younger than those just above them. Health is affected by stress, and stress is a reaction to insults, domination, low status, lack of control. High status and high control, on the other hand, seem to be good for health. A study in Sweden found that people with a PhD live longer than those with a Master's degree, who live longer than those with a Bachelor's degree, who live longer than those with a high school education. Similar effects have been found in other primates. Monkeys are happier and healthier when at the top of social hierarchies; their brains are found to produce more serotonin.

Societies with higher degrees of income inequality have societal institutions whose rules and resource allocations are more skewed in favour of the rich, because they are framed by the rich. For example, the poor pay more than the rich to get access to courts and are less likely to receive a satisfactory outcome. At the same time, these societies have more difficulty in resolving collective action problems, including getting contending groups to make credible commitments to coherent long-term development policies. The much higher coordinating capacity of Scandinavia and Japan compared to India, going back generations, may be linked to their much higher social homogeneity and economic equality.

The impact of inequality on the ability to solve collective action problems is seen in the case of energy. Raising energy prices substantially can cut consumption. But where inequality is high the poor are hit too hard long before the price rises change the behaviour of the rich. Either the government launches administratively difficult schemes to protect the poor (e.g. domestic carbon-trading quotas), or it presents nuclear energy as the painless answer coupled with token energy-saving programmes. It is not hard to guess which choice will prevail (Toynbee 2006).

Societies with high and rising levels of income inequality (including the US and Britain) experience a vicious circle. People in the top fifth, say, of the income distribution become less tolerant of the idea of higher taxes to finance better public services, because they are increasingly able to exit – to go private. The government, whose policymakers come largely from this top quintile, promotes lower taxation, fudging the effects on public services. Over time the collective consciousness changes to regard levels of taxation that were once 'acceptable' as 'unacceptable'. As the quality of public services falls, inequality rises and intolerance of 'more progressive taxation for better public services' also rises.

Within Europe, Scandinavia has much lower after-tax income inequality than the rest. It has also shown better economic and social performance than both the rest of Europe and the US by most of the important yardsticks – economic growth, labour productivity, research and development investment, product and service markets, performance in high technology and telecommunications sectors, rates of employment, physical and social infrastructure and quality of public services (from transport to education and healthcare). Scandinavia's better performance suggests that a relatively equal income distribution is compatible with relatively high economic growth, high labour productivity and entrepreneurial incentives. Yet

European governments and the European Commission remain fixated on the United States as the model of virile capitalism, and look hardly at all to Scandinavia.

In short, this evidence on the impacts of inequality at the national level supports the normative conclusion that income inequality above moderate levels should be reduced via public policy, even if just for the sake of the prosperous. The prosperous can indeed 'do well by doing good'.

Inequality between countries

The liberal argument is even less concerned about widening inequality between countries than about inequality within countries, because we cannot do anything directly to lessen international inequality, as distinct from extreme poverty. But on the face of it, the more globalized the world becomes, the more that the reasons why we should be concerned about within-country inequalities also apply between countries.

Increases in world inequality above moderate levels may constrain world demand and thereby world economic growth, producing a vicious circle of rising world inequality and lower world growth. Widening income inequality within developing countries results in a high marginal propensity to import sophisticated goods and services from rich countries. This sets a basic export imperative for developing countries to compete against each other, generating downward pressure on wage costs and exchange rates. Widening income inequality between countries – in particular the 'missing middle' in world income distribution, only very slowly being filled by the upper percentiles of China's distribution – keeps down the demand for relatively unsophisticated goods of the kind that could be produced in developing countries. This dampener on world demand helps to hold demand for manufactured goods well below world supply capacity, resulting in intensifying competition, overproduction, falling prices and falling profits. Crises of overproduction become more frequent – the only question is where they break out and whose production will be knocked out. As a Korean petrochemical executive said when asked (in the 1980s) whether it was wise for Korea to be undertaking a massive expansion of petrochemical capacity at a time of excess world petrochemical capacity, 'We are pretty sure that if there is blood to be spilled, it will not be ours.'

Rising inequality between countries impacts directly on national political economy in the poorer states, as rich people who earlier compared themselves to others in their neighbourhood now compare themselves to others in the United States or Western Europe, and feel deprived and perhaps angry. Inequality above moderate levels may, for example, predispose the elites to become more corrupt as they compare themselves to elites in rich countries and squeeze their own populations in order to sustain a comparable living standard, enfeebling whatever norms of citizenship have emerged.

Likewise, rapidly widening between-country inequality in current exchange rate terms feeds back into stress in public services, as the increasing foreign exchange cost of imports, debt repayment and the like has to be offset by cuts in budgets for health, education, and industrial policy.

Migration is a function of inequality, since the fastest way for a poor person to get richer is to jump across the border from a poor country to a rich country. Widening inequality may raise the incentive of the educated people of poor countries to migrate to the rich countries, and raise the incentive of unskilled people to seek illegal entry. Yet migration/refugees/asylum is the single most emotional, most atavistic issue in western politics. Polls in western countries commonly show that more than two thirds of respondents agree that there should be fewer 'foreigners' living in their countries (Demeny 2003). For all the resistance, migration into the rich countries will continue to rise, bringing not only a supply of cheap labour but also disease pools from countries with decrepit health systems.

The effects of inequality within and between countries also depend on prevailing norms. Where prevailing norms sanction equality the sense of relative deprivation associated with any given level of inequality is stronger than where power hierarchy and income inequality are thought to be the natural condition of man. The significance for the future is that norms of equity and democracy are being energetically promoted by the prosperous democracies in the rest of the world, at the same time as the lived experience in much of the rest of the world belongs to another planet.

For what it is worth, evidence on the international distribution of happiness (the proportion of people who indicate satisfaction with their lives) could be taken to support the case for more international income redistribution on utility maximization grounds. It turns out that higher per capita income is only associated with higher average happiness in countries below about $15,000 per head (well below the UK, around the level of Spain and Portugal).

The effects of international income inequality on between-country inequality in participation and influence in international organizations are clear, at least in broad terms. In the case of the World Bank, for example, the biggest five shareholders are the United States, Japan, Germany, France and the UK, with almost 40 per cent of the vote, and each has their own executive director (5 out of 24). Forty-two Sub-Saharan African countries have two executive directors between them and 5.2 per cent of the vote. Yet the biggest five shareholders do not borrow from the Bank, whereas the Sub-Saharan African countries are heavily dependent on it. Also, two-thirds of the senior management positions at the World Bank are held by nationals of the non-borrowing countries, which account for less than a fifth of world population. Incidentally, voting shares are worked out using per capita incomes expressed in *market exchange rates* (together with other variables). For all that economists say that PPP$ are more accurate to measure relative welfare, the rich countries are not lining up to reallocate shares to developing countries according to their PPP$ incomes, which are relatively much higher than their market exchange rate incomes (table 5.1).

Finally, the widening inequality between the US and most developing regions apart from East Asia – especially when incomes are expressed in market exchange rate terms rather than in PPP$ – helps the American primacy (or empire) project. It facilitates US intervention in other states to change their political economies, their weapons capabilities or their security alignments, whether bilaterally or through multilateral organizations (Wade 2003a). On the other hand, the high degree of inequality also makes globally concerted action more difficult (e.g. to tighten belts on climate change, to institute international criminal justice). The US at the top and many developing countries near the bottom of the income hierarchy feel inclined to free ride.

The Liberal Theory of Capitalist Politics and Economics

The liberal economic agenda derives from a coherent story about the appropriate role of the state in a market economy; but one which directs attention away from phenomena which question its validity. In the liberal story juridically equal individuals engage in free market exchanges to mutual benefit. The state, seen as external to the economy, acts as the agent of citizens in implementing their collective preferences, providing regulatory and policing functions, particularly with respect to property rights. However, the liberal story stresses that the logic of the state tends to interfere with the logic of the market, rather than support it. Powerholders' grasp for resources impairs exchange and efficiency. The necessary coercive power of the state to enforce contracts and to protect the state and its citizens against external enemies can be turned against citizens in a way that weakens the liberal order, whether by individual public officials seeking 'rents' or by whole agencies of the state. We could call this the 'state-market dilemma': 'markets need states; but states can undermine markets'

(Wade 1995). The liberal story favours sharply limiting the power and resource base of the state, cutting taxes especially at the higher income levels in order to force cuts in public spending (apart from the military, police and prisons).

Underlying this notion of the appropriate role of the state is an assumption that markets – once private property rights and contracts are protected – are self-adjusting, tending towards equilibrium 'by themselves'; and that competition is the driver of efficiency (organizational loyalty is not seen as another driver of efficiency). The perfectly competitive market is the iconic image in liberal thought, the paradigm of a social order that works without power, where no actor is able to shape aggregate outcomes. In a world view founded on distrust of political power, the perfectly competitive market is a beguiling image of a social order with an underlying harmony of interests between its participants.

Looking back over the nineteenth and twentieth centuries we can see that the liberal theory misses or trivializes some of the central drivers of industrial capitalism. For one, it trivializes the problem of order facing a state seeking to expand the economy. On the one hand, the state must provide sufficient predictability and security of property rights that the owners of capital are willing to 'throw [their] property forward in time in the form of new investments which will produce profit only in the future rather than immediately' (Gowan 2005). On the other hand (and this is what liberal thinking misses with its emphasis upon voluntarism), the state must contain the unrest of those without capital, who depend for their livelihood on selling their labour, massed in cities and susceptible to organization. These are much more demanding requirements than those faced by pre-capitalist states. The solution has been to go beyond legally legitimated violence, to identity politics in order to convince the population that the state and its rulers are identical with them, and that they represent the wishes of the people – a very different conception to that in pre-industrial states, where rulers emphasized their distinctiveness from their subjects and their affinity with God(s). Through identity politics, the capitalist state and its rulers try to obscure from view the conflict of interests between those who depend on capital income and those who depend on labour income.

Equally, the liberal story occludes the coordinating and entrepreneurial roles of the modern state in expanding and upgrading the national economy. It does so by assuming that producers face diminishing returns or constant returns, and hence that markets tend towards equilibrium 'by themselves'. In the real world increasing returns to scale and scope, and 'first mover advantages', are pervasive. (First mover advantages refer to the advantages reaped by the early entrants into a new sector or location, in being able to outcompete later entrants, see Chandler 1990.) They drive the results of 'free exchanges' in the direction of monopoly at the sector level, and cumulative advantage for locations with early movers. The presence of early movers in proximity to each other provides 'external economies' for other firms to enter into related activities, creating innovation clusters. But these increasing returns and external economies depend on mechanisms *outside* firms, in which the modern state and state resources have a big role – in providing cheap credit and tax incentives for lumpy or risky investments, supporting R&D, identifying key process or product frontiers important for the economy's future growth, supervising the supply of skilled labour and transport and communications infrastructure, assisting the rundown of 'sunset' industries, providing bankruptcy protection and industrial relations favourable to innovation, and more. This is a role of the state as coordinator and entrepreneur, well beyond the limits of the liberal role; but at the same time it cannot be dismissed with the standard gibe, 'bureaucrats can't pick winners' or 'protection protects the inefficient', because it is not mainly about picking winners or trade protection as such.

The US state has been aggressively hypocritical – using the cover of 'national defence' to mount strategic industrial policy that deploys public resources and authority to enhance US economic capacity in a whole array of frontier industries, while presenting itself as a champion of free markets and a regulatory state as the moral basis for world economic order. And the World Trade Organization, steered by the G7 group of advanced states, has become an instrument for encouraging industrial upgrading in the industries relevant to the advanced countries while discouraging industrial upgrading in the industries relevant to the developing countries. The Uruguay Round agreements – such as Trade-Related Investment Measures (TRIMs), Trade-Related Intellectual Property (TRIPs), Subsidies and Countervailing Measures (SCM) – provide plenty of scope for subsidies of the kind needed to promote high-tech frontier industries, but rule out most of the instruments appropriate for accelerating entry and upgrading in more basic industries (Wade 2003b; Weiss 2005). The advanced economies have been using a whole array of instruments in a neo-mercantilist way to boost national firms and discriminate against foreign firms, including anti-dumping, anti-trust, preferential trade agreements, bilateral investment treaties; both to protect their position at the top of the world hierarchy of income and technology and to improve their own position within the top.[11]

In these terms we can understand the unevenness of development noted earlier, in which a small portion of the world's population living in the advanced industrial states are able to enhance their pre-existing international market dominance, with few new locations (mainly in East Asia) emerging in growth-intensive sectors with increasing returns. The most powerful states seek to expand legible property rights into the jurisdictions of other states with a view to expanding the room for *their* capitals to reap economies of scale and scope. Some of this entails cooperation with other states, legitimized with the liberal claim that free trade and investment benefit all participants. But particularly in relations between already developed states and 'emerging markets', more arm-twisting may be involved. Developed states seek to shape the internal regimes of emerging markets in ways that favour the expansion of the property and profits of their own producers, through both bilateral relations and multilateral organizations (such as the World Bank and the IMF). Debt relationships have proved to be especially useful for this subordination project.

But some sections of the state and of the capitalist and labour classes may resist, seeking to counter the scale and scope advantages of producers based in the developed economies by giving their own producers various forms of assistance to compete and upgrade. The struggles to defend the legitimacy of free trade and investment, and of more powerful states shaping the internal political economies of weaker states, on the one hand, and concerted national development using an array of *non*-free trade and investment policies, on the other, become central to inter-state capitalist politics, and a source of structural, not just contingent conflict between *states* that 'globalization' does not transcend (contrary to the argument of the 'hyperglobalizers').

Conclusions

I began by setting out a liberal argument about appropriate objectives for economic policy, in which reducing income inequality from current levels receives little weight. From the perspective of reality-based rather than faith-based social science I suggested that the argument could be appraised in at least three ways: first, the evidence for the claim that a liberal policy regime is good for economic growth, poverty reduction and income equality; second, the evidence on the impacts of income inequality on other variables; third, the ability of the liberal theory of capitalist politics and economics to grasp central dynamics of twentieth century industrial capitalism.

The liberal theory does not fare well on any of these tests. There is plenty of evidence against the hypothesis that a very liberal policy regime – nationally, internationally – is good for economic growth, poverty and equality. (Only when the comparison is with very inward-oriented and unstrategic policies carried out by patrimonial rulers does it clearly hold.) There is plenty of evidence that, beyond quite moderate levels, further income inequality gives rise to a whole range of undesirable effects. And the liberal theory of capitalist politics and economics suffers from glaring inadequacies for grasping the central dynamics of industrial capitalism and late development.

In particular, I have argued that the dizzyingly steep income pyramid of countries is by plausible measures becoming even steeper, especially when China is taken out. Globalization and market liberalization in 1980–2000 has not raised world economic growth rates compared to 1960–78, and has yielded only a tiny increase in the share of world consumption accruing to those living on less than PPP$1,000 a year.

The credibility of economic liberalism

Why then have economic policy norms shifted worldwide towards liberal policies, when supportive empirical evidence is rather weak? A good part of the answer follows from, 'cui bono?' Those who have the power and influence to shift the norms have seen their own income shares increase handsomely over the 1980s and 1990s. The evidence referred to earlier suggests that economic growth during the 1990s – and presumably the 1980s as well – has benefited mainly two categories of people: those in the upper half of the income distribution of the high-income states, and those who have made it into the swelling ranks of China's middle class. Obviously, the people whose authority and opinions have propelled the drive to liberalism worldwide live high up the income pyramid of the high-income states. They and their reference group have enjoyed a bonanza from liberal globalization.

The high and rising concentration of world income in the hands of the top few percentiles of the income distribution of the high-income states provides the impetus for a shift in national political economies towards the Anglo-American type. US institutional investors (like CAIPERS, the California public employees' retirement system) and hedge funds – benefiting from the US being both the world's largest economy and the most unequal of the high-income ones – have become powerful actors in the world economy at large, including in Japan and Europe. They are using their shareholding power to demand changes in corporate governance law that would allow them more easily to buy up Japanese and European (especially German) companies. They want to buy them because they are cheap compared to US companies. They are cheap because a much lower proportion of the shares of value-added goes to the providers of capital: 8 per cent to equity-holders and creditors and 85 per cent to employees (including managers) in Germany compared with 21 per cent and 68 per cent respectively in Britain. Stock market capitalizations adjust to give roughly equivalent returns, making Japanese and German firms look like real bargains for anyone determined to run them solely to maximize returns on capital.

The liberal ideology is deployed to say that companies *should* be run so as to maximize 'capital efficiency' – and is persuasive to many in the business and political elites even in countries like Japan and Germany awash with savings and in the grip of demand-deficiency deflation, stagnant wages and falling consumer purchasing power and confidence! Even in Japan, the word 'competition' now appears four times more frequently in business rhetoric than the word 'cooperation', whereas before 1990 it was the reverse. And even in Japan the Human Resource departments of major companies now see themselves as handmaidens of the top managers charged with devising incentive systems to get the most out of labour and managing the employment aspects of mergers and acquisitions and divestments, reversing the earlier concern to develop the firm's human resource base and make it a 'learning community'.[12]

Still, the change at the level of norms has not gone as far as this might suggest. Japanese and American managers were asked, 'Do you agree that corporations are the property of the shareholders, and employees merely one of the factors of production?' In the US 67 per cent of managers agreed; in Japan only 9 per cent. That was in 1998. The Japanese percentage would be higher today, but a large gap would persist (Jacoby 2005; Dore 2005). And when a national sample of Japanese was asked (in September 2005), 'Do you prefer a society based on equality or one based on competition?', 64 per cent opted for 'equality', 18 per cent opted for 'competition'. Presumably in the US the proportions would be roughly reversed.

How much inequality is fair?

If inequality is an appropriate target of public policy, can we indicate, in the abstract, a level of inequality that is 'fair' or 'acceptable'? No one in this debate is advocating income equality, or a Gini coefficient of near 0. To give just one instrumental reason, as income distribution moves close to equality there are, one can presume, big disincentive effects on entrepreneurialism, innovation and panache; so economic growth may well slow and perhaps go backwards. No one is presuming that a greater world income equality caused by the developed countries retrogressing towards African living standards would make the world a better place, or that China in the egalitarian communist period was somehow better-off than today, however much liberal polemicists like to paint their opponents with this brush.

In the abstract, one can say little more than that the acceptable degree of inequality should be one which gives sufficient income incentive to take sufficient risk to generate sufficient economic growth to provide sufficient opportunities for the poorer to become less poor. But not so much difference in income outcomes that the rich can translate their income differential into a political oligarchy which sets rules that continuously fortify these differentials and keeps social mobility at low levels.

As the last point suggests, it would be widely agreed that higher levels of income inequality are more damaging for other desiderata the lower the rate of social mobility; conversely, the higher the rate of social mobility the less the damage from relatively high levels of inequality. The empirical studies of the impact of inequality referred to earlier do not control for social mobility, however, not least because little cross-country evidence on social mobility is available.

Policy conclusions

The liberal distinction between equality of income *opportunities* and equality of income *outcomes* is not viable. The bad effects of inequality follow from inequality of outcomes, not just of opportunities. Beyond rather modest degrees of inequality, more inequality of income outcomes makes the reduction of extreme poverty more difficult; causes higher levels of crime; and is associated with lower levels of average health. Further, in many countries some redistribution of income through the tax system – to change *outcomes* – is going to be necessary to improve equality of opportunities. Greater equality of opportunities for education, for example, may well require a more progressive tax structure and less tax avoidance by the rich.

Cultures and political worldviews differ profoundly on where the line between legitimate and illegitimate causes of inequality should be drawn – and hence on which causes of inequality should be levelled out. In the West today gender differences in opportunity are widely seen as illegitimate; but what about inherited wealth, or the transmission from inequality in outcomes in one generation to inequality of opportunities in the next? How can illegitimate differences in opportunities be levelled out without adverse effects on incentives?

Generally it is easy enough to identify policies that would probably improve equality of both opportunities and outcomes. In developed countries more progressive taxation, and earned income tax credits – cash assistance to working families – would help. In developing countries land reform, and more emphasis on expanding domestic demand and relying less on export demand, would help the development of a mass consumer market capable of supporting self-sustaining growth. In the general case there is no necessary tension between redistributive policies financed by progressive taxation, and public goods that help the competitiveness of firms; what firms gain from the public goods (including wage growth restraint in line with productivity growth in exchange for measures that restrain market dislocations) can offset the disincentives from higher taxes.

The harder political economy question is to do with the politics of redistribution. Here a central component of a more egalitarian strategy is the strengthening of political parties, the strengthening of civil society organizations, and the strengthening of the links between civil society organizations and political parties, so as to bring redistributivist priorities onto the political agenda. Compulsory voting as a way of boosting turnout among disadvantaged groups is one option. In the UK, with no compulsory voting, the gap between turnout in the top social classes (AB) and bottom (DE) is large and growing; it increased from 13 per cent in 1997 to 16 per cent in 2005. In the Netherlands, voting was compulsory before 1970 and the turnout gap between top and bottom classes was about 4 per cent; since compulsory voting was abolished in 1970 the gap has soared to 21 per cent (Rogers 2005).

Perhaps the new coalition of prominent developing countries, the G20, can concert their actions to prompt a shift in the consensus on development strategy. The rules of the international development regime need to be changed so as to give developing country governments scope to adopt policies designed to accelerate the economy's move into higher value-added activities, as most of today's developed-country governments did in earlier stages of their economies' evolution; to make a 'cohesive' capitalism with government acting in a 'strategic' economic role (Kohli 2004).

Elites of the G7 states can be expected to resist such attempts in the spirit of Martin Wolf's picture of 'anti-globalists' as 'the enemies mustering both outside and inside the gates'. No wonder, when they preside over a global market economy which delivers to them – and the rest of the top half of the high-income states' income distribution, constituting less than 10 per cent of the world's population – more than half of the world's increase in consumption during the 1990s.

On the other hand, a prolonged period of turbulence between the major currencies – which seems quite likely in view of the size of the current imbalances – may yet prompt the G7 to undertake an adjustment in their economic policies that puts them in touch with their responsibilities. Analysts can help by drawing attention to the body of evidence that is difficult to square with liberal expectations: not only trends in world economic growth, poverty and income inequality, but also the performance of Scandinavia compared to the rest of Western Europe; the performance of Australia compared to New Zealand since the early 1980s (New Zealand underwent a much faster and thorough-going liberalization and has had worse economic performance, to the surprise of open-minded Australian economists); the performance of the 'transitional' economies of Europe and Asia (within regions like Central Europe, Southeast Europe, and the former Soviet Union, those economies that underwent faster liberalization have performed worse than those that underwent slower liberalization) (King 2003); and much else besides. To be persuasive this counter evidence has to be combined into an alternative story about development, one that can plausibly be presented as furthering liberal ends as distinct from liberal means; and the alternative story has to be backed by organizations and social move-ments that matter. Failing that, much of the development policy debate will continue at the primitive level of Wolf's proposition, 'The idea that everything would work well with development if developing countries did not have to liberalize or privatize is just wrong' (as if anyone was arguing for no liberalization or privatization); and will continue to boost a misleading consensus on 'the fundamentals', summarized by Wolf as, 'if governments do the right things, development will normally happen, as China and now India are showing' (Wolf 2005, pp. 40, 42).

Notes

I thank Martin Wolf for good debate. See Wade and Wolf (2002).

1 In the same spirit, studies made in the 1970s and 1980s of the impact of free trade on employment typically measured the impact in *net* flows of jobs and work. The studies unsurprisingly found that the net losses were small, and far outweighed by the gains to GDP from eliminating all trade restrictions. Gains from trade might exceed the losses by 100 to 1. Who could argue with free trade? But the use of net flows conceals the dislocation costs of gross changes – a net loss of only 2 per cent might result from a gross job loss of 10 per cent and a gross job gain of 8 per cent (perhaps at lower wages). See Madrick (2005).

2 When I say that the liberal (or neoliberal) paradigm sets the dominant approach to development strategy, and refer to this approach as the Washington Consensus, I am not talking about academic growth theory. I am talking about the dominant ideas of organizations, media and writers close to policymaking, as academic growth theorists are not.

3 There has been less than full consensus on the issue of how quickly middle-income countries should move to free capital mobility and free trade in financial services.

4 For example, the statement of US Treasury Secretary John Snow, 'Free trade is an essential component of the drive for stronger global economic growth. . . . Developed and developing countries alike need to be prepared to reduce their trade barriers and subsidies. Financial services liberalization offers particular promise, and I look for good offers in this area as a key ingredient for a success-ful conclusion of the Round.' 16 April 2005, at www.ustreas.gov/press/releases/js2385.htm.

5 Some of the ground covered here is covered in more detail in Wade (2005).

Crouch (2005) warns against dichotomous distinctions of the kind I make here.

6 Milanovic's book, *Worlds Apart: Measuring International and Global Inequality*, is essential reading for the debate about world poverty and inequality.

7 The median for the second period is driven down by the former communist countries, many of which experienced negative growth in the 1990s as they underwent Big Bang liberalization.

8 Chen and Ravallion (2004), 'How Have the World's Poorest Fared', is a recent, striking exception. It begins, 'A cloud of doubt hangs over our knowledge about the extent of the world's progress against poverty'.

9 See also the work of James Galbraith and collaborators in the University of Texas Inequality Project at http://utip.gov.utexas.edu.

10 But some recent research sounds a caution. Lindauer and Pritchett (2002, p. 19) conclude from a wide ranging study, 'Estimates in the typical growth regressions are unstable over time and across countries.' See also Mbabzi, Morissey and Milner (2003, p. 113): 'The results are weak: we find no robust evidence that inequality, or indeed growth, are determinants of cross-country variations in poverty . . . any claims regarding growth and poverty or trade liberalization (even globalization) and poverty should be interpreted with extreme caution. . . . If we achieve no more than to convince readers to interpret cross-country evidence on inequality, growth and poverty with extreme caution and to eschew generalizations based on such evidence, we would be content' (p. 137).

11 In the EU many of these neomercantilist instruments are being wielded at the EU level.

12 In a longer discussion I would weave in the important argument of Lakoff (2002). Lakoff takes the explanation much further into moral norms and away from '*cui bono?*'.

References

Bennhold, Karin 2005. 'Richer Companies, Poorer Workers.' *International Herald Tribune*, 10 April.

Chanda, Areendam and Putterman, Louis 2005. 'Effectiveness, Economic Growth, and the Age of States.' In Matthew Lange and Dietrich Rueschemeyer (eds), *States and Development: Historical Antecedents of Stagnation and Advance*. New York: Palgrave Macmillan.

Chandler, Alfred 1990. *Scale and Scope*. Cambridge Mass.: Harvard University Press.

Chen, Shaohua and Ravallion, Martin 2004. 'How Have the World's Poorest Fared Since the Early 1980s?' *World Bank Research Observer*, 19 (2): 141–69.

Crouch, Colin 2005. 'Models of Capitalism.' *New Political Economy*, 10 (4): 439–56.

Demeny, Paul. 2003. 'Population Policy Dilemmas in Europe at the Dawn of the Twenty-first Century.' *Population and Development Review*, 29 (1), March: 1–28.

Demombynes, Gabriel and Ozler, Berk 2005. 'Crime and Local Inequality in South Africa.' *Journal of Development Studies*, 76 (2): 265–92.

Dore, Ronald 2005. 'Deviant or Different? Corporate Governance in Japan and Germany.' *Corporate Governance: An International Review*, 13 (1): 437–46.

Dumenil, Gerard and Levy, Dominique 2004. 'Neoliberal Income Trends: Wealth, Class and Ownership in the USA.' *New Left Review*, 30 (Nov/Dec 2004): 105–33.

Easterly, William 2001. 'The Lost Decades.' *Journal of Economic Growth*, 6 (2): 135–57.

Economic Commission for Latin America 2001. *Panorama social de América Latina 2000–1*. Santiago.

Fajnzylber, Pablo, Lederman, Daniel and Loayza, Norman 2000. 'Crime and Victimization: An Economic Perspective.' *Economia*, 1 (1): 219–78.

Gowan, Peter 2005. 'The Pre-conditions for Transcending the Capitalist Inter-state System.' Working Paper, August. London Metropolitan University, Department of International Relations.

Jacoby, Sanford 2005. *People on Top*. Princeton, NJ: Princeton University Press.

King, Lawrence P. 2003. 'Explaining Postcommunist Economic Performance.' William Davidson Working Paper, no. 559. University of Michigan Business School, William Davidson Institute.

Kohli, Atul 2004. *State-directed Development: Political Power and Industrialization in the Global Periphery*. Cambridge: Cambridge University Press.

Korzeniewicz, Roberto, Stach, Angela, Patil, Vrushali and Moran, Timothy 2004. 'Measuring National income: A Critical Assessment.' *Comparative Studies in Society and History*, 46 (July): 535–85.

Lakoff, George 2002. *Moral Politics: How Liberals and Conservatives Think*, second edition. Chicago, Ill.: University of Chicago Press.

Lindauer, David and Pritchett, Lant 2002. 'What's the Big Idea? The Third Generation of Policies for Economic Growth.' *Economia*, 3 (1): 1–39.

Maddison, Angus 2003. *The World Economy: Historical Statistics*. Paris: OECD.

Madrick, Jeff 2005. 'The Bias in Academic Economics: The Economics Salon.' In Blandine Laperche and Dimitri Uzunidis (eds), *John Kenneth Galbraith and the Future of Economics*. Basingstoke: Palgrave Macmillan, pp. 65–76.

Mbabzi, Jennifer, Morissey, Oliver and Milner, Chris 2003. 'The Fragility of Empirical Links Between Inequality, Trade Liberalization, Growth and Poverty.' In Rolph van der Hoeven and Anthony Shorrocks (eds), *Perspectives on Growth and Poverty*. Tokyo: United Nations University Press.

Milanovic, Branko 2005. *Worlds Apart: Measuring International and Global Inequality*. Princeton, NJ: Princeton University Press.

Reddy, Sanjay G. and Pogge, Thomas W. 2003. 'How *Not* to Count the Poor.' At www.socialanalysis.org.

Rogers, Ben 2005. 'Turnout is Really About Class.' *Guardian*, 14 May.

Sachs, Jeffrey 2005. *The End of Poverty: Economic Possibilities For Our Time*. New York: Penguin.

Suskind, Ron 2004. 'Without a Doubt.' *New York Times Magazine*, 17 October.

Sutcliffe, Bob 2004. 'World Inequality and Globalization.' Oxford Review of Economic Policy, 20 (1).

Toynbee, Polly 2006. 'Good News: Gas Prices Up. Bad News: They'll Fall Again.' *Guardian*, 23 February.

UNDP 2005. *Human Development Report 2005*. New York.

Wade, Robert H. 1995. 'Resolving the State–Market Dilemma in East Asia.' In Ha-Joon Chang and Robert Rowthorn (eds), *The Role of the State in Economic Change*. Oxford: Clarendon Press.

Wade, Robert H. 2003a. 'The Invisible Hand of the American Empire.' *Ethics and International Affairs*, 17 (3): 77–88.

Wade, Robert H. 2003b. 'What Strategies are Viable for Developing Countries Today? The WTO and the Shrinking of "development space".' *Review of International Political Economy*, 10 (4): 621–44.

Wade, Robert H. 2004. 'Is Globalization Reducing Poverty and Inequality?' *World Development*, 32 (2): 567–89.

Wade, Robert H. 2005. 'Globalization, Poverty and Inequality.' In John Ravenhill (ed.), *Global Political Economy*. Oxford: Oxford University Press.

Wade, Robert and Wolf, Martin 2002. 'Are Global Poverty and Inequality Getting Worse? Yes: Robert Wade, No: Martin Wolf'. *Prospect*, (March): 16–21.

Weiss, Linda 2005. 'Global Governance, National Strategies: How Industrialised States Make Room to Move Under the WTO.' *Review of International Political Economy*, 12 (5), December: 1–27.

Wilkinson, Richard 2005. *The Impact of Inequality: How to Make Sick Societies Healthier*. New York: New Press.

Wolf, Martin 2001. 'A Stepping Stone from Poverty.' *Financial Times*, 19 December.

Wolf, Martin 2004. *Why Globalization Works*. New Haven, Conn. and London: Yale University Press.

Wolf, Martin 2005. 'The Case for Optimism.' In Anthony Barnett, David Held and Caspar Henderson (eds), *Debating Globalization*. Cambridge: Polity.

World Bank 2002. *Globalization, Growth and Poverty*. Policy Research Report. New York and Washington, DC: Oxford University Press and World Bank.

World Bank 2003. *World Development Indicators 2003*. Washington, DC: World Bank.

World Bank 2005. *World Development Report 2006*. Washington DC and New York: World Bank and Oxford University Press.

6

Why Inequality Matters

Thomas W. Pogge

I

Looking at the world today, we find unprecedented inequality. On one side, there are those living in the industrialized countries on over US$30,000 per person per year on average, roughly 1,000 million people or about 15 per cent of the world's population. Together, they control about 80 per cent of the global product (World Bank 2005, p. 293).

On the other side, there are those living below the World Bank's international poverty line, which is defined in terms of the purchasing power that US$393 had in the United States in 1993. People are counted as poor if their annual consumption expenditure falls below this line.[1] To be counted as poor today, a household in the US would need to fall below US$540 per person per year.[2] (This corresponds to about £312 per person per year in the United Kingdom.) In poor countries, where money has much greater purchasing power, even the market exchange rate equivalent of $130 (£75) per person per year is generally deemed sufficient to be counted as non-poor.[3] Nonetheless, the World Bank reports that there are well over 1,000 million people in extreme poverty[4] and that they live, on average, over 28 per cent below the poverty line[5] – on roughly $93 (£54) per person per year. These people constitute about 17 per cent of the human population. Together, they control under 0.3 per cent of the global product.

Compared at market exchange rates, the income and consumption expenditure of a typical citizen of one of the affluent countries is then over 300 times that of a typical poor person. This means that, giving away half of her income, any one typical citizen of an affluent country could double the incomes of 150 typical poor people.

Inequalities in wealth are much greater still, because the wealth of affluent people is typically greater than their annual income while the wealth of poor people is typically smaller than their annual income. In fact, the investment income of a few dozen of the world's richest people exceeds the total income of the world's poor.

These enormous inequalities become more disturbing when we consider the deprivations the poor are suffering. The United Nations Development Programme estimates that 850 million human beings are chronically undernourished, 1,037 million lack access to safe drinking water, and 2,600 million lack access to adequate sanitation (UNDP 2005, pp. 24, 44). About 2,000 million lack access to essential drugs,[6] 1,000 million have no adequate shelter and 2,000 million lack electricity (UNDP 1998, p. 49). Some 876 million adults are illiterate.[7] A total of 250 million children between 5 and 14 do wage work outside their household – often under harsh or cruel conditions: as soldiers, prostitutes, or domestic servants, or in agriculture, construction, textile or carpet production.[8]

Roughly one third of all human deaths, 18 million annually, are due to poverty-related causes, readily preventable through better nutrition, safe drinking water, cheap re-hydration packs, vaccines, antibiotics and other medicines (WHO 2004, pp. 120–5). This means that roughly 300 million human beings have died from poverty-related causes in the few years since the end of the Cold War, far more than have perished in all the wars, civil wars and government repression of the entire twentieth century. Nearly 60 per cent of those who die from poverty-related causes are children under 5 (UNICEF 2005, inside front cover). Because lives are much shorter among the very poor, many more than 17 per cent of all lives and deaths occur among them.

The very poor suffer not merely from unfulfilled basic needs for food, water, clothing, shelter, sanitation, minimal health care and minimal education. As a result of their poverty they usually also suffer social exclusion. Their civil and political rights are widely disrespected because they cannot effectively insist on their rights. Often stunted, illiterate, and heavily preoccupied with the struggle to survive, the very poor typically lack effective means for resisting or rewarding public officials, who are therefore likely to rule them oppressively while catering to the interests of other, domestic or foreign agents more capable of reciprocating. Wherever they may live, those who are very poor are generally insecure in their access to nearly all their basic rights and freedoms.

Expanding on an idea introduced by Tom Nagel (1977), I have characterized the global situation today as one of *radical inequality*, defined in terms of five conditions:

1 The worse-off are very badly off in absolute terms.
2 They are also very badly off in relative terms – very much worse off than many others.
3 The inequality is impervious: it is difficult or impossible for the worse-off substantially to improve their lot; and most of the better-off

never experience life at the bottom for even a few months and have no vivid idea of what it is like to live in that way.

4 The inequality is pervasive: it concerns not merely some aspects of life, such as the climate or access to natural beauty or high culture, but most aspects or all.

5 The inequality is avoidable: the better-off can improve the circumstances of the worse off without becoming badly off themselves (Pogge 2002, p. 198).

Let me take for granted here that radical inequality matters morally, that we have moral reasons to seek to reduce it. Still, many who grant this point would prefer to describe what is morally unacceptable in terms of the first and last conditions alone – not as radical *inequality*, but as avoidable *severe poverty* defined in absolute terms. Such people hold that severe poverty is what matters morally. We ought to work to eradicate such poverty insofar as is reasonably possible. This effort may lead to a decrease (or an increase) in inequality as a side effect, but the extent and trend of economic inequality are unimportant.

This line of thought is popular in the affluent countries. It is well-articulated, for instance, by John Rawls who – after endorsing a duty to assist burdened peoples that, but for unfavourable conditions, would organize themselves as liberal or decent societies (Rawls 1999, pp. 37–8) – vigorously rejects any and all more egalitarian principles of global distributive justice (Rawls 1999, pp. 115–19). Widely endorsed among economists, this view is also commonplace in the financial media. In a typical editorial, the *Economist* accepts that 'poverty in an age of plenty is shameful and disgusting' – a case for compassion, not a question of justice – and then sharply condemns 'the widespread and debilitating preoccupation with "global inequality"' (*Economist* 11 March 2004).[9]

What follows is a response to this line of thought.

II

How can we explain that, despite an adequate and growing global average income,[10] severe poverty persists on such a large scale? The experts do not agree. But the explanations they offer tend to focus on national and local factors such as climate, geography, culture, religion, national institutional order and government policies.

It is true that such factors play an important role. We can see this by comparing the trajectories of different countries – South Korea versus Nigeria, for example. And we can observe the relevance of national institutional order and government policies in particular, when we compare different periods in the same country – China before and after Deng Xiaoping's reforms, for instance.

Such examples are often taken to show that global factors play no role in explaining the massive persistence of severe poverty; but this inference is a mistake. Consider this analogy. The fact that the students in a class differ greatly in their learning success shows that these students must be different from one another in some way. There must be student-specific factors that cause some to perform better and others worse. But it does not follow that 'global' factors (affecting the whole class) are irrelevant. It is possible that all students would be learning much more, if the teacher or the classroom or the library were more suitable. And it is also possible that the female students would be learning much more, if the teacher gave them as much attention as he is giving to the boys.

What is true of students is also true of countries. Their success or failure in achieving economic growth and poverty eradication depends on local *and* global factors. Among global factors, the rules structuring the world economy have special importance. These global institutional rules have a *direct* influence on the opportunities of poor countries and on those of their firms and citizens. And these global institutional rules also have an *indirect* impact on important national factors: on national institutional rules and on government policies.

The direct influence is shown, for example, by the international trade rules formulated within the World Trade Organization (WTO). Despite much free-market rhetoric, these rules permit the affluent countries to protect their markets through tariffs, quotas, anti-dumping duties, export credits, and subsidies to domestic producers. Such protectionist barriers greatly restrict the export opportunities of many poor countries, especially with regard to textiles and agricultural products.[11]

The WTO rules also assign monopoly pricing powers to pharmaceutical inventor firms in order to encourage the development of new drugs. As a result, the global poor are doubly excluded from advanced medicines as inventor firms price new drugs far above their cost of production and also shun research into diseases concentrated among the poor. These problems would be avoided if governments cooperated to encourage the development of new drugs in a different way – for example, by paying inventor firms in proportion to the impact of their invention on the global disease burden – while allowing universal free access to new medical knowledge (compare Pogge 2005a).

While the rules of the TRIPs agreement require (on pain of WTO sanctions) that the affluent must be compensated for the use of their 'intellectual property' in medicines, plant species and microorganisms, no rules ask the affluent to compensate for their disproportionate contributions to global pollution and climate change, for example, or for the advantages they continue to enjoy as a legacy of the conquests, genocides and enslavements of the colonial period.

The indirect influence of the global institutional rules on the evolution of world poverty is shown, for instance, by the international resource and borrowing privileges. Under the existing global rules, any person or group possessing effective power in a country is internationally recognized as entitled to sell the country's resources and to borrow abroad, all in the name of the country's people. These privileges are granted to even the most blatantly illegitimate regimes – such as the military juntas in Myanmar[12] – who have come to power by force and continue to rule by force against the clearly expressed will of the overwhelming majority of the population. By being given the privilege to sell the country's resources and to borrow in its name, such rulers can acquire the money they need to pay for weapons and soldiers that help them stay in power. The people are harmed three times over: the natural resources of their country are lost, a national debt is accumulated and the power of their oppressive rulers is enlarged (compare Pogge 2002, chs 4 and 6).

The global rules also greatly facilitate corruption. Public officials in poor countries are routinely bribed by foreign governments and corporations to harm the interests of their own people: to curtail workers' rights, to ignore hazardous pollution, to import unneeded goods at public expense, and so on. There are laws prohibiting such bribery, but they are far too weak to be effective. Those who corrupt officials in poor countries run no serious risk of being punished in their home countries. The global rules also make it very easy to hide corrupt money in the banks of affluent countries. These banks do legally and eagerly assist corrupt rulers and officials of poor countries in transferring vast amounts of money abroad. Bank secrecy is now being cracked to capture the funds of terrorists and their supporters. But the much larger gains from bribery and embezzlement that corrupt rulers and officials of the poorer countries are investing abroad continue to enjoy secrecy and protection (see also Baker 2005). Again, ordinary people in the poor countries are the losers as their assets are stolen and their interests sold out in favour of the interests of foreign governments and corporations.

I conclude from these examples that the design of the global institutional order has a substantial influence on the development of the world poverty problem. Why then are the rules of this order not reformed to facilitate rather than to hinder the eradication of severe poverty? Because global rules that are harmful to the world's poor are often beneficial to the affluent countries and their wealthier citizens. Powerful corporations in the affluent countries benefit from protectionist barriers and pressure their politicians to keep these barriers in place. All people in the affluent countries benefit from the resource privilege, because we can acquire legal title to natural resources from anyone who happens to exercise effective power in a country regardless of whether he acquired or exercises his power against the people's will and regardless of what he does with the proceeds from his resource sales. And the banks of the affluent countries and their shareholders benefit from the influx of corrupt money.

The global institutional rules serve not the interests of the world's poor, but the interests of rich corporations and individuals in the affluent countries and also the interests of the ruling elites of the poorer countries. This fact should not be surprising. The affluent countries and their corporations have a vastly greater ability to influence the design of the global rules than the world's poor do. In the affluent countries, major domestic corporations can exert much influence on the government, for example through contributions to the election campaigns of political candidates and parties. And the governments of these affluent countries, controlling access to the world's largest national markets, can exert overwhelming bargaining power in any negotiations about the global rules. In addition, these governments also have much greater expertise at their disposal, which allows them to foresee the impact that alternative formulations of the rules would have. As reported in the *Economist* (25 September 1999):

> Poor countries are also hobbled by a lack of know-how. . . . Michael Finger of the World Bank and Philip Schuler of the University of Maryland estimate that implementing commitments to improve trade procedures and establish technical and intellectual-property standards can cost more than a year's development budget for the poorest countries. Moreover, in those areas where poor countries could benefit from world trade rules, they are often unable to do so. . . . Of the WTO's 134 members, 29 do not even have missions at its headquarters in Geneva.

The ruling elites of the poorer countries can exert some marginal influence on the design of the global rules – enough influence, often, to demand for themselves a price for their consent. The world's poor, however, can exert no influence at all; they cannot even make their voices heard. To be sure, there are powerful organizations that cast themselves as champions of the poor – the World Bank for example. But these organizations are controlled by the governments of the affluent countries. And this becomes apparent when one looks not at their rhetoric, but at the actual policies of these organizations. The world's poor lack voice and influence, and no one with influence has any incentive to take their needs into account. These unfulfilled needs therefore make no difference to how the global rules are formulated and modified over time.

Economic inequality matters insofar as it affects the design of the common institutional rules and the modifications of this design over time. The more inequality grows, the more the affluent countries, corporations and individuals can shape the global rules in their own favour, through their superior bargaining power and expertise. There is a very real danger of a vicious spiral: inequality enables the rich to shape the global rules in their favour. Such rules allow them to capture a disproportionate share of global economic growth. This in turn gives them even greater influence over the global rules and thus allows them to tilt these rules even further for their own benefit. And the better the rich succeed in shaping the global rules so as to capture a disproportionate share of global economic growth, the smaller the share of economic growth left over for poverty reduction.

Recent global trends illustrate how rising economic inequality and shifting global institutional rules mutually reinforce each other. Figure 6.1 shows how the fruits of recent economic growth have been distributed over the various economic layers of the human population. There is a near-perfect correlation between a group's relative standing at the beginning of the period and its gain in real (inflation-adjusted) terms over the ensuing 11 years. While the populations of the affluent

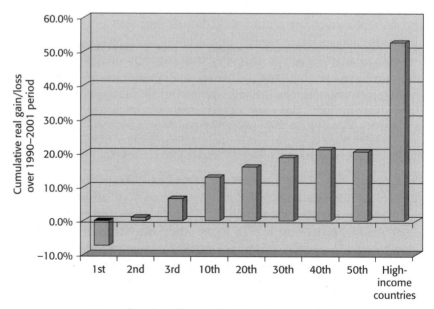

Percentiles of world population based on consumption expenditure

Figure 6.1   Changes in per capita consumption expenditure/GNI among poor and affluent

countries gained 52.7 per cent over the 1990–2001 globalization period,[13] and the median consumption expenditure still rose a respectable 20.7 per cent, the gains at the bottom were puny or even negative as the first (bottom) percentile lost 7.3 per cent and the second gained only 1.0 per cent.[14]

III

Let us return now to the view I want to respond to, the view that the concern with inequality is old-fashioned – motivated by envy perhaps or by some vulgar Marxist ideology – and that what really matters is severe poverty and its speedy eradication through fast economic growth. This is the goal we ought to promote, regardless of what effects such efforts may have on economic inequality.

This view would have some plausibility if economic inequality could be raised and lowered according to the situational assessment of some impartial planner. But, in the real world, this is just not the case. Economic systems, both global and national, are characterized not only by a (generally wholesome) competition under standing rules of the game, but also by a fierce struggle over the design of these rules themselves. The outcomes of this continuous struggle reflect not the well-informed insights of an impartial planner, but the interests, bargaining power and expertise of the various groups of participants.

So generally stated, this point is widely understood. But most people fail to draw two sceptical conclusions it entails. One is that we ought to be sceptical with regard to the descriptions, explanations and policy proposals dispensed by economists and other experts. Economists work with the concept of a *homo oeconomicus*, an individual who, single-mindedly and rationally, seeks optimally to satisfy his preferences. Such imaginary creatures are not good approximations of persons in the real world, but, as various surveys have shown, they do approximate pretty well the kind of people we find in business schools and economics departments – people who cannot comprehend how it could possibly make sense to tip a waiter in a place one does not intend to revisit.

Insofar as they approximate the ideal-type *homo oeconomicus*, the work economists do – what they study and how they study it – will be driven by their career goals. These goals will rarely be served by propagating falsehoods and fallacies, but they will be served by propagating truths that are supportive in preference to truths that are subversive of the standing and policies of those with economic and political power. While economists present themselves as disinterested scientists, they function today more typically as ideologists for our political and economic 'elites' – much like most theologians did in an earlier age. And we ordinary citizens should then not merely learn and benefit from the words of the experts, but also think through the issues on our own as best we can.

Following this prescription, I have studied rather closely the methodology behind the poverty statistics regularly published by the World Bank (see Reddy and Pogge 2006), for example, and also the formulation and interpretation of the widely celebrated UN Millennium Development Goals (see Pogge 2004). The results of these studies are publicly available, and what they reveal about the treatment of the global poor is stunning.

Economic experts do not merely monitor world poverty, they also seek to explain its persistence. There is a wide range of views about why severe poverty persists despite solid growth in the global average income. But virtually all the experts – from Amartya Sen to the economists of the Chicago School – highlight national and local causes for the persistence of severe poverty: causes such as bad governance, sexist culture, conservative religion, unfavourable climate or geography, and so on. To be sure, we rarely find explicit denials that global institutional rules have a substantial influence on the evolution of world poverty, but such global factors are generally downplayed and left aside even though their causal impact, as I have tried to show, is substantial.

In addition to monitoring and explaining world poverty, economic experts also produce recommendations with regard to desirable policies, regulations and institutional arrangements. It is suspicious how often such recommendations, though justified by appeal to the goal of poverty reduction, advocate measures and reforms that will obviously benefit powerful governments and corporations and are likely to increase inequality. And it is disturbing to examine the rather poor record of the recommendations that have actually been implemented (e.g. Stiglitz 2003). Once more it would appear that the content of such recommendations is often better explained by the career goals of the recommenders than by the professed goal of poverty eradication.

These commonsensical observations support the view that we should be sceptical with regard to economic experts and their treatment of the world poverty problem. In contrast to astronomy and mathematics, in this domain we cannot just learn and benefit from the published conclusions of the experts. We must think for ourselves and, as best we can, become experts.

If I may inject here a suggestion to natural scientists and mathematicians: if you want to divert a little of your time to doing something good for the world here and now, you might devote some critical attention to the academic output of economists who, inflated by your prestige, play a key role in the formulation and especially the public justification of political decisions. Drawing on your special talents and training, you could contribute greatly, I think, to deflating the standing of economists' more ideological productions and to making economics more demanding in terms of scholarly rigour and objectivity. This would be a great service to the rest of us who would then – rather than feel compelled to take the pronouncements of the economic experts at face value – be better able to fulfil our responsibilities of citizenship.

There is another sceptical conclusion suggested by the fierce struggle over the design of the economic rules. A well-informed and impartial planner could adjust the scheme of economic rules as needed to ensure that its design continues to be optimal in reference to some weighted set of goals (including poverty avoidance). Taking account of the most advanced understanding of relevant circumstances and causalities, such a planner might raise or lower the overnight interest rate so as to keep in check the risks of inflation and recession. Similarly, she might adjust other parameters of the economy that increase or decrease economic inequality so as to foster economic growth, perhaps, or poverty reduction. Making such adjustments, our planner would enjoy perfect diachronic freedom over the parameters under her control: she would not need to worry that, by lowering the overnight interest rate below 2 per cent now, she would prevent herself from raising this rate to over 6 per cent in the future. Nor would she need to worry that present adjustments leading to a substantial increase in economic inequality would foreclose future adjustments that would bring such inequality back down.

Given the evidence I have presented, we must not assume that real world politics affords such diachronic freedom. It appears that, to the contrary, political decisions about the design of social institutions, policies and regulations are highly path-dependent or rather path-conditioned – especially with regard to economic inequality. How feasible it is, politically, to lower economic inequality to some desired level substantially depends on how much of such inequality there is.

Both sceptical conclusions concur that we must be cautious when we are told that economic inequality does not matter and that, for the sake of poverty eradication, we ought to go along with economic reforms that will raise inequality. We must be cautious firstly, because the support the reform proposal enjoys among politicians and experts is likely to have more to do with the reform's expected raising of inequality to the benefit of the privileged than with its expected lowering of severe poverty. In fact, many advocates of the reform – whatever their public statements – may not seriously believe that it is the best, or even a good way of reducing severe poverty. We must be cautious secondly, because, once inequality has increased, it will be politically much more difficult to reduce it again. This is so because those at the top will then have much greater advantages in bargaining power and expertise as well as much stronger incentives to resist any such inequality reduction. Even more than before, they will be able to dominate the competition over the design of social institutions, policies and regulations in a way that will enable them to cement and even to expand their advantages.

In short, then, I am arguing that inequality matters because it distorts public debate and because it may well be irreversible by cutting us off, politically, from future low-inequality equilibria.

IV

The promoters of the current globalization project hold up China as their poster child, with the World Bank reporting that the number of Chinese living below the international poverty line has fallen by two-thirds or 422.1 million between 1981 and 2001 (see Chen and Ravallion 2004: 153). Are not such spectacular poverty reductions, facilitated by globalization and the export boom it made possible, well worth the cost of rising global inequality?

To answer this question, we need to bear four points in mind. First, there is no solid basis for quantifying the reduction of severe poverty in China. Assessing Chinese households against the international poverty line (defined in terms of 1993 US dollars) requires assumptions about the 1993 purchasing power parity (PPP) of the Chinese currency and about Chinese consumer price inflation. Such assumptions are highly contestable. China has never participated in an official benchmark survey of the International Comparison Program (which publishes PPPs) and PPP estimates for China vary widely. Moreover, statistics about consumer price inflation in China do not adequately reflect either regional variations or the highly atypical consumption pattern of the very poor, who must heavily concentrate their expenditures on basic foodstuffs (see Reddy and Minoiu 2005). That severe poverty in China has declined substantially is beyond reasonable doubt. But the magnitude of this decline is vastly more uncertain than the report's four-digit precision might suggest.

Second, China's poverty reduction has been accompanied by a dramatic increase in intranational inequality. Between 1990 and 2001 alone, the income share of the top decile is reported to have increased from 24.98 to 33.06 per cent, while the income shares of the bottom eight deciles declined. The relative share of the bottom decile declined by 42 per cent (from 3.08 to 1.80 per cent) and the relative share of the bottom three deciles declined by 32 per cent (from 12.69 to

8.58 per cent) (Reddy and Minoiu 2005, p. 7). By international historical standards, this increase in inequality is extremely fast.

Intranational inequality in China, still rising rapidly, raises similar
worries to those I have voiced earlier about the world at large. The most
affluent understand very well that their future wealth is affected by
the social rules. They will therefore generally use their influence on
the design of the social rules towards defending and expanding their
advantages. The richer the top 10 per cent are relative to the rest of the
population, the more their interests will differ from the interests of
the rest and the greater their influence on the design of the social
rules will be relative to the influence of the majority. For these reasons,
large economic inequalities are far easier to create than to eliminate
through ordinary political processes.

Some optimists may contend that either the rich of China or its
political leaders will be so imperturbably focused on the common
good, and on poverty eradication in particular, that the economic
interests of the rich will not deflect the design of China's economic
order. But such optimism strikes me as risky, even naive. Wealth affects
people's perceptions and sentiments, makes them much less sensitive
to the indignities of poverty and much more likely to misperceive their
own wealth as being richly deserved and in the national interest. Also,
wealth and the prestige that comes with it have an influence on many
public officials who are thereby diverted from serving the interests of
ordinary people towards serving the interests of the wealthy (while
perhaps sincerely identifying the latter with the interests of the
nation).

My worries are heightened by our international historical experience. High-inequality countries like those of Latin America have been
highly resistant to structural reforms towards lowering inequality,
because any party in power must cooperate with the powerful
economic elite who can use its economic muscle to do severe damage
to the country's economy and thereby to the government. By contrast,
low-inequality countries like those of Scandinavia find it easy to keep
inequality low. Some citizens are richer than others even there, but
they do not have sufficient power and incentives to manipulate the
political process so as to expand their advantages. The historical
evidence suggests that the increase in economic inequality in China
will eventually level off, but that any reduction in economic inequality below whatever level will then have been reached will be quite slow
and politically difficult to sustain. Any increases in economic inequality – those of the last 20 years and also those of future years – are likely
to be politically irreversible in the foreseeable future.

Third, it is unclear that sharply rising levels of intranational
and international economic inequality were necessary conditions or

necessary side-effects of China's success in economic growth and poverty reduction. The argument that they were remains to be made. Here it is worth noting that, had inequality in China been kept in check, less economic growth would have sufficed to achieve the same poverty reduction. Thus, suppose that China had, over the 1990–2001 period, grown its economy in a different way that would have left the national income share of the bottom three deciles undiminished (at 12.69 per cent). And suppose China's growth rate in per capita gross national income would then have been fully 2 percentage points lower each year. On these assumptions, the real income of the bottom three deciles would still have been over 20 per cent *higher* in 2001 than it was in fact.

Fourth, much of China's export boom has come at the expense of the other poor countries. It is therefore a grave mistake to conclude from China's success, as many have done, that all poor countries could have done, or could still do, similarly well. To be sure, the world economy as presently structured is not a constant-sum game, where growth is fixed so that some can get larger shares of it only if others get smaller ones. Nonetheless, outcomes are strongly interdependent. Export opportunities into the affluent countries' markets are limited by the protectionist barriers – quotas, tariffs, anti-dumping duties, export credits and subsidies – already discussed. China's exporters could succeed only by out-competing exporters from other poor countries, thereby lowering export prices for all exporters. More recently, China's huge imports have raised prices of raw materials (crude oil most notably), thus slowing the development of other poor countries dependent on imports of the same natural resources. These interdependencies surely go some way towards explaining why, outside China, the reported number of people below the international poverty line has actually been stagnant, even slightly rising (see Chen and Ravallion 2004: 153).

V

The claim that inequality matters, morally, is often supported by highlighting the miseries of *relative* poverty. As has been shown by some excellent empirical work done in the UK, people who are doing worse economically than their peers also fare worse on many measures of human well-being, including happiness, health and longevity (see Wilkinson 1986 and 1996; Black et al. 1990). Without meaning to detract from this line of argument, I have here sought to develop another.

Many believe that absolute poverty matters and inequality does not. Addressing such people, I have tried to show that their view is incoherent – that, if absolute poverty is worth caring about, then so is inequality. High inequality tends to bias the range of publicly available information about the poverty problem, the range of publicly available explanations of its persistence, and the range of reform proposals offered to address it. These distortions impede effective poverty eradication. High inequality also strengthens the incentives and political power of those who have a vested interest in resisting serious poverty eradication efforts. For these reasons, the avoidance of severe poverty, which may be easy in a low-inequality system, becomes politically very difficult in a high-inequality system, even if *per capita* income is much higher in the latter. This is true of individual countries as well as of the world at large.

We want to reduce absolute poverty, of course; and we want economic and technological progress. But we ought to think carefully how we can achieve them while keeping economic inequality in check. And we should be prepared to make sacrifices in the rate of growth if we can thereby also reduce probably irreversible increases in economic inequality. From a moral standpoint, the achievements of a global or national institutional order are measured not by the luxuries enjoyed by a few, but by the extent to which it enables all its present and future participants securely to fulfil their needs and live in dignity.

Notes

1 Chen and Ravallion (2004, p. 147) – defining this international poverty line in terms of $32.74 per month in 1993 PPP prices. As the authors explain, this poverty line has superseded an earlier one defined in terms of $30.42 per month in 1985 PPP prices. Although the two lines are strictly incomparable, the old $1 a day label is still frequently used in reference to the new line.
2 See www.bls.gov/cpi/home.htm (accessed 27 July 2006).
3 This assumption is questionable because the consumption of the global poor does not mirror the composition of international consumption expenditure on which PPPs are based. What they do consume – basic foodstuffs mainly – is cheaper than it would be in the US, but generally not as much cheaper as PPPs suggest. See Reddy and Pogge (2006) and Pogge (2004) for a thorough critique.
4 Chen and Ravallion (2004, p. 153) – reporting 1,089 million.
5 Chen and Ravallion (2004, pp. 152 and 158) — dividing the poverty gap index by the headcount index.
6 See www.fic.nih.gov/about/plan/exec_summary.htm (accessed 27 July 2006).
7 See www.uis.unesco.org.
8 See ILO (2002, pp. 9, 11, 17, 18) and www.ilo.org/public/english/standards/ipec/simpoc/stats/4stt.htm (accessed 27 July 2006).
9 At www.economist.com/opinion/displayStory.cfm?story_id=2499118.
10 The global average income is about $6,300 (£3,630) per person (World Bank 2005, p. 293) or, at market exchange rates, 68 times the average income below the international poverty line ($93/£54).
11 These asymmetrical trade barriers are so blatantly unfair, and so blatantly contrary to the official free-market rhetoric of the promoters of the current

globalization project, that they have come under fire even from many officials of the affluent countries and of their international organizations. See for instance the forceful critique by then World Bank Chief Economist Nick Stern: 'Cutting Agricultural Subsidies',13 February 2003. At www.globalenvision.org/library/6/309 (accessed 27 July 2006). Still, the barriers remain while those who maintain them keep blaming one another.

12 Where the NLD party led by Aung San Suu Kyi won over 80 per cent of parliamentary seats in the 1990 elections, but was ever since prevented from taking power by the SLORC and SPDC military juntas.

13 GNI per capita, PPP (current international $s), from the World Bank´s *World Development Indicators* which are available to subscribers only.

14 Consumption expenditure gains for various (lower-half) percentiles of world population can be calculated by means of the World Bank´s interactive *PovcalNet* software, available at http://iresearch.worldbank.org/PovcalNet/jsp/index.jsp (accessed 27 July 2006, calculated 7 October 2005).

References

Baker, Raymond 2005. *Capitalism's Achilles Heel*. New York: John Wiley and Sons.

Black, Sir Douglas, Morris, J. N., Smith, Cyril, and Townsend, Peter 1990. 'The Black Report.' In Peter Townsend and Nick Davidson (eds), *Inequalities in Health*. London: Penguin.

Chen, Shaohua and Ravallion, Martin 2004. 'How Have the World's Poorest Fared Since the Early 1980s?' *World Bank Research Observer*, 19: 141–69. At http://wbro.oupjournals.org/cgi/content/abstract/19/2/141 (accessed 27 July 2006).

Economist 1999. 'White Man's Shame.' *Economist*, 352 (8138), 25 September: 89–90.

Economist 2004. 'A Question of Justice?' 11 March.

ILO (International Labor Organization) 2002. 'A Future Without Child Labour.' At www.ilo.org.

Milanovic, Branko 2002. 'True World Income Distribution, 1988 and 1993: First Calculation Based on Household Surveys Alone.' *Economic Journal*, 112 (476): 51–92.

Nagel, Thomas 1977. 'Poverty and Food: Why Charity is Not Enough.' In Peter Brown and Henry Shue (eds), *Food Policy: The Responsibility of the United States in Life and Death Choices*. New York: Free Press.

Pogge, Thomas 2002. *World Poverty and Human Rights: Cosmopolitan Responsibilities and Reforms*. Cambridge: Polity Press.

Pogge, Thomas 2004. 'The First UN Millennium Development Goal: A Cause for Celebration?' *Journal of Human Development*, 5 (3): 377–97.

Pogge, Thomas 2005a. 'Human Rights and Global Health: A Research Program.' In Christian Barry and Thomas Pogge (eds), *Global Institutions and Responsibilities*, special issue of *Metaphilosophy*, 36 (1–2): 182–209, to be reissued as an expanded anthology. Oxford: Blackwell Publishers.

Pogge, Thomas 2005b. 'Severe Poverty as a Violation of Negative Duties.' *Ethics and International Affairs*, 19 (1): 55–84.

Rawls, John 1999. *The Law of Peoples: With 'The Idea of Public Reason Revisited'*. Cambridge, Mass.: Harvard University Press.

Reddy, Sanjay G. and Minoiu, Camelia 2005. 'Chinese Poverty: Assessing the Impact of Alternative Assumptions.' At www.columbia.edu/~sr793/techpapers.html (accessed 27 July 2006).

Reddy, Sanjay G. and Pogge, Thomas W. 2006. 'How *Not* to Count the Poor.' In Sudhir Anand and Joseph Stiglitz (eds), *Measuring Global Poverty*. Oxford: Oxford University Press. At www.columbia.edu/~sr793/techpapers.html (accessed 27 July 2006).

Stiglitz, Joseph 2003. *Globalization and Its Discontents*. New York: Norton.

UNDP 1998. *Human Development Report 1998*. New York: Oxford University Press. At http://hdr.undp.org/reports/global/1998/en (accessed 27 July 2006).

UNDP 2005. *Human Development Report 2005*. New York: UNDP. At http://hdr.undp.org/reports/global/2005 (accessed 27 July 2006).

UNICEF 2005. *The State of the World's Children 2005*. New York: UNICEF. At www.unicef.org/publications/files/SOWC_2005_(English).pdf (accessed 27 July 2006).

WHO 2004. *The World Health Report 2004*. Geneva: WHO Publications. At www.who.int/whr/2004. (accessed 27 July 2006)

Wilkinson, Richard G. (ed.) 1986. *Class and Health: Research and Longitudinal Data*. London: Tavistock.

Wilkinson, Richard G. 1996. *Unhealthy Societies: The Afflictions of Inequality*. London and New York: Routledge.

World Bank 2005. *World Development Report 2006*. Washington, DC and New York: World Bank and Oxford University Press.

7

Global Inequality and Global Macro Economics

James K. Galbraith

INEVITABLY the study of economic inequality is conditioned by the preconceptions of the economist, and the taxonomic history of the discipline powerfully reinforces those preconceptions. The classical economics separated theories of value and distribution from theories of growth; much of the functional analysis of wages, profits and rent could be carried out with reference to a stationary or steady state. Though in Marx distribution and growth did merge, the marriage was brief, and in the neoclassical revival their divorce was complete.

Keynes and Kalecki rejected the determining power of the labour market over wages and employment, and their theory of investment and profits was bound up with prospects for growth. But Keynesians after Keynes didn't read Keynes, or if they did they lacked the nerve to push his revolution to its full extent. And so they contented themselves with modelling aggregative variables such as income and the interest rate, unemployment and inflation. This allowed microeconomists to retain control over the theory of distribution, and the result was the postwar compromise division of introductory economics into a semester of micro and a semester of macro. These were ostensibly the same subject, but as any undergraduate could see they had essentially nothing in common.

After gathering strength for some decades, the microeconomists ventured forth to reclaim the entire subject – to oblige macroeconomics to accept a microeconomic foundation. They succeeded, as the world knows. In most treatments nowadays, the same forces – supply and demand, relative supply and relative demand, aggregate supply and aggregate demand – determine all essential economic outcomes; it is only a matter of defining the appropriate framework for the market. Macroeconomics has practically been swallowed up. Even the term has been surplused in some circles, and resold second-hand to a subdiscipline concerned with statistical analyses of econometric time series.

In consequence we have today essentially the same 'monocotyledonous' wage doctrine that Veblen poked fun at back in 1898. Relative wage rates are governed by marginal productivities, and these are determined by the relative supply and relative demand for labour of various grades. Supply and demand are largely governed by such factors as technology, trade and within specific national labour markets by the various institutional arrangements that either impede or facilitate the adjustment of relative wage rates to the market-clearing equilibria. In a well-functioning economy, markets will clear, unemployment will be minimal, and the pattern of relative wages will reflect the efficient levels. In an economy beset by rigidities, unemployment will be visible, and relative wage rates will be distorted by the offending institutions. Given predominant views of 'skill bias' in technological change and the substitutability of foreign for domestic labour, it is expected that such distorted economies will show greater economic equality than the efficient ones. Having made a commitment to particular social structures, such economies face the trade-off between equity and efficiency in a particularly acute and intractable form.

Today's well-bred economist has essentially no alternative to thinking along these lines. It is my purpose here to provide one. My argument is simple and empirical. The presence of *any* strong global pattern to changing inequalities in pay – whatever its source or precipitating causal factor – would refute the view that relative wages are determined wholly by the interactions of firms and workers in local or even national labour markets. It would show that they are, at the least, strongly conditioned by forces sweeping around the world. Such forces are, by definition, *macroeconomic*.

Suppose such a pattern exists. The question then becomes: what lies behind it? Once such a question is posed, the lines of causality are reversed, *ipso facto*. At that point, the study of macroeconomic change becomes an essential component of any effort to understand inequality outcomes. Depending on the size and relative importance of the pattern, compared to local variations, it may emerge as the *central* element in any such effort.

Fifty years ago, Simon Kuznets articulated the prototype of my view, holding that in general the processes of intersectoral transition would govern the evolution of pay inequality as economic development progressed. Thus the famous hypothesis of the inverted 'U'. Inequality would rise as the differential between city and countryside came to dominate the development landscape, and then decline as industrialization deepened and social democracy took hold.

Kuznets' hypothesis implies that most countries in the world eventually should surmount the agro-industrial transition point, and be found on the downward sloping portion of a Kuznets surface. Once that is the overall case, then in general strong growth should reduce inequality, while recessions and economic crises, which reduce income levels, should increase it.

These are not the only relationships compatible with a general version of Kuznets' view. Kuznets surely understood that smaller countries, some specialized in commodities such as oil, would not follow the same intersectoral path as the United Kingdom or the United States. He would have appreciated that the emergence of sectors specializing in technology goods would conspire to lend a procyclical bias to inequality in the most advanced countries (such as the US, UK and Japan). Countries that sell into investment and export booms would tend to experience rising pay inequality as incomes rise and falling inequality when incomes fall. (In other work Pedro Conceição and I have called this the 'augmented Kuznets hypothesis.') Finally, Kuznets would surely have agreed that in a globalized economy, global forces are capable of imposing themselves over the purely national relationship between inequality and income.

The modern microeconomic position in these matters thus requires that the Kuznets hypothesis in its general form be rejected. There can be no consistent relationship, of any shape, between *levels* of income and *levels* of inequality, no global pattern to the movement of inequality. And this is the present mainstream position. The most widely subscribed theories hold that inequality is a matter of policy choice, idiosyncratic to each country and its political system.

The mainstream today links the choice of inequality level to the prospects for economic growth, but it divides into two rivulets on the direction of the effect. The first, associated with the authors of the 1994 *East Asian Miracle* report, holds that egalitarian policies (especially land reform and universal education) are preconditions for accelerated growth, on the grounds that they improve work incentives and capacities. The second holds that increased *inequality* of income and wealth generates economies of concentration in leading sectors, and that this is a motor of accelerated growth. Both positions are supported, in the main, by theoretical hypothesis and casual empiricism, though an occasional article claims to find systematic support in the data for one or the other (e.g. Forbes 2000). On all of this, more presently.

The principal empirical support for the new mainstream view lies simply in the apparent absence of contradictory evidence, which would take the form of consistent support for the Kuznets hypothesis, in modern data. The main modern source for this has been until recently the 'high-quality' subset of the Deininger–Squire (DS) data set of world inequality measures, published by the World Bank. But as a crucible for testing Kuznets, this source of information is defective in two critical respects.

First, DS is a very difficult data set from which to draw systematic conclusions. It combines measures of inequality of highly diverse types, including income and expenditure, household and personal income, income gross and net of tax. It combines these measures in an overall panel that remains sparse, with fewer than 800 country-year observations over nearly 50 years in the most widely used version. These measurements are unbalanced, with far more coming from advanced countries such as the United States, the UK, Japan and Taiwan, than from most of the countries of the developing world. Moving from this foundation to general statements about the evolution of inequality in the world economy requires steps to reconcile the differing data types, and steps to fill in the gaps, usually by interpolating over long intervals. Without additional sources of information, this is very difficult to do with any confidence in the result.

Second, even if DS were reliable, it is not a record of measures of inequality in *pay*. While many economists find measures of *household income inequality* attractive for welfare reasons, Kuznets himself was concerned only about disparities in the rewards to labour; he considered other sources of income to be unnecessary complications. In this, Kuznets was entirely within the theoretical tradition of professional economics, according to which the distribution of labour income is governed by principles entirely separable from those governing the distribution of capital assets and political entitlements. Indeed economics has no theory governing the latter, which can take any form at all, but it is the distribution of pay, capital income and entitlements together that determine the overall distribution of *income*. Thus it is possible for a Kuznets relationship to exist in *pay* and yet be unobservable in *income*. If that is the case, the relationship nevertheless exists. The distribution of non-labour income (and the distribution of all income across households of varying sizes and compositions) may mask the Kuznets relationship, but it cannot render it invalid for the purposes Kuznets intended, of assessing whether intersectoral transitions and global macroeconomic forces are central determinants of changing inequality in the structure of remuneration.

Evaluating the Kuznets hypothesis broadly stated thus requires additional data. It would in principle require actual measurements of inequalities in pay, on a balanced, comparable and annual basis, for many if not most of the countries of the world. However, until recently no such data set has existed and indeed none was thought possible by those few analysts (if any) who considered the question.

The breakthrough – I will not minimize it – of the work of the University of Texas Inequality Project lies in seeing a way to construct precisely such a data set, and to do so from inexpensive and readily available raw materials. Our work is based on a sequence of assumptions, each of which has turned out, on close examination and checking against related evidence, to be remarkably robust.

We begin with the well-accepted argument of Henri Theil (1972) that the between-groups component of a Theil inequality measure provides a lower-bound estimate of total inequality. We *infer*, first, that where a consistent group structure (sampling frame) exists through time, change of the between-groups component is usually a robust indicator of change in the dispersion of the entire distribution. We *discover*, second, that where a consistent group structure exists in measurements taken in different countries, the between-groups components are again reasonably robust measures of the relative degree of inequality in the different places. We *surmise*, finally, that observed changes in a consistently measured part of an overall dispersion is likely, though not certain, to be consonant with changes of the dispersion as a whole.

In practical terms, these inferences together imply that one can construct an entire worldwide data set for pay inequality from the between-industries component of a Theil statistic measured across manufacturing sectors for most economies. And the data permitting such a calculation are readily available from the UNIDO Industrial Statistics, a respected but generally neglected data source. First, data for individual countries are consistently available through time, generally on an annual basis from 1963 through 1999. Second, data are in a common classification scheme across countries, permitting between-groups components of the Theil statistic to be compared. Third, and most surprisingly, while the dispersion of manufacturing pay is more volatile than the dispersion of pay as a whole or the dispersion of incomes, the correlation across types of inequality measures is high, and one can therefore use the manufacturing pay dispersions as a robust indicator of the behaviour of broader but often elusive economic distributions.

Galbraith and Kum (2003) present the UTIP-UNIDO data set of manufacturing pay dispersions, with about 3,200 country-year measurements over the period 1963 to 1999. Galbraith and Kum (2005) extend this work to show the correlation of these measures to a matched subset of about 500 observations from DS, and then show how pay inequality measures can be used as instruments, alongside other variables, to fill out a balanced and dense data set of *estimated* measures of gross household income inequality. The result is called the Estimated Household Income Inequality data set, and along with UTIP-UNIDO it is freely available on the website of the University of Texas Inequality Project, at http://utip.gov.utexas.edu.

The emphasis here is on the patterns revealed by the UTIP-UNIDO measures, and their relationship to the Kuznets hypothesis. We proceed in three stages: patterns of change within individual countries, patterns of change across regions of the world through time, and global patterns.

Patterns within Countries

Figure 7.1 shows inequality in China and Hong Kong.[1] In both places, inequality remained nearly constant from the start of the reform period around 1979, through until the economic slowdown and inflation that led to the insurrection and repression of 1989, associated in the West with Tiananmen Square.[2] Following that period, our measurements show a steady increase in inequality in both China and Hong Kong.

Inequality remained constant in the early reform period because the impetus to rapid growth came from agricultural reform, greatly increasing the real income of the peasantry. After Tiananmen, the Chinese government loosened central control and inaugurated the 'open-door policy'. The loci of most rapid growth shifted to the coastal areas and the cities, and in particular to Guangdong province, in the South, and to Shanghai and to Beijing – the seat of government where the rebellion had most threatened the regime. Here incomes grew dramatically in the years that followed. The spillover to Hong Kong can be accounted for partly as a question of migration, partly because Hong Kong handles most of Guangdong's exports, and partly because the opportunities to become richer in certain sectors in China were then amplified (for instance, via the property bubble) in Hong Kong.

Figure 7.2 shows the especially interesting cases of Iran and Iraq, neither of which are rich in survey data. Both countries experienced the oil boom of the early 1970s. But in Iraq this led to a marked decline

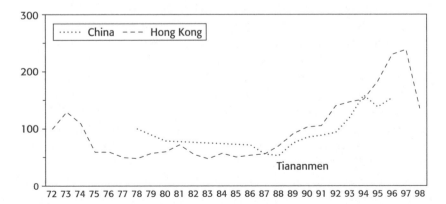

Figure 7.1   Inequality in China and Hong Kong

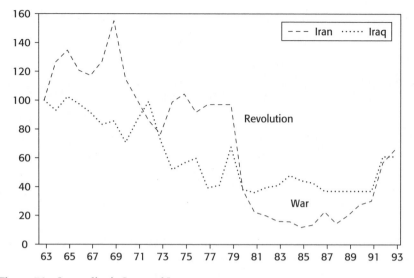

Figure 7.2   Inequality in Iran and Iraq

in our measure of inequality, reflecting the transformation of the country (under the Baathist regime, in the early years of Saddam Hussein's power) into an urban, middle-class nation with the strongest health and welfare services in the Middle East at that time. In Iran, no similar transformation occurred. There came the abrupt revolution of 1979, which deposed the Shah and installed the Islamic Republic. At that point, a radical equalization was imposed (with considerable violence) and it shows up with striking clarity in the figure. The two countries then went to war, maintaining popular mobilization and low inequality until the war ended in 1988. After that, Iran liberalized to some degree, and both countries saw sharp increases in inequality at the time of the 1991 Gulf War.

The Southern Cone of Latin America provides a third case; figure 7.3 presents the examples of Chile and Argentina, as well as Brazil. Notice that in Chile in 1973 and Argentina in 1976, turning points in measured inequality occurred. These were the years of military *coups d'etat* against Salvador Allende and Isabel Perón, and the start, in both countries, of repression against leftists and the 'dirty war'. The experiences of the two countries then diverge in 1982. This was a year of war (the Falklands) and the collapse of military government in Argentina, but of a banking crisis in Chile, whose military remained in power for another eight years. Chile began recovering from its extreme crisis in the mid-1980s, and inequality declined. Argentina entered a new period of crisis under the radical government of Raul Alfonsin, which deteriorated into hyperinflation. By the time that Alfonsin resigned prematurely in 1989, cumulative increases in inequality in the two

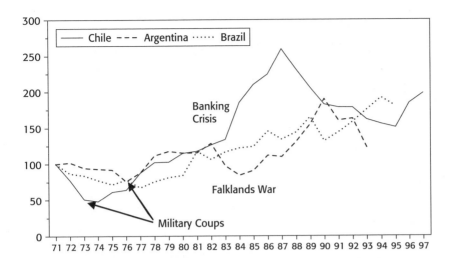

Figure 7.3   Inequality in the Southern Cone

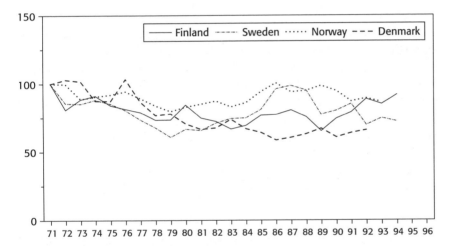

Figure 7.4   Inequality in Scandinavia

countries had again converged. Notice that throughout this period, Brazil too experienced rising inequality.

A striking counter-example to the general pattern of rising inequality occurs in the Scandinavian countries, where our measure of inequality remained largely stable in most cases, and actually fell substantially in the case of Denmark. Figure 7.4 illustrates the pattern. No iron law dictated that inequality had to rise, even in the 1980s.

A few hundred miles away, in Central Europe, we find yet another pattern in the data. Measured pay inequality in the communist countries of Poland, Czechoslovakia and Hungary was stable through the 1970s and 1980s, reflecting the planned and command nature of the

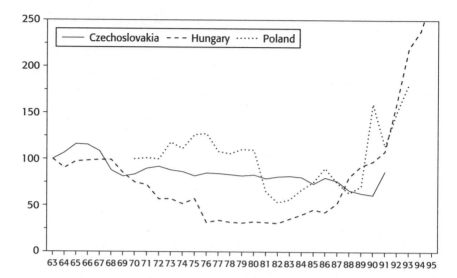

Figure 7.5   Inequality in Central Europe

economic regime. When the regime collapsed, in 1989, inequality immediately sky-rocketed, as wages rose in some sectors but fell sharply for the less skilled, many of whom also lost their jobs (see figure 7.5).

Before 1989, inequality in Central Europe was the lowest in the world – no doubt, so low as to interfere with economic efficiency and work incentives. After 1989, inequality rose to levels prevalent in the poor countries. But while this is true, these figures merely show the evolution of inequality within each country. We have not yet established that these same measures can be used to produce valid comparisons of inequality from one country to the next.

Comparing Inequality between Countries

It is not obvious that one can use the between-groups component of Theil's T statistic to compare inequality meaningfully from one country to the next. Theil's T is not bounded between zero and one, as the Gini coefficient is;[3] measures taken from populations of different sizes are normally different on that ground alone. Moreover it's obvious that if one moves from a coarse to a fine classification scheme (for instance, from a two-digit to a four-digit industrial classification, or from a between-states to a between-countries measure with US geographic data), a larger part of the total inequality will be observed as lying 'between-groups' in the finer scheme. The between-groups component of Theil's T statistic will thus necessarily be larger in that case, even though population inequality is unchanged.

Table 7.1 Low, middle and high inequality countries ranked by UTIP-UNIDO		
Low inequality	**Medium inequality**	**High inequality**
China	Israel	Swaziland
East Germany	Pakistan	Yemen
Cuba	Uruguay	Uganda
Czechoslovakia	Myanmar	Ghana
Denmark	Ecuador	Oman
Sweden	Somalia	Jamaica
Seychelles	Argentina	Cameroon
Romania	Venezuela	Congo
Macao	El Salvador	Trinidad and Tobago
Norway	Haiti	Mozambique
Netherlands	Zimbabwe	Kuwait

But in fact, the existence of a common classification scheme takes care of this problem. We chose to work with the UNIDO Industrial Statistics initially because it is an inexpensive, reliable source of harmonized data covering many countries. We then found that the between-groups Theil's T statistics computed across industrial categories for the ISIC categories yielded measures that provide remarkably plausible cross-country comparisons. This came as a surprise. There is no compelling mathematical reason for it.

Yet we know the comparisons are plausible for three reasons. First, the measures are consistent across frontiers: countries that are economically integrated, with low barriers to trade and capital movement (as in Europe) tend to show similar inequality measures, even where those countries are markedly different in overall size (for instance, Denmark and Germany). Second, the measures correspond broadly to those of the Luxembourg Income Study, a 'gold standard' in measures of household income inequality. The LIS achieves a high level of comparability across countries by careful comparison of large microdata sets, but with only a handful of annual observations for each country and at a great cost of effort. Third, our measures correspond to casual expectation. They are low in socialist and social-democratic countries, higher in capitalist democracies, higher in middle-income developing countries, and generally speaking much higher in the dualistic economies of the low-income developing world.

Table 7.1 gives partial evidence on UTIP-UNIDO rankings. The table presents three columns of countries for which at least ten observations are available, the lowest or most equal, those in the middle of the range and those at the top. There is a clear consistency in the measurements. (Note that data for China in this particular version terminate in 1986.)

Table 7.2 UTIP-UNIDO inequality measures: distribution of observations by region and time								
Continent	Before 1965	1966–1970	1971–1975	1976–1980	1981–1985	1986–1990	1991–1995	1996–1999
Africa	28	91	111	122	116	87	97	40
Asia	36	78	92	104	109	102	82	33
Europe	55	104	110	115	120	122	103	47
South America	11	21	27	35	41	46	43	17
Central and North America	24	48	62	58	67	55	49	20
Oceania	6	12	15	15	19	20	16	5

We infer that our measures of inequality across industrial pay, even though measured quite crudely across broad categories from a standard international data set, were in many ways reliable proxies for measures that others had spent far more time and money working to produce. So far as we know, this is merely a practical reality, a feature of economic life. It must reflect the fact that differences in industrial structure are highly influential in determining the larger differences in inequality characteristics of different countries. It must reflect the fact the ISIC categories, while crude, are sufficiently fine to capture large parts of the actual inequalities in the pay and also the income structure of most countries, along with the fact that the standardization of the group structure at 29 industrial categories holds the computed statistic within a definite range.

Table 7.2 gives the coverage of the UTIP-UNIDO measures of inequality in manufacturing pay, for regions and five-year intervals around the world. As the table makes clear, the coverage is consistent and reasonably uniform around the world – including many hard to survey countries of Africa, Asia and Central America – though it does taper off in the earlier years (before many countries had consistent reporting systems, or perhaps simply in some cases for failure to go back and fill in blanks in the historical record), and in the most recent period – no doubt due to lags in the reporting of recent data to UNIDO or in the preparation by the latter of the finished data set. Still, we have, for the first time, a snapshot of changing patterns of inequality within countries across the entire world, on a nearly annual basis over nearly 40 years.

Overall, the UNIDO source permits calculation of inequality measures for nearly 3,200 country-year observations, covering over 150 countries during the period 1963 to 1999. We then match this data to real gross domestic product (GDP) per capita, from the Penn World Tables version 5.6. Including only countries with four or more observations on both variables, this matching reduces our data to

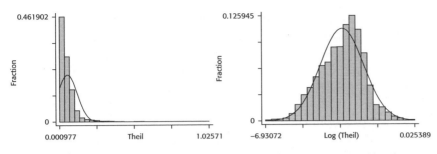

Figure 7.6   Distribution of the UTIP-UNIDO inequality measures: raw and log form

2,836 country-year observations. The coverage of observations in region and time is tabulated in Table 7.2. Observations are annual for virtually all of the Americas, Europe and Asia; only in Africa and for small island countries do we face significant gaps in coverage.

Figure 7.6 gives a picture of the distribution of the UTIP-UNIDO inequality measures. Note that the raw values of the T statistic are grouped heavily to the left and diminish sharply as one moves to the right: there are many low observations and a handful of larger ones. Since the T statistic has a lower bound at zero, this distribution approximates what would be most likely if our measure were sampling from some random, larger universe of inequality numbers, generated by a process of random percentage change, over time, in the inequality statistic. This is reassuring. It suggests, among other things, that there is nothing particularly strange or distorted about our collection of numbers. We find that the logarithm of our statistic is 'nearly normal' in its distribution, which is what the underlying numerical properties of the index would lead one, under a simple rule and in the absence of any particular contradictory information, to expect. Figure 7.6 gives both the distribution of measures and their log transformation.

Now let's look at the distribution of inequality measures over the entire world. The left-hand panel of figure 7.7 presents a simple series of the average of our (log) UTIP-UNIDO pay inequality measures, annually for developed (OECD) and less developed (non-OECD) countries, together with bands indicating the standard error (variation) of the series. From this, we can see that in general, within-country inequality measures are higher for developing countries, and that the gap in pay inequality between developed and developing countries remains nearly steady over four decades. The stability of the error bands tells us that our series is comparatively regular across countries from year to year; there may be fluctuations from country to country, but on the whole the range across countries remains remarkably constant.

Looking at the trend of these measures, we arrive directly at a central finding, which is that inequality in manufacturing pay in both

OECD and non-OECD countries, on average, rose sharply from the early 1980s. The pattern is unambiguous. It is clear. It is consistent. It is uncomfortable. It is unmistakable. It is flatly contradictory to the idea, expressed by Sala-i-Martin and taken up by Stanley Fischer, that the years since 1975 have seen general declines in world inequality – outside the effect of rising average incomes in China and India on the global distribution. This is the first critical generalization of our work.

Why is this pattern clear to us and not to others? The right-hand panel provides an answer. When the same procedure is applied to the DS data, great fluctuations both within and between groups are found. In 1964, 1966 and 1982, but not in other years, non-OECD countries appear to enjoy less income inequality on average than OECD countries. And since the early 1980s, while the poorer countries appear to have experienced increased income inequality, the rich countries appear to have not. This is despite the fact that pay inequalities increased in both groups of countries, despite the fact that the industrial sectors are generally much larger in the OECD countries, despite the fact that from the early 1980s onward the developed countries were hit by policies, under Reagan in the United States and Thatcher in Great Britain, that explicitly aimed to reduce labour income and raise the share and the power of the rich.

The DS results can occur in a data set, but not in real life. As it turns out, they are due mainly to large changes in the composition of the data set from one year to the next. In a low-inequality year DS may be reporting on a handful of East European countries, while in a high-inequality year the sample might be weighted to Africa or Latin America. So the comparison is, in a sense, unfair. It does not necessarily mean that any particular number in the DS collection is wrong. But it is by no means obvious how one can effectively overcome the gaps in coverage, in order to make the DS data into a meaningful measure of world developments. As Milanovic (2002a) showed, the one attempt to

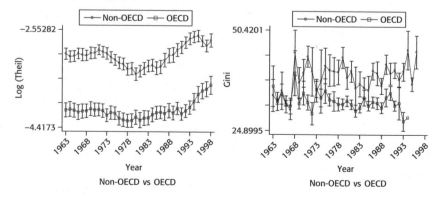

Figure 7.7   Trends in global inequality: contrasting views

do so (Sala-i-Martin 2001), was shot through with approximations and interpolations. Sala-i-Martin's method, in short, was designed so that it could not, in general, have picked up the influence of the year-to-year trends apparent in the left-hand panel. But are those trends in fact significant for income inequality? We think so. But that fact, let us remind ourselves, has yet to be established.

Regional and Global Trends

The next step is to examine patterns of *change* in the global pay inequality data over a series of six-year windows. To permit as complete a picture as possible in a world of incomplete data, we use an average value for the three years immediately surrounding the start and the finishing dates of each window. This allows us to capture the major patterns of change in the data and to see, at a glance, where and when rising inequality began, and how it moved around the world. This approach will also permit us to identify significant exceptions to the trend.

Figure 7.8 presents the pattern as we have it for the 1960s, specifically from 1963 to 1969. The map is spotty, owing to the relatively fragmentary character of the records for the earliest years of the data set. In any event, the important characteristic of the map is that there is no clearly discernible pattern. Our measure of inequality rises in some

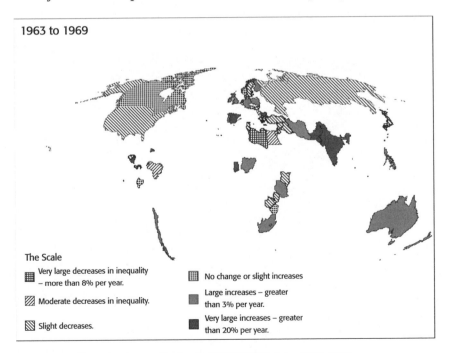

1963 to 1969

The Scale

▦ Very large decreases in inequality – more than 8% per year.

▨ Moderate decreases in inequality.

▧ Slight decreases.

▦ No change or slight increases

■ Large increases – greater than 3% per year.

■ Very large increases – greater than 20% per year.

Figure 7.8 Changing inequality in the UTIP-UNIDO data, 1963–1969

countries and falls in others, and that is about as much as one can reasonably and reliably say.

In the 1970s the plot thickens, the data grow more comprehensive, and a distinct pattern emerges of rising inequality in the richest industrial countries, and indeed, across the world, of countries that rely mainly on imported oil. Meanwhile among oil exporters, especially across North Africa and the Middle East, the case is different; our measure of inequality in these regions undergoes a systematic decline.

Is it too much to infer the obvious? The oil shocks of the early 1970s created boom conditions in the producing countries, recession among the major consumers. Where economies boomed, pay inequalities declined: low-wage workers gained more rapidly, in proportionate terms, than those at the top of the scale. This may be simply a demand effect. With rapid growth, the hours worked of the most contingent members of the workforce tend to grow, while those who already had secure employment are less favourably affected. With recession, conversely, those at the bottom of the pay scale are more vulnerable to reduced hours and intermittent layoffs than those at the top, and inequalities widen. In any event, for our purposes the precise mechanism is not important. As figure 7.9 shows, there is a pattern in the data by this point which is very difficult to assign to any other general cause,

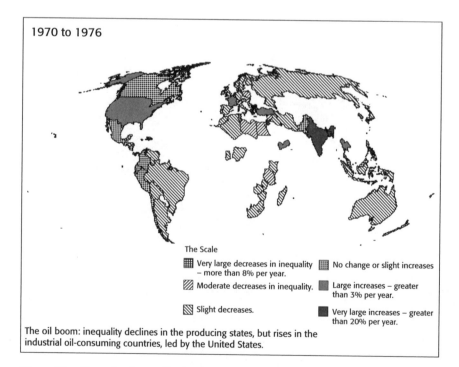

Figure 7.9   Changing inequality in the UTIP-UNIDO data, 1970–1976

than the worldwide shift in relative purchasing power that occurred in favour of exporters of oil and other commodities during the inflationary 1970s. Meanwhile in certain developing countries (notably Brazil and Argentina), rapidly expanding bank debts kept up a momentum of economic growth despite the higher bill for imported oil.

The commodities boom of the 1970s gave way, of course, to the debt crisis and economic collapse of the early 1980s, and this pattern is clearly reflected in figure 7.10. Inequality rises most sharply in Latin America, notably Brazil, Chile, Peru and Mexico: the epicentres of the debt crisis. Though our information is less good, inequality also appears to be rising sharply in Africa at this time, and in parts of Asia. But there are notable exceptions. Iran and Iraq, in the grip of revolution and war, defy the trend. So do India and China. The common distinguishing feature of all four countries is their prior insulation from the developing world's rush to dependence on borrowing from commercial banks, and their consequent protection from the financial upheavals that followed. China in particular had remained entirely autarkic through 1979, while India's external debt was concentrated on long-term, concessional loans from the World Bank's International Development Agency. Both countries maintained strict capital control through this period which had prevented debt entanglement by entities outside the government. For the rest of the world, we may term this period the Age of Debt.

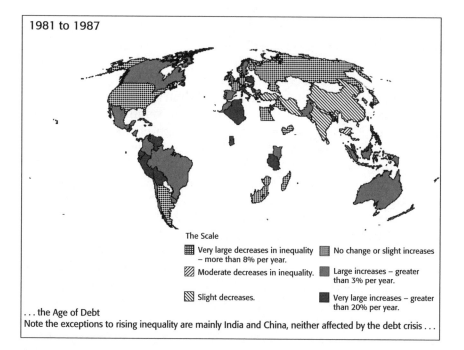

1981 to 1987

The Scale

▦ Very large decreases in inequality – more than 8% per year.   ▦ No change or slight increases

▨ Moderate decreases in inequality.   ▪ Large increases – greater than 3% per year.

▨ Slight decreases.   ■ Very large increases – greater than 20% per year.

... the Age of Debt

Note the exceptions to rising inequality are mainly India and China, neither affected by the debt crisis ...

Figure 7.10   Changing inequality in the UTIP-UNIDO data, 1981–1987

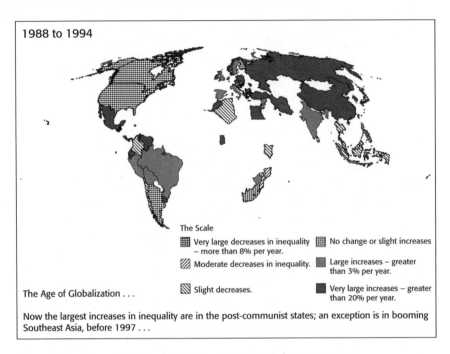

Figure 7.11   Changing inequality in the UTIP-UNIDO data, 1988–1994

Finally, in the late 1980s, a wave of reform swept the socialist world, leading ultimately to the collapse of communist governments in Europe and then of the Soviet Union itself. In this period, rising inequality is almost everywhere. But it is greatest in those countries which had previously registered the most exaggerated degree of equality in their pay structures: the former Soviet Union and its neighbours. Figure 7.11 illustrates the pattern observed through to 1994.

While a few countries show declining inequality in this period (some, like Mozambique, with data that are surely open to question) only one region shows a pattern of increasing equalization consistently across countries at this time. That is Southeast Asia – notably Malaysia, Thailand, Indonesia and Singapore – then in the grip of a boom driven by foreign direct investment (FDI). This boom came to an end in the crisis of 1997. Consistent worldwide data are not yet available for the years since the crisis, so we are as yet unable to measure the effects of those events on global inequality. Nevertheless, what we have so far is, by far, the most complete and consistent global pattern of changing inequalities within countries yet measured.

The general patterns of change observed in this data point to the predominant influence of regional and of global economic forces on conditions within countries. The effect of these forces depends, of course, on the circumstances into which they are projected. High oil prices lower inequality in producing countries and raise them among the consumers. High interest rates – the proximate cause of the debt crisis in 1981–2 – raise inequality in debtor countries but leave those who have sheltered themselves from the whirlwind of global finance comparatively unscathed. Globalization – falling trade barriers and the freeing of the capital account – increases inequality as the barriers that once shielded an industrial middle class in developing and social-ist countries come down. Against this, the force of FDI can keep inequality at bay for a time – though only for a time, and only in coun-tries small enough, and tied closely enough to rapidly expanding export markets for FDI to have a large effect on national conditions.

These patterns lead to another important question. What is the rela-tionship between inequality and the *level* of national income? Is there a systematic relationship between the level of one and the level of the other, as Simon Kuznets argued five decades ago? Or, alternatively as modern theorists prefer to believe, is the correct relationship between the *level* of inequality and the *rate* of economic growth?

Re-examining the Kuznets Hypothesis

Kuznets' famous argument was based on straightforward consider-ation of the central processes of development, and in particular of the *intersectoral transition* from agriculture to industry. In the northern states of the United States, notably, the starting point had been a rela-tively egalitarian society of agrarian freeholders; these were prosper-ous by then-prevailing world standards but they still had much lower real incomes, on average, than could be had in the emerging industrial cities. Thus as the industrial revolution took hold, capitalism opened a vast urban-rural income gap, and overall inequality in the society rose primarily on this account. Thus Kuznets argued that the initial transition towards industrial development would be accompanied, in general, by rising inequality in the distribution of income.

Later on – especially with the mechanization of agriculture – the centre of economic gravity would shift entirely to the cities. And with a declining relative rural population the entire evolution of inequality would come to be determined by relationships inside the cities (and later, the suburbs). In these relationships, countervailing power, modern industrial relations, democratization and the rise of the welfare state would assure, past a certain point, declining inequality in the overall structures of pay. From this, Kuznets inferred that the rela-tionship between income and inequality would follow an inverted 'U' shape: first rising, and then falling, as the ordinary processes of indus-trialization unfolded.

Whether Kuznets' view of the initial conditions of agrarian life were a realistic portrayal of the general case is very much open to doubt. They surely did not characterize either feudal Europe or the American South. There is also no special reason to assume that the income level at which the transition from agriculture to industry begins would necessarily correspond, over long historical intervals, from one country to another. Thus the inverted U may or may not be found in any particular set of modern data. For that matter, it may or may not be found in the historical data, if we were to obtain superior measures of the relative incomes prevailing between farms and cities, and within cities themselves, in the long process of industrialization.

But this is not the true test of Kuznets' procedure. What Kuznets offered was a *general* method for coming to some state of expectation concerning the pattern of inequalities that one might reasonably expect. That method consists of assessing inequality primarily as a matter of an appropriate pattern of intersectoral transitions. The key to the analysis lies in identifying the principal sectoral structures relevant to the problem, and the key characteristics of each. Kuznets' particular case was of the transition from egalitarian agriculture to a mixed industrial economy, followed by the decline of the rural population share and the democratization of industry. But other patterns can easily exist, and these too will yield 'Kuznets relations' of varying forms. If Kuznets is right in general terms, such patterns – if correctly identified – are the key to understanding why inequality sometimes rises and sometimes declines. They will, as a general rule, involve some consistent pattern of evolution of inequality as income levels change.

Fifty years after Kuznets, the development literature continues to make reference to his inverted-U hypothesis, but his larger rooting of the causal force in intersectoral transitions has been for the most part forgotten. Rather, the test of the inverted U curve has become a statistical exercise, largely free of historical and institutional context. And in the meanwhile, the available evidence – mostly Deininger and Squire – has been deployed to argue that no Kuznets relationship, indeed no systematic relationship between income levels and inequality of any kind, exists. Various studies have, to be sure, found curves of one form or another in various subsets of the DS data. But the evidence is weak, and no general pattern has been widely accepted.

In 1994, important work associated with the World Bank and published as a report entitled *The East Asian Miracle* advanced a very different claim. EAM argued that reductions in inequality were *preconditions* to the growth surge experienced especially in Korea, China, and Taiwan. The underlying theoretical relationship tied the expected return on education, economic engagement (and entrepreneurial activity) to the distribution of current returns. In a more equal society (it was said) people feel a closer connection between work and reward and are therefore more strongly motivated to effort. Thus, policies that reduced inequality – land reform and universal public education, in particular – would lead towards more rapid growth.

The EAM argued for redistribution within a market-oriented policy framework emphasizing personal incentives and micro-structural causal factors. In this, the EAM study embraced neoclassical economics without entirely going over to neoliberal policy ideas. The essence of the argument, however, was to neglect institutional forces and inter-sectoral transitions in favour of an argument about personal behaviour in the labour market. Unfortunately, once the venue is conceded, the decision in the case may be determined, and in ways that the plaintiff's attorney may not be able to control. So it happened here.

In the late 1990s, a contrary position emerged. This one held that *rising* inequality could set the preconditions for more rapid growth. This argument was essentially similar to the view of Victorian polit-ical economists, who believed in the concentration of wealth as the motor of capital accumulation, and therefore the indispensable social role of the upper class. In the new version, the relevant theory of growth was based on the idea that concentrations of knowledge, savings, capital and entrepreneurship provide the seedbed for the transition to advanced development. In an influential article in the *American Economic Review* in 2000, Kristen Forbes claimed to have found evidence for this position in (where else?) the high-quality subset of the DS data.

The EAM and the Forbes positions were, of course, diametrically opposed. One held that the relationship between initial inequality and later growth slopes downward; the other held that the relationship slopes upward. Yet in their view of the character of the causal relation between inequality and economic growth, they shared an important element of common ground. Both held that there exists an important causal link between the *level* of inequality and a subsequent *rate* of economic growth, which is to say, between an initial *state* and a later *rate of change*. Whichever way this connection ran, it is plainly incom-patible with Kuznets' idea, which connects the level of inequality to the level of income, and the evolution of inequality to intersectoral changes in the pattern or stage of economic development.

To see this point, consider two countries perched side by side in income–inequality space. Let's say, for instance, they are both in the midst of a rural to urban transition, and both are therefore experiencing high inequality at the peak of the inverted U. Under the original Kuznets formulation, therefore, both would expect to enjoy declining inequality as development progresses and incomes increase. Both would therefore descend the downward-sloping surface of the

Kuznets inverted U, and divergences in future inequality would depend largely on divergences in future income performance.

Under either the EAM or the Forbes model, however, the Kuznets relationship – even if it existed at some one point in time – would quickly evaporate. Let's suppose the EAM hypothesis were correct. Let's further suppose one of the two countries were to embark on a programme of land reform and public education. At that point, inequality would fall. This would happen first, *before* there was any growth in income. The socially progressive country would therefore fall off the Kuznets curve. Only with time, as growth accelerated and income levels grew, might the inverted U relationship be even partly restored (and that assumes that the growth of incomes would not, itself, reverse the earlier decline in inequality). At any moment of time, moreover, *any number* of countries might be in the off-curve position, that of embarking (or renewing) egalitarian commitments as a precondition to more rapid growth. There is therefore no reason to believe that a stable, general downward-sloping relationship between inequality and income levels would persist in the data.

Under the Forbes hypothesis, contrariwise, a country that enacted neoliberal reform would first experience rising inequality, and then rising incomes. The further evolution of that country would be entirely off the Kuznets curve. And since, again, at any moment any number of countries might be in the process of implementing reform, there is no reason to expect an enduring relationship between income levels and inequality measures. As general matter, therefore, the truth of either proposition relating levels of inequality and later rates of growth precludes finding a Kuznets-type relationship between levels of inequality and levels of income. Put another way, the finding of a Kuznets relationship of any kind – whether sloping downward or upward or curved in any predictable respect – between the levels of income and the levels of inequality would constitute strong evidence against both the EAM and the Forbes propositions.

But when we correlate levels of manufacturing pay inequality and levels of national per capita income, what do we find? We find, in fact, that a stable and persistent relationship exists! There is a strong negative correlation in the UTIP-UNIDO data: higher incomes are associated with lower inequality, generally speaking. This is by itself decisive evidence against either thesis linking an initial state of inequality to a later rate of growth – though it is, to be sure, somewhat more decisive against the Forbes version than against that of the EAM report.

The finding of a negative relationship between income and inequality in a dense global data set based on manufacturing pay is broadly consistent with Kuznets' general method and also loosely consistent with his specific historical thesis. It is important to remember that the

UTIP-UNIDO data measure only inequalities in the structure of manu-facturing pay. And the measures are for a specific historical period, 1963–99, which was associated with deepening industrialization in much of the world. We therefore should not be expected to observe many countries in the initial phases of industrialization, undergoing a large rural to urban transition (here, China is a major exception). Instead, most of the information we observe is of a type that Kuznets would have expected to display a downward-sloping relationship between income and inequality, and most of it does.

An important qualification concerns the behaviour of a relatively small number of advanced industrial countries – the US, the UK and Japan – and a somewhat larger number of small oil producers, mainly in the Persian Gulf. In these cases, rising incomes have led in recent years to rising inequality. The effect is to give our version of the Kuznets curve a slight upward loop on the right-hand side of the scale. We believe that in the case of the most advanced industrial countries, a principal reason for the upward slope lies in the fact that the most advanced sectors supply capital goods and therefore have strongly pro-cyclical patterns of employment and pay. Thus when growth acceler-ates, pay differentials widen in such countries.

We find that a broad relationship between the level of income and the level of inequality – when measured, as Kuznets intended, in struc-tures of pay – exists, contrary to the implications of recent theoretical models. But on closer examination, something else important emerges from this data: that is, the Kuznets relationship is not stable over time. Rather, taken over the entire period of observation, it has tended to shift outward, so that more recent years are characterized by higher levels of inequality, for a given level of real per capita national income.

Figure 7.12 illustrates this relationship with the visual device of a regression plane. Inequality is on the vertical axis, per capita GDP on the left horizontal, and a 'time' variable on the right horizontal. The downward slope of the plane as the figure recedes into the distance captures the core relationship between inequality and income. But it is well to notice that the plane is not horizontal in the third dimen-sion. Instead, it is tilted upward, indicating that inequality has tended to rise, year on year, even when changes in the income level are controlled for. This is something new. It represents a common element, or *global tendency*, in the data.

It is possible, moreover, to gain a considerably more precise view of the character of this global tendency, by estimating a regression model with inequality as the dependent variable, per capita income as the depend-ent variable, and vectors of dummy variables or categorical effects, one for each country and one for each year. This is a two-way fixed effects

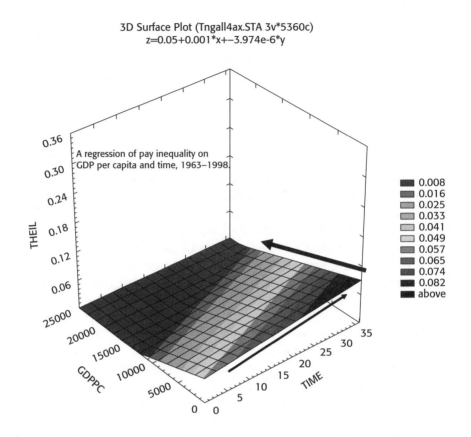

3D Surface Plot (Tngall4ax.STA 3v*5360c)
z=0.05+0.001*x+−3.974e-6*y

A regression of pay inequality on
GDP per capita and time, 1963–1998.

The downward sloping income–inequality relation holds, but with an upward shift
over time...

Figure 7.12   A downward-sloping Kuznets surface in pay data

model. The resulting vector of time effects shows the pattern of the
common tendency, relative to the final year in the sample, as figure 7.13
illustrates, and the arrows provide a schematic of the major movements.
We find that, over all, there was no global trend in inequality during the
1960s. From 1973 through 1980, on the other hand, inequality declined:
the years of the oil shocks, the commodities boom and the global
buildup of commercial debt sponsored strong economic growth and
relatively rapid growth of pay for less well-paid workers.

Then came the U-turn of the 1980s. From 1981 through to the end of
the millennium – the years of debt crisis, communist collapse and
neoliberal globalization – inequality within countries rose relentlessly
as a global pattern. And what is more, this pattern is essentially
identical to that observed when one measures the dispersion of
incomes *between* countries. The inset gives this pattern, as calculated
by Milanovic (2002) from the Penn World Tables, using only average
GDP per capita.

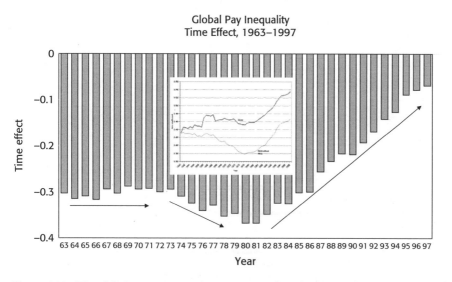

Figure 7.13   The global macroeconomic movement of pay inequality

What is the interpretation of this remarkable matching of trends? The simplest one, and by all odds the most appealing, is *that they measure the same events*. The UTIP-UNIDO measures capture a global pattern in the evolution of inequalities within countries, and in particular a sharp turnaround and increase from 1981 onwards. These data measure the gap, across industries, between the well- and the poorly-paid. The Milanovic/Penn World Tables measure captures the gap between rich and poor across countries. But these developments could, and probably do, have a common cause. Surely a force that widens the income difference between the rich and the poor within any given country should also widen the income difference between a country comprised mainly of rich people and a country comprised mainly of poor people. The fact that this appears to have been the case is merely a confirmation that UTIP-UNIDO and the Penn World Tables are reliable sources of information.

How important is the global component of inequality change? Figure 7.14 provides the answer. The left-hand panel, as before, reflects the data as they are. The right-hand panel is a simulation of what the UTIP-UNIDO inequality measures would show if the global component of rising inequality were removed. The evidence is clear: the whole of the worldwide rise in inequality in the years of globalization and neoliberalism is attributable to the common worldwide pattern. It was, in other words, a global macroeconomic event.

The fact that these patterns are common across countries establishes an important forensic fact. It cannot be the case, as most writing on the subject and in particular the 'new theories' relating inequality to subsequent growth persistently allege, that inequality is merely the

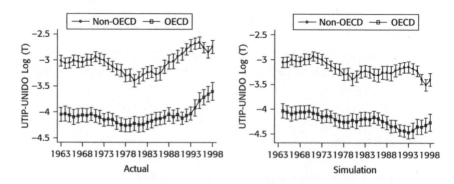

Figure 7.14   Actual change in pay inequality and simulation with global component removed

reflection of policy choices taken within countries. If that were true, we should expect no global pattern: countries have differing preferences and should be expected to act on reformist impulses at differing times. This is not, however, what we observe. To the contrary, we find that there is a consistent global pattern to the movement of inequality, and this pattern transcends domestic political choice. Presumably, few countries would deliberately choose to lower their growth rate or to slip further behind in average per capita income, but this occurred, as the divergence in the Milanovic measure reveals.

There must be a common external cause. And this brings us to the critical question: what did cause the decline in global inequality, both within countries and between them, from 1973 to 1980, and the long, sordid increase in the two decades that followed?

As it happened, changes in global financial governance occurred on precisely the dates now revealed to be the critical turning points in the inequality data. Up until 1973, the world lived under the globally stabilizing financial order of the Bretton Woods system, created in 1944 to provide a framework within which countries could pursue reconstruction and development, with short-term financial assistance from the International Monetary Fund and long-term development aid from the World Bank. Capital movements between countries were generally controlled, and international commercial banking played a minor role in global finance. This system began to break down when Richard Nixon ceased to exchange dollars for gold in central bank settlements in 1971, and it fell apart altogether in 1973.

From 1973 through the end of the decade, commercial banks financed global development on exceptionally favourable terms. In a time of rising commodity prices (notably oil, but also cotton, coffee, copper and other mainstays of developing-country agriculture and mining), real interest rates facing the developing world were effectively less than zero. It was a great moment to borrow and spend, and the developing countries did so with abandon. As a result they grew rapidly – and, moving down the inverted U of the Kuznets curve, inequalities within those countries generally fell. But it was also to prove the last hurrah.

From 1979 forward, with the arrival of Margaret Thatcher (and economic monetarism) in power in Britain, and then the appointment of Paul A. Volcker to chair the Federal Reserve Board in the United States, and then again the election of Ronald Reagan in 1980, the global economic climate changed. Interest rates soared, the pound and the dollar rose, commodities slumped, and the currencies of Latin America and Africa collapsed. Imports were slashed, and what was experienced as recession in the global North was full-blown depression in the global South. Now, with declining per capita incomes, the Kuznets process went into reverse, and inequality rose sharply. But it was not only a Kuznets process. Everywhere, with high interest rates, creditors gained on debtors. Everywhere, with a rising dollar, those who held dollar assets gained on those who did not. Everywhere, with collapsing local currencies, those who could sell to the outside world gained on those whose market was largely internal. Everywhere – and continually for 20 years, with just the limited exceptions already mentioned – global inequalities rose.

Notes

This article is based partly on joint theoretical work with Pedro Conceição and joint empirical work with Hyunsub Kum, and on many conversations with the University of Texas Inequality Project (UTIP) team.

1   The Chinese data in this diagram is partly from UNIDO, and partly from information gleaned from the State Statistical Yearbook, which we believe to be consistent with the information provided by UNIDO.
2   Most observers now believe that the major casualties of the 4 June incidents occurred in battles between the army and the city population of Beijing during the march into the square, and not in the Square itself, which most protesters had left by the time the army arrived.
3   The bounds for Theil's T are zero and ln(n), where n is the size of the population, and the upper bound is approached when one person has all of the income. In principle the upper bound for the between-groups component of Theil's T is no different, since one can imagine a two-group division of any 'totally unequal' population into one group with population 1/n and all of the income, and the other with population $(n-1)/n$ and no income. But in practice an industrial group structure never approaches this bound.

References

Aghion, P. and Howitt, P. 1998. *Endogenous Growth Theory*. Cambridge, Mass.: MIT Press.

Atkinson, A. and Brandolini, A. 2001. 'Promise and Pitfalls in the Use of Secondary Data-Sets: Income Inequality in OECD Countries as a Case Study.'

Journal of Economic Literature, 34: 771–99.

Atkinson, A., Rainwater, L. and Smeeding, T. 1995. *Income Distribution in OECD Countries: Evidence from the Luxembourg Income Study*. Paris: OECD.

Barro, R. J. 2000. 'Inequality and Growth in a Panel of Countries.' *Journal of Economic Growth*, 5: 5–32.

Bénabou, R. 1996. 'Inequality and Growth.' In B. S. Bernanke and J. J. Rotemberg (eds), *NBER Macroeconomics Annual 1996*. Cambridge, Mass.: MIT Press, pp. 11–74.

Birdsall, N., Ross, D. R. and Sabot, R. 1995. 'Inequality and Growth Reconsidered: Lessons from East Asia.' *World Bank Economic Review*, 9 (3), September: 477–508.

Conceição, P. and Galbraith, J. K. 2001. 'Towards a New Kuznets Hypothesis: Theory and Evidence on Growth and Inequality.' In J. K. Galbraith and M. Berner (eds), *Inequality and Industrial Change: A Global View*. Cambridge: Cambridge University Press, pp. 139–60.

Deininger, K. and Squire, L. 1996. 'A New Data Set Measuring Income Inequality.' *World Bank Economic Review*, 10 (3): 565–91. At http://econ.worldbank.org.

Deininger, K. and Squire, L. 1998. 'New Ways of Looking at Old Issues: Inequality and Growth.' *Journal of Development Economics*, 57: 259–87.

Easterly, W. and Sewadeh, M. 2001. *Global Development Network Growth Database*. World Bank. At http://econ.worldbank.org.

Fields, G. 1980. *Poverty, Inequality, and Development*. New York: Cambridge University Press.

Fields, G. 1994. 'Data for Measuring Poverty and Inequality Changes in the Developing Countries.' *Journal of Development Economics*, 44: 87–102.

Fields, G. and Jakubson, G. A. 1994. *New Evidence on the Kuznets Curve*. Mimeo. Ithaca, NY: Cornell University.

Forbes, K. 2000. 'A Reassessment of the Relationship between Inequality and Growth.' *American Economic Review*, 90: 869–87.

Galbraith, J. K. 1998. *Created Unequal: The Crisis in American Pay*. New York: Free Press.

Galbraith, J. K. 2002. 'A Perfect Crime: Inequality in the Age of Globalization.' *Daedalus*, Winter: 11–25.

Galbraith, J. K. and Berner, M. (eds) 2001. *Inequality and Industrial Change: A Global View*. Cambridge: Cambridge University Press.

Galbraith, J. K. and Kum, H. 2003. 'Inequality and Economic Growth: A Global View Based on Measures of Pay.' *CESifo Economic Studies*, 49 (4): 527–56.

Galbraith, J. K. and Kum, H. 2005. 'Estimating the Inequality of Household Incomes: Toward a Dense and Consistent Data Set.' *Review of Income and Wealth*, 51 (1), March: 115–43.

Galor, O. and Tsiddon, D. 1997a. 'The Distribution of Human Capital and Economic Growth.' *Journal of Economic Growth*, 2: 93–124.

Galor, O. and Tsiddon, D. 1997b. 'Technological Progress, Mobility and Economic Growth.' *American Economic Review*, 87 (3): 363–82.

Li, H., Zou, H. and Squire, L. 1998. 'Explaining International and Intertemporal Variations in Income Inequality.' *Economic Journal*, 108: 26–43.

List, J. and Gallet, C. 1999. 'The Kuznets Curve: What Happens After the Inverted-U?' *Review of Development Economics*, 3 (2): 200–06.

Milanovic, B. 2002a. 'The Ricardian Vice: Why Sala-i-Martin's Calculation of World Income Inequality are Wrong.' At SSRN: http://ssrn.com/abstract=

403020.

Milanovic, B. 2002b. 'True World Income Distribution, 1988 and 1993: First Calculation Based on Household Surveys Alone.' *Economic Journal*, 112 (476): 51–92.

Sala-i-Martin, X. 2001. 'The Disturbing "Rise" in Global Income Inequality.' Mimeo, March.

Sala-i-Martin, X. 2002. 'The World Distribution of Income (estimated from individual country distributions.' Mimeo, May.

Theil, H. 1972. *Statistical Decomposition Analysis: With Application to the Social and Administrative Science*. Amsterdam and London: North Holland.

UNIDO (United Nations International Development Organization) 2001. Industrial Statistics Database.

UTIP (University of Texas Inequality Project) 2001. At http://utip.gov.utexas.edu.

Veblen, Thorstein 1948. 'Why is Economics Not an Evolutionary Science?' In Max Lerner (ed.), *The Portable Veblen*. New York: Viking Press.

8

Global Inequality, the 'Great Divergence' and Supranational Regionalization

Grahame F. Thompson

Introduction

THIS chapter examines the relationships between growth of the inter-national economy, international inequalities and 'globalization'. First it assesses what has happened to economic growth rates during the latest round of globalization. Then it turns to the underlying character of international inequalities over the longer term to ask whether the disappointing recent record on global growth is likely to be reversed as – and if – globalization in its present form continues. Finally, and as a response to the previous analysis, it explores an alternative characterization of the international economy, and provides an explanation for what may actually be driving it. This suggests that the way forward for addressing international inequalities could be one based upon the emergent consolidation of supranational regional trading blocs rather than 'globalization' as such.

Global Economic Growth

One of the often celebrated arguments of those who champion global-ization is that this is the only way that economic growth can now be secured and international inequalities addressed. They argue that global integration and interdependence are a fact and in the long term this is beneficial to all concerned. Indeed the only sensible programme – at both the domestic and international level – is to embrace these facts and push for ever faster adoption of those policies that will quicken the pace of globalization and further its consolidation. But is the basic idea that globalization has actually led to higher growth rates really the case?

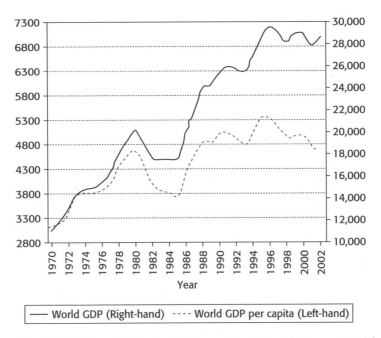

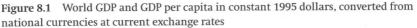

Figure 8.1 World GDP and GDP per capita in constant 1995 dollars, converted from national currencies at current exchange rates

Source: Freeman (2003), figure 16.1, p. 153

A significant step in challenging this much rehearsed view on globalization was provided by the analysis of the ILO World Commission on the Social Effects of Globalization (ILO 2004). This showed that in every decade since 1960 the mean per capita world GDP growth rate had consistently fallen, from 3.5 per cent in the 1960s to 1.5 per cent in 2000–3 (ILO 2004, figure 10, p. 36). Much the same message emerges from figure 8.1, which records world real GDP and GDP per capita between 1970 and 2002. Real per capita GDP stagnated from the late 1980s, while aggregate GDP failed to consistently increase after 1995.

Finally, figure 8.2 compares country growth rates (by quintile groupings) between 1960–80 and 1980–2005. Apart from the lowest quintile (where there was a slight increase in growth rates between the periods), the other four quintile groupings show a decrease in growth as between the two periods.

Several different ways of presenting GDP growth rates derived from a number of different sources are presented in the above analysis so as to build a robust overall picture. And a consistent message results: the most recent period of the growth of globalization (roughly since the mid-1970s) has not seen a renewed bout of global economic growth. Indeed, quite the opposite, with a continuing decline of growth rates and stagnating real incomes. Thus the much repeated claim that

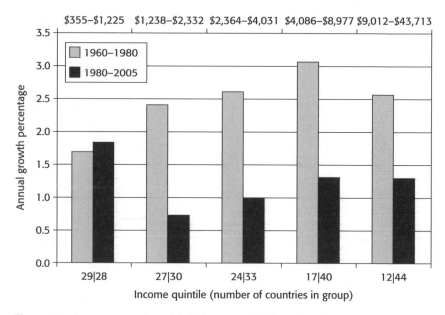

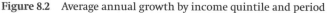

Figure 8.2   Average annual growth by income quintile and period

Source: Weisbrot et al. (2005), figure 1, calculated from Penn World Tables 6.1, April 2005 IMF World Economic Outlook

globalization has proved itself by providing definite growth benefits for all is seen to have been a hollow one on this evidence at least.

The results of this analysis provide the backdrop to much of the discussion that follows, which is sceptical in relationship to many of the claims made on behalf of globalization. Indeed, as will become clear, the burden of the overall argument is to challenge any strong claim that there is such a global economic system firmly in place, at least as commonly understood. But before that there is the question of international inequalities and these occupy the next three sections.

What is Global Inequality?

The economist Stanley Fischer has drawn attention to two separate but contradictory trends in international inequality (Fischer 2003). First, he points to the fact that international inequality *between countries* was *increasing* over the period 1980–2000. In order for *between*-country inequality to have *decreased*, countries that were poor in 1980 would have had to experience higher rates of growth than rich countries. On the other hand, if countries that were already rich in 1980 grew faster than poor countries, then between-country inequality would increase. The evidence presented in figure 8.2 confirms the faster growth of the top two quintile groups of countries than all but the bottom quintile group since 1980. Thus, judging by this between-country inequality data, the last two decades have seen an increase in global inequality.

But what about over a much longer time period? How might we expect the pattern of inequalities to develop as growth and income change? One of the first general theoretical approaches to the relationship between income distribution and growth was originally advanced in the 1950s by Simon Kuznets (Kuznets 1955 – note that this was developed in the context of the evolution of inequalities within a single country not across countries). He suggested this would take the form of an inverted 'U' shape. In the early stages of industrialization labour would move from the low productivity – but also originally low inequality – agricultural sector to the higher productivity – but also initially medium inequality – manufacturing sector. Thus as per capita income grew (as a result of higher productivity) overall inequality would also grow. This would account for the upward-sloping part of the curve. And this result holds as long as inequality *between* the sectors is substantially greater than the inequality *within* them. Eventually, this condition would be eroded however. Workers would now mainly find themselves in the new manufacturing sector, the economy reaches a point where factor movement was equalizing returns across sectors, and inequality decreases as incomes grow since efficiency increases and productivity differences begin to decline within the new manufacturing sector, overwhelming any lingering differences between sectors. The curve then begins to turn downwards.

The empirical grounding for the Kuznets curve was found in the experiences of countries like the UK, Germany and the USA (the countries for which, in the 1950s, there were long enough data runs to test the hypothesis). But as more data from a larger number of countries became available empirical support for the existence of the curve declined. (Some studies even found a reverse of the inverted 'U' shape, that is an actual 'U' shape, for example Anand and Kanbur 1993.) Indeed, as we will see in a moment, contrary to Kuznets' predictions, inequalities have remained high in the advanced (OECD) countries, and have even increased there in recent years. In addition, these advanced countries have experienced at best only modest growth rates. This, and other evidence (e.g. Ravallion and Chen 1997), led to the suggestion that the relationship between growth and inequality is more like a linear inverse relationship: the higher the inequality the lower the growth rate, the greater the equality the higher the growth rate.

However, the existence of a Kuznets-type curve has recently been revived, this time in an explicit international context. Figure 8.3 shows the results of Robert Barro's (2000) analysis based upon a large panel data set of countries. It shows the relationship between country Gini coefficients (after filtering out the estimated effects of control

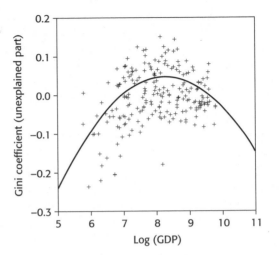

Figure 8.3   Gini coefficient versus log (GDP)

Source: Barro (2000), figure 4, p. 25

variables like different schooling levels, degree of openness and dummies for the basis of data collection) and the log of their per capita GDP. The peak occurs at a per capita GDP of US$3,320 (at 1985 US dollars) and the curve is stable for different years (1960, 1970, 1980 and 1990).

Other things being equal, then, and *if* poorer countries were to develop to incomes beyond US$3,300 per capita, we might expect internal income equality to eventually fall. However, it is worth recalling that this Kuznets relationship only emerges after the *main determinants* of growth have been filtered out in Barro's analysis, that is those of education, openness and controlling for different methods of generating the inequality data.

Getting back to the picture presented by Fischer, this changes when we consider the same countries he deals with but weighted by their share of world population. In particular China and India are such large countries in population terms and were near the lower end of the income spectrum at the beginning of the period, so their higher than average growth rates tipped the balance in favour of a between-country *decrease* in inequality over the period 1980 to 2000. In effect, this re-weighted between-*country* inequalities to produce a measure of between-*persons* inequality on a global scale, which was then found to be decreasing.

Fischer's argument is that if poor countries grow more rapidly than rich countries, then inequality will eventually fall. But the absolute gap will only start to close a long time into the future – that is, assuming that the poor countries concerned *continue* to grow more rapidly than the rich.

To complicate matters further, according to Fischer's analysis, most

Gini index for income inequality

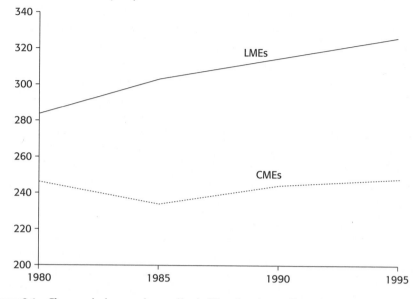

Figure 8.4   Changes in income inequality in liberal and coordinated market economies, 1980–1995

Source: Luxembourg Income Study at www.lisproject.org/keyfigures/ineqtable.htm

countries saw an *increase* of *within*-country income inequality, that is, inequality measured across the individuals of a given country during the period 1980–2000. This is confirmed by the data shown in figure 8.4, which breaks advanced countries down into two groups, liberal market economies (LMEs) and coordinated market economies (CMEs), both of which show a growth in the Gini coefficient between 1985 and 1995.

India and China also saw a rise in inequality during this period. But despite these increases of within-country inequality, both countries also saw a big drop in the absolute levels of poverty, as measured by the number of people living on less than US$1 a day.

A second more contentious point stressed by Fischer is that globalization is not to blame for global poverty; it can help rather than hinder the poor, if it has a positive influence on economic growth. But, as we have seen above, such growth benefits have yet to arrive. However, according to Fischer, the problem has not been too much globalization but rather that not all poor countries were able to take advantage of it. Fischer lays the blame for this on both rich and poor nations alike: rich nations did not open up their agricultural and textile markets (in particular) enough to benefit the poorer countries; and the poor countries have not sufficiently explored the possibilities of increasing their trade with one another.

All this is highly contentious of course, as the other chapters in this volume point out. Clearly, one of the great difficulties with these debates is to get a consistent grip on the bare facts of international inequality. Here there are just no easy answers. There are, first, different measures of inequality. For instance inequality between countries can be measured in terms of a ratio, or in terms of an absolute gap. More importantly, there are different aspects to any pattern of inequality and different measures aim to represent different aspects of that pattern. Then there are the conflicting and often overlapping start dates or periods over which changes are analysed.

Global income data are usually assembled on the basis of country income data. In turn, country income data can be derived from income surveys among individuals or this can be done on the basis of households surveys. Alternatively, income data can be generated directly from national accounts. Then, to get to the global picture of income inequality requires study of *both* the between-country inequality *and* the within-country inequality – and combining these somehow – as well as allowing for the fact that countries are not equal in terms of their share of the world's population or income. Further to this, there are all the complications associated with how to convert income measures in national currencies into a common internationally recognized currency, whether this be US dollars or PPP equivalent units.

I leave it to others to debate these issues in detail (e.g. Milanovic 2005) though I have discussed them elsewhere (Thompson 2004b). The general conclusion to that discussion was that there is no single, correct way to measure global inequality – a complex phenomenon like inequality cannot be adequately described by a single measure – and that there are no simple answers to the question of whether the world is becoming more or less equal. From the point of the present chapter, however, the emphasis yet again on the global arena for such a discussion is questionable. This will become clear later when the supranational regional and still continued domestic orientation of economic activity is outlined. In addition, there are good reasons to remain suspicious of treating all countries as essentially the same – so that a single inter-country equation can be used to adequately specify structural relationships on a global level. There are such differences between the socioeconomic organizational characteristics of economies that to treat them as all structurally equivalent is analytically suspect, I would suggest. Thus, the pursuit of a single measure (or even multiple measures) designed to answer the question of what has happened to global inequalities since the inception of the latest round of globalization is at best a difficult task, if not an impossible or inappropriate one.

Convergence or Divergence?

Given the above comments it may be better to divide the international system into different groups of countries. One traditional way of doing this is to have two sets; a set called the 'advanced' or 'developed' countries, and another called the 'developing' or 'non-industrialized' countries.[1] The first group have consolidated their position as high-income earners, and there has been some considerable convergence between them over a long period of time. The other 'group', the less developed, do not have so much in common – there has been great diversity between them and they have not so obviously converged, indeed in many ways they have diverged amongst themselves. These countries have, on average, seen growth rates slower than the richer countries. But they have also seen some strikingly different patterns. A few have converged on the leaders since the end of World War II (e.g. Korea, Singapore, to some extent Taiwan), others have stagnated, while still others have had a mixed record of take-offs, stalls and nose dives. In addition a few of the original convergence group have departed from that group, like Argentina and South Africa, to become 'troubled middle-income' countries. But what has been even more striking is that the core of the original convergence group made up of the Atlantic economy states and temperate ex-colonies like Australia and New Zealand have consolidated its position and seen a marked stability in its membership. What is more, while this group has tended to 'converge' in terms of growth, productivity and living standards, it has in turn 'diverged' from the other group – and, as it has been described, 'diverged, big time' (Prichett 1997). Cases where poor countries, and especially the least developed countries, actually gain significantly on the leaders are historically rare. In most poor countries there are strong forces for stagnation. Of course, the recent experiences of China and India may be about to break this pattern, but see below.

One question this raises is whether 'globalization' has made any difference to these patterns and trends (Dowrick and DeLong 2003). In fact, it seems not. If globalization is understood as the progressive liberalization and opening of economies to international trade and investment, then in the first round of globalization between 1870 and 1914, whilst it consolidated the original convergence club in the manner just described, it did not extend this beyond that charmed circle. It brought great structural change and economic integration to the other economies, but the relative gap in income and productivity and the gap in industrial structure vis-à-vis the industrial core of the world economy continued to widen.

During the interwar period globalization and integration were in retreat as tariff barriers were raised, autarkic economic blocs emerged, international investment shrank, the Great Depression hit and world trade collapsed. But, interestingly, there was some global convergence of 'between-country' GDP per capita, and the 'convergence club' actually expanded slightly during this period (Milanovic 2002, 2005; Dowrick and DeLong 2003). Thus while 'globalization' retreated international 'convergence' grew.

The post-World War II period was very much one in which the international system first recovered from the disintegration of the interwar period. It also brought both a slight expansion in the size, and a shift in the location, of the 'convergence club'. As mentioned above, a number of East Asian economies 'joined' and a number of the older members from Latin America 'retreated' from the club. But the basic core membership remained. And as just suggested, there was no dramatic convergence in between-country income differences even as the second period of 'globalization' matured after the 1970s.

What this suggests is that convergence is a phenomenon somewhat independent of international economic integration or globalization. Greater trade, migration, or capital flows, have no discernable effect on the catch up of poorer countries. In effect, poorer countries would just as likely 'catch up' with the subset of rich convergence club countries whether there is international economic integration and globalization or not. But why has this structural divide between the convergence club and the rest persisted for so long?

Investment and productivity

At root this has to do with the gap in productivity between the two groups, but it might be expected that this would have been eroded as capital moved to exploit the cheaper wage costs in the developing countries, or labour moved towards the developed-country group to exploit the higher wages to be had there. Neither of these processes seem to have happened to the extent that might have been expected, however. The recent period of globalization has not seen capital resources flowing to the less developed economies of Africa, Latin America or even Asia to any great degree. Table 8.1 shows the stock of foreign direct investment (FDI) in these regions, expressed as a share of GDP, from the turn of the twentieth century to 1990. In all cases this share was greater in 1914 than it was in 1990. There has been a massive growth of FDI in the period since 1970 but it has been *intra-developed country flows*: the convergence club has invested in itself.

The international inequalities in respect to capital stocks and flows have been neatly summed up in the following quote:

Table 8.1 FDI in Latin America, Asia and Africa, 1900–1990

	Foreign investment as a share of GDP						
	1900	1914	1929	1938	1967	1980	1990
Latin America	1.20	2.71	1.26	0.87	0.33	0.33	0.47
Asia	0.17	0.40	0.23	0.26	0.11	0.15	0.32
Africa	1.33	1.17	0.24	0.35	0.23	0.34	0.74
Total	0.44	0.89	0.45	0.41	0.2	0.24	0.42

Total stock of foreign investment at 1900 US prices expressed as a ratio of country grouping GDP (except for Argentina the dates are 1900, 1913, 1929, 1938, 1970, 1980 and 1989, and the ratio calculation is at domestic prices).

Source: Twomey (2000), compiled from various tables

Table 8.2 World trading relations: direction of trade (percentages of world merchandise trade), 1998

	Destination		
Origin	High-income countries	Low- and middle-income countries	World
High-income countries	58.5	17.3	75.8
Low- and middle-income countries	17.0	7.1	24.2
World	75.6	24.4	100.0

These numbers may not add up to the totals because of rounding of figures to one decimal place. The figures are for trade in goods only; trade in services (which is less well recorded) is not included.

Source: World Bank (2002)

In 1990, the richest 20 percent of world population received 92 percent of gross portfolio capital inflows, whereas the poorest 20 percent received 0.1 percent. The richest 20 percent of the world population received 79 percent of foreign direct investment, and the poorest 20 percent received 0.7 percent. Altogether, the richest 20 percent of the world population received 88 percent of gross private capital inflows, and the poorest 20 percent received 1 percent. (Easterly and Levine 2001, p. 205)

Trade

In addition, despite the growth of some developing countries, and although countries that trade more generally grow more, only a small part of world trade involves developing countries. This can be seen clearly from table 8.2 above which reports on the direction of world merchandise trade for 1998. A little less than one-quarter of world merchandise exports originated in the developing countries, while just over three-quarters originated in high-income countries. Since the ability to export ultimately also determines the ability to import, these figures broadly represent the picture of world trade in general, and things have not much changed since 1998.

Migration

Another element in this picture of continued divergence is that of labour migration. This has become one of the most controversial aspects of the globalization debate. In the recent period it has tended to focus around the issue of the effects of migration on the relative distribution of incomes within the advanced countries. In this case, it is the effects on *unskilled* migration from the 'South' to the 'North' that often captures the attention and the headlines. Does this added supply of unskilled labour from the 'South' undermine the wages of the 'Northern' unskilled workers, for instance, and how much is it respon- sible for the increase in wage/income inequality in the USA or Europe? Has it been responsible for the growing 'within-country' inequality between wage earners in these countries?

It is important to point out that whilst there has been some labour migration in the international system, most of this has been limited to skilled migration from the least developed countries (LDCs) to the rich countries. It is skilled workers who earn relatively less rather than more in poor countries, so there is an incentive for them to migrate (Easterly and Levine 2001, p. 206). But overall, international migration has been limited (with the partial exception of migration into the USA, though this has also favoured skilled migration). The story of migra- tion in the twentieth century has been one of *intra*-national migration, from rural to urban areas, not so much *inter*-national migration as in the nineteenth century (which helped to establish convergence in the Atlantic economy as mentioned above).

And this connects to the effect of *trade* in respect to labour remu- neration in various countries. As the Northern countries have imported more from the Southern ones, what is the 'skill' content of the goods and services so traded? Commodities and services 'embody' relative skill intensities. So trade and migration are to some extent substitutes in terms of the way 'within-country' and 'between-country' inequalities can emerge and evolve. A good deal of low-skilled manu- facturing has been driven out of the advanced countries and relocated in the less developed countries, the output of which is then sold back to the advanced countries. Thus instead of unskilled labour migrating to the Northern advanced countries to produce low-skilled goods there, it is in effect 'imported' there via the skill intensity of the prod- ucts that are exported to those countries from the less advanced ones. Thus to find out the effect of growing integration and globalization on the unskilled wages in the Northern countries requires not only the direct effects of migration to be assessed but also the indirect effects of the skill intensity of trade as well.

Technology and innovation

In addition, this emphasis on labour skill intensity raises issues about the role of *technology* in these international trade, migration, investment, growth and inequality relationships. The demand for different skill mixes is the response to different technologies and to the changing dynamic of technological advance. Furthermore, technological advantage is often thought to move from one country to the next – in particular as a response to the trade and investment opportunities offered by the different factor availabilities and factor price movement in different countries. In the long run, other things being equal, the convergence of the factor price of labour across countries could bring per capita incomes close together. As trade lowers the developing countries' skilled wages, and increases the more developed countries' (MDC's) skilled wages, this boosts the LDC's technical progress because the cost of innovation declines there, and lowers the MDC's technical progress as the cost of innovation has increased there, so trade leads to *convergence*. But once again, this depends upon empirical factors since we could just as easily assume that trade leads to the premium on skilled labour in developing countries to be lowered, which reduces the incentive to acquire skills there, and hence could lower their growth rate. So, under these alternative circumstances, trade leads to further *divergence*. It all rather depends upon the effects of trade on the skill premium and technical advance in different types of countries, which is difficult to predict a priori. But as we have seen above, the net empirical result has been a trend more towards divergence rather than convergence.

An important test of some of these issues arose in the 1990s in respect to the rather sudden integration of the US economy into the international economic system in the 1980s and 1990s as the amount of trade relative to US output (the trade to GDP ratio) soared for the USA and a number of its industries were increasingly threatened by overseas competition. This happened at the same time as medium-skilled and unskilled wages fell in the USA (the skill premium increased). Migration added to these pressures. In addition, this was a time of very rapid technological advance in the US economy (the widespread introduction of information and communication technologies – ICTs), also leading to a sudden change in the demand for different skills and significant relative wage changes. So what was the relative importance of these various factors in leading to the overall result of a sharp decline in the fortunes of the less skilled US workers in particular? The consensus opinion after much empirical work was that about 10 per cent was due to migration, 20 per cent due to trade, and the remaining 70 per cent due to technical advance (see Cline 1997; Hirst and Thompson 1999, ch. 4).

However, it is important to remember that many of these expectations and trends do not seem to have actually emerged in practice since the basic long-term divergences discussed above have continued to exist. Easterly and Levine (2001) suggest that there are major external economies associated with technological spillovers that concentrate economic activity around existing areas, and indeed attract new activity to those existing locations. External economies are those economies that make it cheaper for firms to produce their own output but which are not generated internally by their own increase in size, say, but arise because of the growing size of the whole industry or economy in which the firm operates. Thus each firm can benefit by the existence and growth of certain other firms, which help it to reduce its own costs. One source of these economies could be the development of specialized labour training facilities and a local skilled labour market that provides trained workers for a number of firms making similar products in an area. Another source could be organizational innovations (process technologies) that leak between firms so all benefit from the innovations originally found in one firm. And similar benefits can arise from profit-motivated product technological innovations, which, as they are exploited by other firms, set in motion an escalation of further innovation which further boosts output and productivity growth.

The result of all of this is that a virtuous circle of growth and innovation could be sparked off so that the first possibly lucky accident leads to a continuing cycle for the originating group of companies or countries who are propelled along a higher growth path, while the rest are left behind. And it becomes very difficult to break into this cycle: the virtuous circle keeps those already advantaged at an advantageous position which reinforces the inequalities associated with the 'divergence, big time' characterizing the international system.

Could Globalization be the Cause of Inequalities?

The idea that globalization can cause inequality might be surprising. However, between-country reductions in inequality can coexist with increases in within-country inequality. And the above analysis emphasized the important role in calculations of global inequality played by just two, albeit very large, countries – namely, China and India – and the absence of any convergence between many developing countries and the OECD convergence club.

Only a few countries appear to account for the larger portion of the increases in world trade and international investment. They suggest that far from being a *general* process that has affected economies the world over, economic globalization has in fact been important in integrating only a few countries in the world economy. Other data support this general point. The World Bank estimates that exports of manufactured goods rose from 25 per cent of poor country exports in 1980 to 80 per cent in 1998. This integration was concentrated in 24 developing countries (including China and India), which were home to 3 billion people. These countries doubled the ratio of trade to national income and their per capita incomes rose by an average 5 per cent a year. Yet for another 2 billion people in the developing world, including much of Africa, the ratio of trade to national output fell and income per head shrank. Similarly, more than half of the foreign investment inflows to developing economies are concentrated in just five countries.

This is particularly striking for developing countries, even the so-called 'globalizers' that benefited from large increases in per capita incomes between 1980 and 1997. Prominent examples in this group are countries like India and China. Even as growth rose and poverty fell, inequality increased. Systematic investigation into the influence of trade on inequality by Ravallion (2001) showed that, while on average (that is, across all countries) there was no relation between participation in trade and inequality within a country, in low-income countries increasing trade was always associated with greater within-country inequality.

In these countries foreign investment may also play a role in contributing to income inequalities. While foreign firms are notorious for shifting their production to lower-cost locations in search of profits and have questionable practices in their treatment of legal and environmental regimes in many countries, foreign firms almost always raise wages in the economies and sectors that they enter. This is a well-established empirical fact, and one confirmed in most studies on foreign investment and wage rates.

Globalization or Regionalization?

This section lays out some data and arguments designed to answer the question as to whether the international economic system is developing along paradigmatic global lines or supranational regional lines. As will become clear, drawing a sharp contrast between these two trajectories for the international economy is not altogether appropriate: they overlap and there still remains considerable distinct nation-state based international economic activity as we will see. Thus the case is a mixed one. But, given the overriding emphasis placed upon the ubiquity of global forces and of globalization as the main tendential features of contemporary economic relationships – something accepted as the conventional wisdom by almost all journalists, policy-makers, politicians, activists and most academics working in this field – the burden of the following analysis is to suggest a counter case. It presents an argument that there are strong tendential features that might lead us to think of the international system forming into supra-national regional blocs in contrast to its 'globalization', and that these moves towards such a 'regionalization' are as strong as, if not stronger than, those leading towards further globalization. As will become clear, this section assembles a somewhat eclectic set of evidence to make its case, the implications of which are not altogether unambiguous even in their own terms.

To start with, three sets of data are presented in figure 8.5 that address the trade relationship between the USA, China and the rest of East Asia. Figure 8.5a shows the trajectory of exports to the ASEAN countries from the USA and from China. The obvious point to note is that USA exports to ASEAN peaked in the late 1990s and went into decline in the early 2000s, while China's exports to these countries continued to rise. Figure 8.5b looks at Japan's imports from the USA and from China, where imports from China continued to expand rapidly in the 1990s and early 2000s, while imports from the USA declined in value terms. Finally, figure 8.5c focuses on the imports of the Northeast Asian economies from the USA and from Japan. Whilst their imports from the USA stagnated over the late 1990s and early 2000s, there was a surge in imports from Japan.

What are the overall implications of these trends? Whilst these data are not comprehensive they do indicate to two main points (which have also been noted by other analyses): first the USA is loosing out on its exports to the East Asian region generally; secondly there seems to be growing trade integration between the Northeast Asian economies (including China) and Japan and the ASEAN countries. Thus a regional trade bloc could be forming in East Asia, thereby tending to exclude imports from the USA (though *exports to* the USA from this proto-bloc continue to remain strong, leading to well-known trans-Pacific trade tensions).

The increasing 'isolation' of the US economy from the rest of the international economy can be seen from the data presented in table 8.3. This shows correlations in the fluctuations of several real variables between the USA and Europe, Japan and Canada over two different time periods. In the case of USA–Europe and USA–Japan, there is a significant *reduction* in the correlations for all four variables

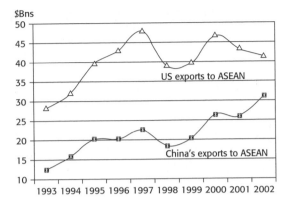

Figure 8.5a   US and Chinese exports to ASEAN, 1993–2002 ($bn)

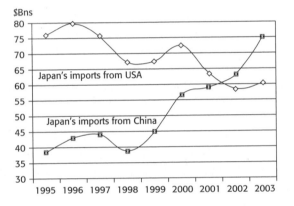

Figure 8.5b   Japan's imports from USA and China, 1995–2003 ($bn)

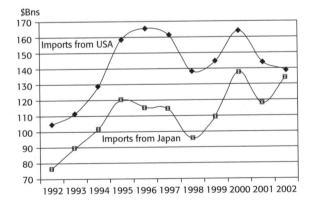

Northeast Asia includes China, Hong Kong, Korea, Taiwan and Japan.

Figure 8.5c   Imports of Northeast Asia from USA and Japan, 1992–2002 ($bn)

Source: Data in IMF, Direction of Trade Statistics, Annual Issues; 2003 data from Statistical Handbook of Japan

Table 8.3 Correlations of real variable fluctuations between the USA and other economies (1972–2000)		Output	Consumption	Investment	Employment
Europe	1972–1986	0.71	0.48	0.61	0.60
	1986–2000	0.31	0.06	−0.03	0.01
Japan	1972–1986	0.61	0.38	0.59	0.39
	1986–2000	−0.05	−0.01	−0.17	−0.30
Canada	1972–1986	0.76	0.38	0.01	0.54
	1986–2000	0.84	0.66	0.43	0.87

Source: Adapted from Heathcote and Perri (2002), table 6, p. 7

between 1972–86 and 1986–2000, implying an increasing 'divergence' of business cycles in global economic activity. On the other hand, between the USA and Canada the movement is in the opposite direction, with significant increases in correlations and convergence. Thus NAFTA seems to be working in these cases, with the consolidation of a North American bloc.

Another important feature of the international economy and the case for 'globalization' concerns the role of MNCs. Here the pertinent question for our purposes is 'Are MNCs genuinely globalizing their economic activity?' The conventional wisdom is that they are but this is strongly contested by the work of Alan Rugman (and co-authors). In several important books and articles (Rugman 2000, 2005a, 2005b; Rugman and Verbeke 2004a and 2004b; *MIR* 2005) these analyses have demonstrated that the vast majority of the top 500 MNCs either still remain 'national' in their operating characteristics, or are at best supranationally regional in their strategic outlook. Only 9 of the 500 were truly 'global' in Rugman's terms, with at least 20 per cent of their sales in all three parts of the triad of North America, Europe and East Asia, but less than 50 per cent in one of these regions alone. In fact, the vast bulk of the MNCs were still 'domestically' orientated with at least 80 per cent of their sales in their home territory or region.[2] What is more, Rugman's analysis suggests that this supranational regionalization of MNCs is becoming stronger rather than weaker.

There are also other quantitative approaches to international economic activity which have reached similar conclusions to Rugman's, but based on the supranational regionalized nature of trade activity. For instance, Su (2006) takes a network approach to trade flows. On the basis of four cross-sectional analyses for the years 1928, 1938, 1960 and 2000, Su finds that trade is regionally distributed rather than global in each case, and that this regional pattern has increased in intensity over the most recent cycle (1960–2000).

Table 8.4 Relationship of market region and borrower domicile

Panel A: Percentage of syndicated loan volume in each market due to borrowers in each domicile

Borrower domicile	US market	European market	Asian & SW Pacific market
United States	97.7	3.2	2.6
Europe	0.5	81.8	1.0
Latin America	0.2	6.3	0.3
Canada	1.0	0.6	0.0
Asia & SW Pacific	0.1	1.9	94.4
Other	0.5	6.2	1.7
Total	100.0	100.0	100.0

Panel B: Percentage of syndicated loan volume issued by borrowers in each domicile appearing in each market

Borrower domicile	US market	European market	Asian & SW Pacific market	Total
United States	98.5	1.2	0.3	100.0
Europe	1.7	98.0	0.3	100.0
Latin America	6.0	93.0	1.0	100.0
Canada	80.5	19.4	0.1	100.0
Asia & SW Pacific	0.9	6.9	92.2	100.0
Other	15.1	79.0	5.9	100.0

Data are for all multi-lender loans reported in Loanware as made in the three markets during 1992–2002. Panel A examines the composition of each market in terms of borrower domicile, whereas Panel B examines the market choices of borrowers from each domicile, one at a time.

Source: Carey and Nini (2004), table 1, p. 31

Returning for a moment to companies, a slightly different approach to Rugman's question about global or regional orientation of activities is provided by looking at the markets in corporate loans and securities. In table 8.4 the percentages of syndicated loans over the period 1992–2002 that are raised in one of the triad markets either by borrowers from different countries or that appear in the market when raised by borrowers from different domiciles is shown in Panels A and B respectively. On both counts it is clear that the international market for syndicated loans over this period is resolutely 'regional' rather than 'global'. There is hardly any cross-borrowing by actors from one international market to another outside of their home region. But while 80 per cent of loans raised by Canadian borrowers are from the US market, for instance, interestingly Latin America companies predominantly borrow from Europe. Asian and Southwest Pacific borrowers remain closely tethered to their home regional markets.

In part these results confirm the continued 'home biases' found in the international securities markets more generally, as reported in table 8.5. But what about the *trends* in international securities

Table 8.5 Home bias: portfolio allocations of lenders in each region

Borrower region	Lender region			Global weight
	US	Europe	Other	
US	91	39	31	64
Europe	6	51	12	22
Other	3	10	57	14
Total	100	100	100	100
Memo: lender-region share	49%	35%	16%	

Data are for all multi-lender loans reported in Loanware as made in the three markets during 1992–2002 that include information about participating lenders' shares of the amount of the loan. If loans with missing shares are included, results are similar, except that lenders from the Other region have shares of 40, 14 and 46 per cent in loans to US, European and other borrowers, respectively (for loans without share data, we assume each lender takes an equal share).

Source: Carey and Nini (2004), table 3, p. 32

trading? Figures 8.6a and 8.6b concentrate upon the shares of US and foreign equities in US and world portfolios.

Figure 8.6a shows that the proportion of US equities in total world portfolios remained steady between 1990 and 2003, though there was a slight rise of the US equity share in foreign portfolios (by about 4–5 per cent). (The 'adjusted' trend shown in both parts of this figure takes account of US investors exposure to foreign markets by the fact of US MNCs having a significant presence abroad.) In figure 8.6b the share of foreign equities in world portfolios has also remained steady, while that of the US share has risen slightly (by about 3 per cent). The general point to make in relation to these data is that there is only a slight trend growth of US equities in world portfolios, but that there is no sharp increase in foreign equity trading on the world's stock exchanges overall. Anywhere close to a truly global market for shares has yet to emerge.

Finally, in relationship to the globalization of company activity and its consequences, figure 8.7 switches to the returns on company stocks observed in the domestic and international spheres. If we were to ask what is driving any co-movement of company stock returns across national stock markets (and there is some evidence that this has happened since the mid-1980s) there are a number of possible explanations: coincidental country effects (like macro economic variable shocks), international financial integration, real integration, sector or industry effects, temporary idiosyncratic effects, and so on. Figure 8.7 provides evidence on these relationships based on fluctuations in the stock returns of a sample of 10,000 firms from 42 developed and emerging market countries operating in 40 industry sectors (Brooks and Del Negro 2002). The approach is to regress a value-weighted cross section of international stock returns on a number of global, country and industry variables.

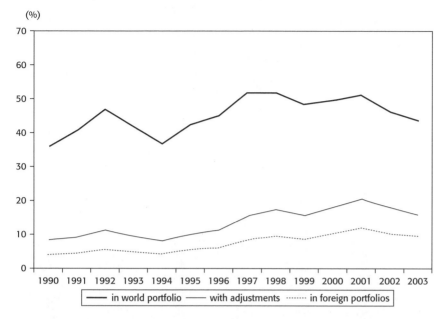

Figure 8.6a   The share of US equities in world and foreign portfolios

Source: Cai and Warnock (2004), figure 1

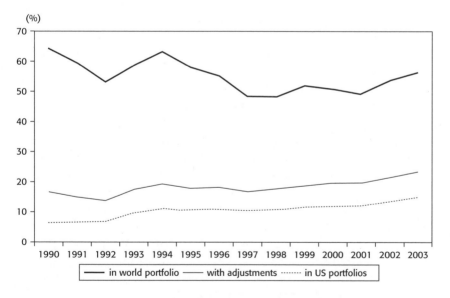

Figure 8.6b   The share of foreign equities in world and US portfolios

Source: Cai and Warnock (2004), figure 2

Temporary or idiosyncratic effects are not reported here.[3] For the rest, however, the emphasis is upon country effects, industry effects and diversification effects (which is a surrogate measure for global financial integration). What the results show is that specific *country*

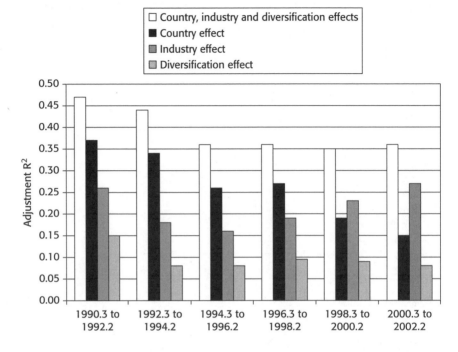

Figure 8.7   The relative importance of country, industry and diversification effects in global stock returns

Source: Adapted from Brooks and Del Negro (2002), figure 1, p. 43

effects have fallen in importance in explaining stock market return fluctuations – and this trend is a consistent result across a number of comparable studies. On the other hand, there is no great increase in the importance of *global financial integration* (as measured by the international diversification of balance sheet portfolios and income statements). Overall, however, there is some indication that between 1990 and 2002 at least the international correlation between stock market returns *decreased*. And many studies have found a similar result – a decrease in international financial integration since the late 1980s accompanied by a growing importance of what has happened just in the USA in explaining the actual trends because of its particular relationship to other countries (see discussion and references in Brooks and Del Negro 2002 and in Klingebiel 2002).

So far in this section we have concentrated on international trade and company activity. But what about financial activity more generally? Elsewhere I have concentrated on the financial aspect of the international system, presenting evidence and arguments that this is also either still national in orientation, or likely to develop further along supranational regional lines (Thompson 2004b; Thompson 2005). Here I just introduce some further evidence to this effect, which is shown in table 8.6.

Table 8.6 World bond market portfolio (end 2001) %

	Total bonds outstanding – % in world bond portfolio	Local currency bonds outstanding	
		% in world bond portfolio	% of country's total bonds
Developed countries	93.1	86.9	93
Euro area	22.0	19.5	89
UK	4.2	3.1	74
Japan	15.5	15.3	99
USA	46.2	45.3	98
Emerging markets	6.9	5.4	78
Latin America	1.7	0.8	48
Emerging Asia	3.8	3.5	91
China	1.3	1.3	97
India	0.4	0.4	97
World total	100	92	92

Local-currency denominated debt is the sum total of the long-term debt components ('Domestic Debt Securities') and local currency proportions of 'International Bond and Notes by Country of Residency' as both reported to the BIS. This is supplemented by data on other long-term debt for countries and Brady Bonds. It includes US$ 2.5 trillion of foreign currency, denominated primarily in US dollars, euros and sterling.

Source: Calculated from Burgen and Warnock (2004), table 1, p. 29

The global bond market is huge (towards the end of 2000 outstanding accumulated government and corporate bond issues were well over US$30,000 billion). But this market is dominated by two currencies of issue: at the end of 2002, 49.3 per cent in US dollars and 24.6 per cent in euros (Japanese yen was 9.6 per cent) (see Thompson 2006, table 4).

So where are these bonds issued and held? Table 8.6 answers this at a number of levels. Just over 93 per cent had been issued in the developed world leaving just under 7 per cent for the emerging markets, including China and India. And local currency bonds continue to be held in their country of origin, and bonds denominated in local currencies also dominate overall country portfolios. All in all then, there is still no serious 'global market' in bonds despite the often cited extent of East Asia's holding of US Treasury bonds. Compared to the total of all bonds issued, these holdings remain small (though they may present problems in themselves for the countries concerned in such government borrowing and lending).

To sum up this presentation of evidence on the character of international economic activity, again the approach has been to present a range of often overlapping data drawn from different sources to try to establish a robust general result. What are the implications of these data for the idea that everything economic is now global in character? They indicate that this idea is suspect on a number of counts. First, the bulk of economic activity still remains closely tethered to national territories and is not footloose internationally. Second, any economic activity that is resolutely 'international' in character is less globally configured than it is supranationally regionally based. The question needs to ask, therefore, why this is the case. Here we might learn something from the way the patterns of international trade (and investment) are analysed.

The Empirics of International Trade and Investment

The usual empirics of international trade (and investment to a lesser extent) are modelled via the operationalization of a gravity equation. In this, trade between two countries is seen as a positive function of the income of wealth of the countries and a negative function of the cost of trading or the distance between the two. In addition to these two variables, a further set of 'control' variables are introduced to account for cultural, geographical and institutional similarities/differences between countries that might also affect the amount of trade between them (see the equation below).[4] And it is these cultural, institutional and geographical variables that have been found to have become increasingly important in determining overall trade flows. The variables used in the equation are as follows: (BOR) – sharing a border; (LAN) – language differences; (COL) – past colonial ties; (BLOC) – belonging to a common trade bloc; (LAW) – legal differences; (CUR) – sharing a common currency.

$$Tij = a + b\left(\frac{GDPi}{Pi}\right) + c\left(\frac{GDPj}{Pj}\right) - d(Dij)$$
$$+ e(BORij) + f(LANij) + g(COLij)$$
$$+ h(BLOCij) + k(LAWij) + l(CURij) + u$$

As income grows, income as such becomes less important (indeed, with a coefficient of less that 1, that is a proportionate increase in income per capita leads to a less than proportionate increase in international trade). On the other hand distance remains a formidable deterrent to international trade, and other economic activity. Typical equation coefficients with respect to (international) distances are shown in table 8.7.

In addition, there is evidence that trading partners are becoming closer rather than further away, which is the opposite to what might be expected in an era of 'globalization' (Carrere and Schiff 2004). Of course, it is the relationship between cost and distance that is the

	Trade ($\partial = -1.25$)	FDI ($\partial = -0.42$)	Equity flows ($\partial = -0.85$)	Technology (R&D stocks)
1,000 km	0	0	0	0
2,000 km	58	25	45	35
4,000 km	82	44	69	72
8,000 km	97	58	83	95

Table 8.7 The effect of distance on economic interactions (international bilateral transactions). Percentage reductions in the value of magnitudes relative to 1,000 km

∂ are elasticities of transactions with respect to distance.

Source: Calculated from Venables (2002)

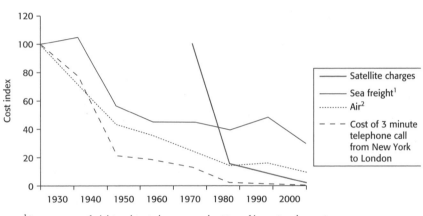

[1]Average ocean freight and port charges per short ton of import and export cargo
[2]Average air transport revenue per passenger mile

Figure 8.8   Decreasing costs of transport and communication

Sources: Busse (2003), also cited in IMF WEO 2005/HM Treasury (2005), chart 5, p. 6

major determinant of the trade coefficient in the table, and the dramatic reduction in freight rates that may have fuelled any growth of long-distance trade since the 1970 slowed considerably towards the end in the 1990s (see figure 8.8).

Thus we might expect a slowing down of 'globalization' as a result of these trends. There is a limit to how far the physical barriers presented by distance and cost can be overcome, hence the incentive to trade (and invest) closer to home on a regional basis.

And this is bolstered by the effects of some of the other 'cultural' or 'institutional' variables shown in the equation that are important in explaining the coefficients for trade and the other dimensions shown in table 8.7. Legal differences (LAW) are a major factor, language differences (LAN) are important, past colonial ties (COL – important for migration) are another key factor. Then there are 'geographical' variables like sharing a border (BOR) and whether the countries belong to a common trade bloc (BLOC). Finally, the sharing of a common currency (CUR) can be a major stimulant to trade and other interactions. Many of these influences favour local solutions to economic relationships over global ones.

Conclusions

Several points can be made in conclusion based upon the above analysis. In the first place, it is not at all clear that 'globalization' has proceeded to the extent often thought by popular or even academic opinion. Such that there has been any dramatic increase in the internationalization of economic activity it has demonstrated an important supranational regional dimension. Indeed, this may be the dominant trend. If so, then inequalities might be better tackled on this supranational regional basis rather than by looking for further global responses to it.

Indeed, it was during the period of global retrenchment in the inter-war period that some 'convergence' between countries emerged, adding to the argument that globalization as such may not be an effective mechanism to encourage the amelioration of inequalities. The forces for continued divergence remain strong, even where globalization is active. Recognizing this, and tackling these divergences through concerted regional action may provide an answer.

And here, expecting MNCs to provide the mechanism for the global transfer of technology and innovation could also prove a false hope. MNCs continue to concentrate their activities in the home base or regionally amongst the TRIAD group of convergence countries. The only economies to have yet developed an 'autonomous' innovation regime in the post-World War II period have been Japan, Korea and possibly Taiwan. All of these did this very much as a 'bootstraps' exercise without relying on foreign capital to kick-start their innovation processes.

This is not an argument for the development of antagonistically poised trading blocs in the international system, but it is one that seeks to find a way forward for the reduction of international inequalities through other means than the further globalization of responses. As we have seen, the conditions for this global response may have diminished recently as distance and transport costs re-assert their constraints on the further development of long-distance economic interactions. Regional configurations could also be stimulated by these developments.

Notes

1   Whether this is still an appropriate division in a 'globalized' world is challenged by Payne (2005), who argues that the pattern is now much more diverse and multilayered. In part, the analysis in the main text supports this view. But given there remains such a vast difference between the incomes of the very poor and those of the very rich, with not much in between (an absent 'global middle-class' – Milanovic 2005), a division along these lines still seems worthwhile.

2   Rugman concentrates on sales in his analysis to the (relative) neglect of assets, employment and sourcing. There is some strong support that assets are also supranationally regionally distributed (Rugman 2005b), but sourcing is completely neglected. Some companies, for instance may sell most of their output 'nationally' but source their raw materials, components and intermediate or retail products 'internationally'.

3   In fact these can be by far the most important in terms of coefficient value, consistently accounting for some 50 per cent of the variance in the equation formulations found in this and other studies. This alone casts some doubt that there is a systematic relationship between international stock returns since half of the fluctuation is due to unidentified (non-systematic) variables.

4   Other variables can be added here, of course. Two of the most important not considered in this short exposition would be a country size variable and one to measure factor endowments.

References

Anand, S. and Kanbur, R. 1993. 'The Kuznets Process and the Inequality–Development Relationship.' *Journal of Development Economics*, 40 (1): 25–52.

Barro, R. J. 2000. 'Inequality and Growth in a Panel of Countries.' *Journal of Economic Growth*, 5: 5–32.

Brooks, R. and Del Negro, M. 2002. 'Firm-Level Evidence on Globalization.' Washington, DC: IMF, Financial Studies Division.

Burgen, J. D. and Warnock, F. E. 2004. 'Foreign Participation in Local-Currency Bond Markets.' International Finance Discussion Paper 2004-794. Washington, DC: The Federal Reserve Board.

Cai, F. and Warnock, F. E. 2004. 'International Diversification at Home and Abroad.' International Finance Discussion Paper 2004-793. Washington, DC: The Federal Reserve Board.

Carey, M. and Nini, G. 2004. 'Is the Corporate Loan Market Globally Integrated? A Pricing Puzzle.' International Finance Discussion Paper 2004-813. Washington, DC: The Federal Reserve Board.

Carrere, C. and Schiff, M. 2004. 'On the Geography of Trade: Distance is Alive and Well.' Policy Research Working Paper, no. 3206. Washington, DC: World Bank.

Cline, W. 1997. *Trade and Income Distribution*. Washington, DC: Institute for International Economics.

Dowrick, S. and DeLong, J. B. 2003. 'Globalization and Convergence.' In Michael D. Bordo, Alan M. Taylor and Jeffrey Williamson (eds), *Globalization in Historical Perspective*. Chicago, Ill.: University of Chicago Press.

Easterly, W. and Levine, R. 2001. 'It's Not Factor Accumulation: Stylized Facts and Growth Models.' *World Bank Economic Review*, 15 (2): 177–219.

Fischer, S. 2003. 'Globalization and Its Challenges.' *American Economic Review*, 93 (2): 1–30.

Freeman, A. 2003. 'Globalization: Economic Stagnation and Divergence.' In A. Pettifor (ed.), *Real World Economic Outlook*. Basingstoke: Palgrave Macmillan, figure 16.1, p. 153.

Heathcote, J. and Perri, F. 2002. 'Financial Globalization and Real Globalization.' NBER Working Paper, no. 9292. Cambridge, Mass.: NBER.

Hirst, P. Q. and Thompson, G. F. 1999. *Globalization in Question: The International Economy and the Possibilities of Governance*, second edition. Cambridge: Polity Press.

HM Treasury 2005. 'Global Europe: Full Employment Europe.' HM Treasury, October 2005, chart 5, p. 6.

ILO 2004. *A Fair Globalization: Creating Opportunities for All*. Report of the World Commission on the Social Effects of Globalization. Geneva: ILO.

Klingebiel, D. 2002. 'Capital Markets and Financial Integration in Europe: Discussion of Firm-Level Evidence on Globalization.' Mimeo, World Bank.

Kuznets, S. 1955. 'Economic Growth and Income Inequality.' *American Economic Review*, 45 (2): 1–28.

Luxembourg Income Study, 2000. 'Income Inequality Measures'. At www.lisproject.org/keyfigures/ineqtable.htm.

Milanovic, B. 2002. 'Income Convergence During the Disintegration of the World Economy 1919–39.' Washington, DC: World Bank.

Milanovic, B. 2005. *Worlds Apart: Measuring International and Global Inequality*. Princeton, NJ: Princeton University Press.

MIR (*Management International Review*) 2005. 'Special Issue on Regional Multinationals.' *MIR*, 45 (1): 5–166.

Payne, A. 2005. *The Global Politics of Unequal Development*. Basingstoke: Palgrave Macmillan.

Pritchett, L. 1997. 'Divergence, Big Time.' *Journal of Economic Perspectives*, 11 (3) Summer: 3–17.

Ravallion, M. 2001. 'Growth, Inequality and Poverty: Looking Beyond Averages.' *World Development*, 29 (11): 1803–15.

Ravallion, M. and Chen, S. 1997. 'What Can New Survey Data Tell Us about Recent Changes in Distribution and Poverty?' *World Bank Economic Review*, 11 (2): 357–82.

Rugman, A. M. 2000. *The End of Globalization*. London: Random House Business Books.

Rugman, A. M. 2005a. 'Regional Multinationals and the Myth of Globalization.' Paper to the Centre for the Study of Globalisation and Regionalisation (CSGR) Annual Conference, Warwick University, 26–8 October 2005.

Rugman A. M. 2005b. *The Regional Multinationals: MNEs and 'Global' Strategic Management*. Cambridge: Cambridge University Press.

Rugman, A. M. and Verbeke, A. 2004a. 'A Perspective on Regional and Global Strategies of Multinational Enterprises.' *Journal of International Business Studies*, 35: 3–18.

Rugman, A. M. and Verbeke, A. 2004b. 'Regional Transnationals and Triad Strategy.' *Transnational Corporations*, 14 (3): 1–20.

Su, Tieting 2006. *Globalization and Trade: World Trade Networks 1920–2000*. London: Routledge.

Thompson, G. F. 2004a. 'Are There Any Limits to Globalization? Trade, Capital Flows and Borders.' In N. Karagiannis and M. Witter (eds), *The Caribbean*

Economies in an Era of Free Trade. London: Ashgate.

Thompson, G. F. 2004b. 'Global Inequality, Economic Globalization and Technological Change.' In W. Brown, S. Bromley and S. Athreye (eds), *Ordering the International: History, Change and Transformation*. London: Pluto Press.

Thompson, G. F. 2005. 'Is the Future "Regional" for Global Standards?' *Environment and Planning A*, 37 (11), November: 2053–71.

Thompson, G. F. 2006. 'Economic Policy Making in Europe since the Advent of the Euro.' In C. Hay and A. Menon (eds), *Handbook of European Politics*. Oxford: Oxford University Press.

Twomey, M. J. 2000. *A Century of Foreign Investment in the Third World*. London: Routledge.

Venables, A. J. 2002. 'Geography and International Inequalities: The Impact of New Technologies.' *Journal of Industry, Competition and Trade*, 1 (2).

Weisbrot, M., Baker, D., and Rosnick, D. 2005. 'The Scorecard on Development: 25 Years of Diminished Progress.' At www.cepr.net/publications/development_2005_09.pdf.

World Bank 2002. *World Development Indicators 2002*. Washington, DC: World Bank.

9

Spatial Disparities and Economic Development

Ravi Kanbur and Anthony J. Venables

Introduction

AMIDST a growing concern about increasing inequality, the spatial dimensions of inequality have begun to attract considerable policy interest. In China, Russia, India, Mexico and South Africa, as well as most other developing and transition economies, there is a sense that spatial and regional disparities in economic activity, incomes and social indicators, are on the increase. Spatial inequality, defined as inequality in economic and social indicators of well-being across geographical units within a country, is a dimension of overall inequality, but it has added significance when spatial and regional divisions align with political and ethnic tensions to undermine social and political stability. Also important in the policy debate is a perceived sense that increasing internal spatial inequality is related to greater openness of economies, and to globalization in general.

Inequalities between continents and countries are of course 'spatial', but our focus in this chapter is on spatial disparities between regions within a country. In contrast to between-country comparisons, this is an area where there has been remarkably little systematic documentation of facts concerning what has happened. Correspondingly, there is insufficient understanding of the determinants of spatial disparities in a globalizing world. As a result, the policy discussion tends to take place in something of an analytical vacuum. To address this gap the World Institute for Development Economics Research of the United Nations University (UNU-WIDER) launched its project, 'Spatial Disparities in Human Development'. The project invited submissions of papers to a series of five conferences, covering broad methodological topics as well as with specific regional focus. All the papers selected for conference presentation were then further subjected to academic peer review, and only those that passed these quality standards were published. In all, there are six such volumes, with more than 40 peer-reviewed papers.[1] This chapter summarizes some of the main themes and conclusions from the studies.

A small number of the studies in the project are purely methodo-logical, focusing on techniques for measuring and analysing spatial inequality. But most of the studies are empirical in nature. Between them, the papers provide information on different dimensions of spatial disparities in no fewer than 58 developing and transition economies[2]. Some of the papers are country case studies. Others are comparative, covering several countries. Some countries (like China, Mexico or Russia) are covered by more than one paper, each emphasizing a different aspect of spatial inequality. For 26 countries, one or more papers make use of information from two points in time, allowing an assessment of the evolution of spatial disparities and the determinants of this evolution.[3]

The papers published in the six volumes of the project represent one of the most comprehensive collections of detailed analysis on spatial disparities in development. They comprise a rich source of empirical information and methodological techniques for understanding spatial inequality and its evolution in the development process. It would be impossible to summarize the rich and diverse country-specific findings in the papers. However, we can attempt to draw out some of the main findings by asking the following three questions:

1 How big are spatial disparities, and what has been happening to them?
2 What explains the levels and trends in spatial inequality?
3 What are the appropriate policy responses to spatial inequality?

Let us take each of these questions in turn.

Levels and Trends in Spatial Disparities

Interpersonal inequality within a country can be divided into within- and between-group elements. For the purposes of the studies in this pro-ject the group is defined spatially, as a region or perhaps as an urban–rural distinction. The researcher can then construct measures of inequality between regions, such as a Gini coefficient, just as such meas-ures can applied between individuals within a country or region. Indeed, for a particular inequality measure (the generalized entropy measure) it is possible to measure the proportions of overall inequality due to inter-regional and intra-regional inequalities. Researchers typically find that up to 25 per cent of overall inequality is between regions, the remainder being accounted for by interpersonal inequalities within regions.

Using these and other measures the overall conclusion from the wealth of information presented in the studies undertaken in the project is that spatial inequality is high and, in many countries, rising.

While there is tremendous country heterogeneity, the case is illustrated by the following examples:

1 In Africa, in 6 out of the 12 countries studied by Sahn and Stifel (2003), the percentage of people below a poverty line constructed on the basis of information about households' asset holdings is more than 50 percentage points greater in rural areas than in urban areas. The smallest rural–urban difference is 30 percentage points. Similarly, school enrolments, and the ratio of girl to boy enrolments, is much higher in urban than in rural areas.

2 In Peru, the incidence of poverty in districts at sea level was 46.1 per cent in 1997, while for districts at an altitude greater than 3,500 metres above sea level it was 63.3 per cent (Escobal and Torero 2005).

3 In Indonesia, in 1993, the rural poverty incidence was 46.5 per cent in West Kalimantan, but only 10.7 per cent in Yogyakarta (Friedman 2005).

4 In China, in 2002 rural per capita income in Shanghai province was 6,224 yuan, but only 1490 yuan in Guizhou province (Wan and Zhou 2005).

5 Using community level data on public services, Anderson and Pomfret (2005) show considerable inequalities in the provision of public services in Central Asia. For example, in Tajikistan, 'Gorno-Badakhshan, the most isolated region, has poor roads, low-quality and inadequately heated schools, and low availability of water, sewer and garbage disposal systems.'

These examples can be multiplied many times from each of the countries studied in the project. Spatial inequalities are high. But how are they evolving over time? Once again there is country heterogeneity, but the overall conclusion is inescapable. For the 26 countries for which the studies used data over time, spatial inequalities have by and large been on the increase. The following examples are illustrative.

1 In Africa, Sahn and Stifel (2003) conduct tests of rural–urban convergence in achievement indices for eight different welfare indicators. They conclude that 'there is only convergence in cases of enrolment and stunting; and when we exclude Nigeria, there are no cases of convergence, while there is statistically significant divergence in cases of asset poverty and enrolments.'

2 In Mexico, using the appropriate statistical tests, García-Verdú (2005) finds convergence across regions in adult literacy, but not in per capita GDP or infant mortality.

3 Forster, Jesuit and Smeeding (2005) examine changes in the regional patterns of inequality in the Czech Republic, Hungary, Poland and

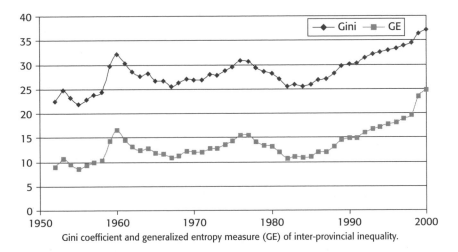

Gini coefficient and generalized entropy measure (GE) of inter-provincial inequality.

Figure 9.1   The evolution of regional inequality in China.

Source: Kanbur and Zhang (2005)

Russia using data from the Luxembourg Income Study for the 1990s. They find that 'capital cities and major urban areas are mainly winners, while regions which are longer distances from their rich western neighbors characterize losers.'

4 Friedman (2005) highlights another dimension of regional dispar-ity, that the poverty-reducing impact of growth differs from region to region in Indonesia – 'poverty has been much more responsive to growth in rural Java and Bali than in the more remote areas of Kalimantan, Maluku, and Irian Jaya with other regions such as Sumatra and Sulawesi falling somewhere in between.'

5 For China, Kanbur and Zhang (2005) estimate inter-povincial inequality over 1952–2000 (see figure 9.1). Regional inequality was low in the first years of communist rule when land reform was intro-duced, but rose precipitously during the Great Leap Forward. It then fell back, until the effects of the Cultural Revolution started an increase in inequality that peaked in 1976. Following this, the trans-ition from the Cultural Revolution to the period of rural reform saw a decline in inequality through until the mid-1980s. Since then decentralization and opening the economy to trade and investment has brought a steady increase in inequality between regions.

Explanations of High and Rising Disparities

Why do spatial disparities arise in developing countries? The economic geographer's distinction between first and second nature geography is helpful. First nature simply says that some regions are favoured by virtue of their natural characteristics. These may be proximity to rivers, coasts, ports and borders, or endowments of climate or natural resources. Evidently these factors account for some of the success of coastal China relative to the interior, border states of Mexico relative to the South, and low altitude regions of Peru relative to mountains.

Second nature emphasizes the efficiency gains from proximity. Interactions between economic agents (firms and consumers) are more efficient in densely packed areas than when people are widely dispersed. There are a number of reasons for this, usually organized under three headings, and extensively analysed in the 'new economic geography' (see Fujita and Thisse 2002). The first is technological externalities; firms learn from the co-presence of other firms in related activities, so are able to innovate and implement new technologies more efficiently. The second is 'thick' labour markets. In regions of dense economic activity labour markets work more efficiently, having lower costs of job seeking and better matching of firm's labour requirements to available labour skills. Incentives for workers to acquire specialist skills may also be greater, as workers are more likely to be able to find employers demanding those skills. The third heading is specialization and the size of the market. Firms that locate close to large markets can operate at a larger size, gaining advantages of increasing returns to scale. Their scale of operation will attract suppliers of intermediate goods and services. This may lead to the development of specialist supply networks, increasing further the attractiveness of the region for firms.

The effect of these spatially concentrated efficiency gains is to cause cities and booming regions to have high productivity, and this in turn attracts more people and firms into the city or region. These agglomeration forces can therefore create virtuous circles of self-reinforcing development in some cities or regions, while other regions lag behind. Thus, first nature geography may give a region an initial advantage, which then becomes amplified by second nature agglomeration forces. Provision of public services may be a further amplification force; for reasons of both efficiency and political economy, public services may be concentrated in urban areas which are both relatively easy to serve and politically influential.

What determines the strength of these forces? How do they depend on aspects of the economic environment such as openness to trade, the stock of labour skills, the quality of infrastructure and the policy environment? Many of the studies in the UNU-WIDER project address the question of explaining high and rising spatial disparities. Again, it would be impossible to summarize in any simple way the rich range of conclusions from each of these studies, but we can highlight two central causal factors – public infrastructure and openness to international trade.

1 For Africa, many of the social indicators used by Sahn and Stifel (2003) in their documentation of rural–urban disparity, such as school enrolments and neonatal care, are direct reflections of the inequality in the distribution of public schools and health.
2 Again for Africa, the importance of 'remoteness' in explaining poverty is established by Christiaensen, Demery and Paternostro (2005), this remoteness being a function not just of distance but lack of transport connections to the capital city and the coast.
3 For Peru, Escobal and Torero (2005) conduct a statistical analysis in which explanatory variables are introduced in sequence to explain regional income variations in Peru. 'First nature' geographic variables such as altitude, soil type and temperature are first introduced and provide good explanation. But when infrastructure variables are introduced the explanatory power of the geographic variables weakens and almost disappears. What this suggests is that public infrastructure plays a powerful role in explaining levels and changes in spatial disparities.
4 Similar conclusions can be drawn from the work of Ravallion (2005) on China. Using appropriate statistical techniques, he establishes that there are indeed spatial agglomeration forces at play in explaining changes in individual level incomes, and the crucial role of local infrastructure (as well as local natural endowments) in explaining successful income growth. The implication is that spatial disparities will have a tendency to rise, which of course is what is found by the studies in this project.
5 For India, Lall and Chakravorty (2005) show the propensity of private sector firms to locate away from 'lagging and inland regions', which are of course the regions with poor infrastructure and poor connections to the coast and the major urban clusters.

Spatial disparities have risen over the last two decades according to the studies in this project. The last two decades have also seen considerable opening up of economies to international trade. Are these two phenomena related? Predictions from theoretical economic geography are ambiguous. On the one hand, trade is likely to have the effect of breaking down some long-established inward-looking centres of activity; inward-looking centres of import-substituting production become less viable. But on the other, trade facilitates the development of new coastal or border located clusters. The empirical studies in this project appear to support the idea that trade has on balance increased spatial disparities, as new export-oriented areas of economic activity have seen the most rapid economic growth.

1 Kanbur and Zhang (2005) find that a variable measuring China's trade openness provides at least partial statistical explanation of increasing regional inequality in China since the start of the economic reforms in 1978.
2 For Mexico, Rodriguez-Pose and Sanchez-Reaza (2005) examine pre- and post-NAFTA patterns of regional growth, and find that 'trade liberalization and economic integration have not provoked a reduction in territorial disparities, but have led to greater polarization.' A similar result is found by García-Verdú (2005).
3 For Vietnam, Jensen and Tarp (2005) carry out a number of simulation experiments based on a model of trade. They find that 'Comparing the poverty impact of trade liberalization between urban and rural areas, it appears that the number of poor expands more rapidly in rural areas compared to urban areas. Trade liberalization will therefore tend to worsen the rural poverty headcount bias in Vietnam in the short to medium term.'
4 For Africa, the evidence on openness is more indirect. Te Welde and Morrissey (2005) find that in West Africa, foreign-owned firms tend to locate in the capital city, pay higher wages and employ more skilled workers, thereby exacerbating inequality vis-à-vis rural areas. McCormick and Wahba (2003) find that in Egypt, 'there is a regional bias in the location of firms and jobs created by returnees compared with non-migrants, in favor of the capital city.'
5 The growth effects of trade are often spatially concentrated, and in addition there is evidence that more remote areas benefit less from growth in terms of its poverty reduction impact (Friedman 2005 for Indonesia, and Christiaensen, Demery and Paternostro 2005, for Africa), leading to a divergence in poverty rates across the regions of a country.

Appropriate Policy

There are several reasons why policymakers should be concerned about spatial inequalities in economic and social indicators of well-being. First, inequality *between* a nation's regions is one component of overall national inequality across individuals (the other component being of course inequality across individuals *within* each geographical unit or region). When spatial inequality goes up then, other things being equal, so does national inequality. Second, inequality *between* a nation's regions may be of concern in and of itself, especially when the geographical regions align with political, ethnic, language or religious divisions. Yet spatial inequalities may also be associated with high levels of efficiency, or may be a manifestation of rapid growth. Openness to the outside world, which is well recognized as a long-term source of efficiency and growth, can lead to spatial concentration of activity. Spatial agglomeration brings the benefits of increasing returns to scale and thus helps efficiency and growth, but these agglomeration forces are also associated with market failures. The positive and negative externalities associated with clustering and congestion mean that there is no presumption that unregulated activity gives the most efficient outcome. The growth of megacities suggests that agglomerations can become too large, so there may be an efficiency case for decentralization of activity to new centres.

The evidence presented in the UNU-WIDER project is clear, spatial inequalities are high and rising. What then should be the policy response, bearing in mind the trade-offs involved? The theory, evidence and causal analysis presented in this project suggests a two-pronged approach to addressing the problem of rising spatial inequalities while still reaping the gains from agglomeration and international trade. The first component of the strategy is to remove barriers to the deconcentration of economic activity. These can be political and institutional obstacles, such as the need for firms to locate near political and administrative centres. The strategy also requires the development of economic and social infrastructure to facilitate deconcentration, and to help interior and poorer regions benefit from integration into the global economy. Such investments can also start growth poles in lagging regions – new centres of activity can develop and reach a scale where they benefit from a virtuous circle of agglomeration. The second component is to facilitate, or at least not impede, the migration of individuals and households to areas of high and rising well-being. Such redistributions of population are beneficial to the individuals concerned, and are an inherent part of the structural change associated with development. This two-sided approach stands the best chance of gaining the most from the efficiencies of agglomeration and openness, without running into the potential destabilization of rising spatial inequality. Here are some examples of support for these components from the studies in this project.

1 For China, Ravallion (2005) argues that 'results provide support for the types of poor-area development programs that have been supported by the Government of China since the mid-1980s. . . . [T]he present results also point to the importance of local endowments of human and physical infrastructure to the microgrowth process. When combined with data on the costs to the government's

budget of alternative interventions, these empirical results will hopefully also inform public choices on how best to balance agricultural development initiatives with infrastructure development, so as to assure maximum growth of living standards in poor areas.'

2 For India, Lall and Chakravorty (2005) turn their findings on the determinants of firm investment in poor regions into a policy question of how industrial development can be induced to reach the lagging regions. The answer seems to be not industrial ownership by the state in lagging regions (on which the record has not been good) but infrastructure provision to start a virtuous cycle of agglomeration.

3 For Africa, Christiaensen, Demery and Paternostro (2005) conclude as follows: 'The recent microeconomic evidence on poverty dynamics has shown that some regions, by virtue of their sheer remoteness, have been left behind as growth has picked up. Households with limited access to markets and public services have not benefited from growth in the 1990s. The provision of public goods (notably infrastructure services – from the Ethiopian case, especially roads and from the Ugandan case, electricity) is crucial to help poor households benefit from the opportunities created by economic policy reforms and growth.'

4 For China, there is a considerable literature on how restrictions on migration from one area to another have prevented the poor from benefiting fully from the growth of the coastal regions, leading to a dramatic increase in spatial inequality (Kanbur and Zhang 2005). Of course migration does take place, leading to the large number of illegal workers on the streets of the major cities. A freer regime of migration, suitably phased in to address the problems of urban congestion, would constitute the second component of a strategy to manage rising spatial inequalities in China (the first component being, of course, a more spatially equitable investment strategy for public infrastructure).

5 For Brazil, Timmins (2005) applied a statistical methodology for estimating the power of agglomeration forces while taking into account migration. He found that migration mitigates these forces considerably, so much so that without taking migration into account there may be a considerable overestimate of the benefits of agglomeration returns.

6 The case of Chile, studied by Soto and Torche (2004) for the project, also highlights the importance of impediments to migration, not so much through physical restriction as through fiscal incentives. They find that lack of convergence in Chile in the 1980s and 1990s is associated with low levels of regional migration and that this phenomenon is in part the result of government social policies.

These include restrictions on the sale or rent of subsidized houses, effectively tying families to their original location and, thus, inhibiting migration.

The broad outline of appropriate policy for managing high and rising spatial disparities is thus clear. The case for policy interventions to ensure a more spatially equitable allocation of infrastructure and public services, and for policies to ensure freer migration, has been made powerfully in the papers in the project. But of course the broad outline still needs to be developed in a detailed and country-specific manner. The benefits of infrastructure allocation need to be weighed against the costs, so both will have to be quantified. Migration has equity benefits, but these have to be set against possible congestion costs in receiving regions, and the risk of further undermining the economic base of sending regions. In order to make these trade-offs in an evidence-based way, we will need a deeper and more detailed understanding of the determinants of spatial inequality, and how exactly policy interventions in infrastructure and other areas will impinge on it. The studies undertaken in the UNU-WIDER project and described in this chapter have made a start. A full research and policy agenda lies ahead.

Notes

1   The volumes are as follows, in chronological order. (1) Ravi Kanbur and Anthony J. Venables (eds), *Spatial Issues in Africa*, Special Issue of the *Journal of African Economies*, 12 (4), December 2003. (2) Ravi Kanbur and Anthony J. Venables (eds), *Spatial Inequality and Development*, Oxford University Press, January 2005. (3) Ravi Kanbur and Anthony J. Venables (eds), *Spatial Inequality and Development*, Special Issue of *Journal of Economic Geography*, 5 (1), January 2005. (4) Ravi Kanbur, Anthony J. Venables and Guanghua Wan (eds), *Spatial Inequality and Development in Asia*, Special Issue of *Review of Development Economics*, 9 (1), February 2005. (5) Ravi Kanbur, Luis F. Lopez Calva and Anthony J. Venables (eds), *Spatial Inequality in Latin America*, Symposium in *Cuadernos de Economía (Latin American Journal of Economics)*, 42 (124/125), December 2004/May 2005. (6) Ravi Kanbur, Anthony J. Venables and Guanghua Wan (eds), *Spatial Disparities in Human Development*, United Nations University Press, November 2005.

2   The countries are as follows. *Africa*: Benin, Burkina Faso, Burundi, Cameroon, Central African Republic, Chad, Comoros, Côte d'Ivoire, Egypt, Ethiopia, Ghana, Kenya, Madagascar, Malawi, Mali, Mauritania, Mozambique, Namibia, Niger, Nigeria, Rwanda, South Africa, Senegal, Tanzania, Togo, Uganda, Zambia, Zimbabwe; *Asia*: Bangladesh, Cambodia, China, India, Indonesia, Malaysia, Nepal, Pakistan, Philippines, South Korea, Turkey, Vietnam; *Latin America*: Argentina, Bolivia, Brazil, Chile, Colombia, Ecuador, Mexico, Peru; *Transition Economies*: Czech Republic, Hungary, Kazakhstan, Kyrgyz Republic, Poland, Russia, Tajikistan, Turkmenistan, Ukraine, Uzbekistan. A small number of the papers also provide some spatial information on a number of

developed countries: Austria, Belgium, Canada, Finland, France, Germany, Greece, Japan, Spain, Switzerland, United Kingdom, United States.
3   These countries are: Brazil, Burkina Faso, Cameroon, Côte d'Ivoire, China, Egypt, Ethiopia, Ghana, India, Indonesia, Kenya, Madagascar, Mauritania, Mexico, Niger, Nigeria, Peru, Philippines, Russia, Senegal, South Africa, Tanzania, Togo, Uganda, Zambia, Zimbabwe.

References

Anderson, Kathryn and Pomfret, Richard 2005. 'Spatial Inequality and Development in Central Asia.' In Ravi Kanbur, Anthony J. Venables and Guanghua Wan (eds), *Spatial Disparities in Human Development: Perspectives from Asia*. Tokyo: United Nations University Press.

Christiaensen, Luc, Demery, Lionel and Paternostro, Stefano 2005. 'Reforms, Remoteness and Risk in Africa: Understanding Inequality and Poverty During the 1990s.' In Ravi Kanbur and Anthony J. Venables (eds), *Spatial Inequality and Development*. Oxford: Oxford University Press.

Escobal, Javier and Torero, Maximo 2005. 'Adverse Geography and Differences in Welfare in Peru.' In Ravi Kanbur and Anthony J. Venables (eds), *Spatial Inequality and Development*. Oxford: Oxford University Press.

Forster, Michael, Jesuit, David and Smeeding, Timothy 2005. 'Regional Poverty and Income Inequality in Central and Eastern Europe: Evidence from the Luxembourg Income Study.' In Ravi Kanbur and Anthony J. Venables (eds), *Spatial Inequality and Development*. Oxford: Oxford University Press.

Friedman, Jed 2005. 'How Responsive is Poverty to Growth? A Regional Analysis of Poverty, Inequality and Growth in Indonesia, 1984–99.' In Ravi Kanbur and Anthony J. Venables (eds), *Spatial Inequality and Development*. Oxford: Oxford University Press.

Fujita, M. and Thisse, J. 2002. '*The Economics of Agglomeration*.' Cambridge: Cambridge University Press.

García-Verdú, Rodrigo 2005. 'Income, Mortality, and Literacy Distribution Dynamics Across Sates in Mexico: 1940–2000.' *Cuadernos de Economía*, 42 (42), May: 165–92.

Henderson, J. Vernon and Gun Wang, Hyoung 2005. 'Aspects of Rural–Urban Transformation of Countries.' *Journal of Economic Geography*, 5 (1) January: 23–42.

Jensen, Henning Tarp and Tarp, Finn 2005. 'Trade Liberalization and Spatial Inequality: A Methodological Innovation in a Vietnamese Perpsective.' *Review of Development Economics*, 9 (1), February: 69–86.

Kanbur, Ravi and Rapoport, Hillel 2005. 'Migration Selectivity and the Evolution of Spatial Inequality.' *Journal of Economic Geography*, 5 (1), January: 43–58.

Kanbur, Ravi and Zhang, Xiaobo 2005. 'Fifty Years of Regional Inequality in China: A Journey Through Central Planning, Reform and Openness.' *Review of Development Economics*, 9 (1), January: 87–106.

Lall, Somik Vinay and Chakravorty, Sanjoy 2005. 'Industrial Location and Spatial Inequality: Theory and Evidence from India.' *Review of Development Economics*, 9 (1), February: 47–68.

Lin, Songhua 2005. 'International Trade, Location and Wage Inequality in China.' In Ravi Kanbur and Anthony J. Venables (eds), *Spatial Inequality and Development*. Oxford: Oxford University Press.

McCormick, Barry and Wahba, Jackline 2003. 'Return Migration and Geographical Inequality: The Case of Egypt.' *Journal of African Economies*, 12 (1), December: 500–32.

Ravallion, Martin 2005. 'Externalities in Rural Development: Evidence for China.' In Ravi Kanbur and Anthony J. Venables (eds), *Spatial Inequality and Development*. Oxford: Oxford University Press.

Rodriguez-Pose, Andres and Sanchez-Reaza, Javier 2005. 'Economic Polarization Through Trade: Trade Liberalization and Regional Inequality in Mexico.' In Ravi Kanbur and Anthony J. Venables (eds), *Spatial Inequality and Development*. Oxford: Oxford University Press.

Sahn, David and Stifel, David 2003. 'Urban–Rural Inequality in Living Standards in Africa.' *Journal of African Economies*, 12 (1), December: 564–97.

Soto, Raimundo and Torche, Aristides 2004. 'Spatial Inequality, Migration and Growth in Chile.' *Cuadernos de Economía* 41 (124), December: 401–24.

Te Welde, Dirk Willem and Morrissey, Oliver 2005. 'Spatial Inequality for Manufacturing Wages in Five African Countries.' In Ravi Kanbur and Anthony J. Venables (eds), *Spatial Inequality and Development*. Oxford: Oxford University Press.

Timmins, Christopher 2005. 'Estimable Equilibrium Models of Locational Sorting and Their Role in Development Economics.' *Journal of Economic Geography*, 5 (1), January: 59–83.

Venables, Anthony J. 2005. 'Spatial Disparities in Developing Countries: Cities, Regions, and International Trade.' *Journal of Economic Geography*, 5 (1), January: 3–22.

Wan, Guanghua and Zhou, Zhangye 2005. 'Income Inequality in Rural China: Regression-based Decomposition Using Household Data.' *Review of Development Economics*, 9 (1) February: 107–20.

10

More Inequality and Fewer Opportunities? Structural Determinants and Human Agency in the Dynamics of Income Distribution

Gøsta Esping-Andersen

Introduction

FOLLOWING decades of income compression, the advanced societies are now experiencing a surge of income inequality. This historical U-turn has caught the social sciences by surprise because it contradicts the prevailing consensus that, following Kuznets (1955), saw the advanced economies as inherently driven towards greater income compression. In a parallel way, postwar sociologists like Martin Lipset and Daniel Bell envisioned a new 'middle-class' society where merit and effort would reign victoriously, sweeping aside the lingering residues of class privilege.

Until the 1990s it appeared as if the new tide of inequality was confined to the Anglo Saxon countries – and mainly to the US and the UK. This suggested that the phenomenon was idiosyncratic, the by-product of these countries' unregulated labour markets, decaying trade unions and weak welfare states (Katz and Autor 1999; Gottschalk and Smeeding 1997; Atkinson 1999). The most recent data at our disposal show that the tide is ever more universal. This suggests that we must turn our attention, once again, to structural explanations.

The structural interpretation of inequality originates with Pareto's Law that claimed that income distributions are inherently driven towards a convergent equilibrium, both across time and societies.[1] As such, inequalities will be pretty impervious to public manipulation or institutional change. As Brandolini (2005) argues, Pareto deliberately used scientific 'laws' to stifle the egalitarian reformists of his time. Fortunately for the latter, Pareto's Law fared poorly when tested against good data. A half century later, Kuznets' theory was equally structural in nature, providing yet again no rationale for redistributive intervention. But since it optimistically saw economic growth and more equality as perfect companions, there was ample room for manoeuvre for social reformists. Additionally, human capital theory helped promote an active role for public intervention in the process of market distribution.

As ever more advanced countries now experience a resurgence of inequality, idiosyncratic explanations are giving way to a third round of structural interpretations. Globalization has, unsurprisingly, occupied centre stage in the popular mind although most economists lean towards a more *endogenous* – but equally structural – theory based primarily on technological change that, in turn, biases labour demand in favour of skills. This interpretation enjoys abundant empirical support but it may very well be based on too narrow a focus. It is very centred on changes in (male) wage distributions and this, in turn, implies an individualized rather than household-based analysis. The lack of attention to household-level distributions may bias our understanding because it fails to consider the impact that two major revolutions in contemporary social behaviour may have on the income distributions. Firstly, to paraphrase Claudia Goldin (2004), we are witnessing a revolution in women's economic roles. Secondly, demographic change is creating new patterns of family formation, more marital instability and a radically new household structure.

Income Inequality and Life Course Dynamics

The link between income inequality and opportunities has always been, at best, ambiguous and, at worst, utterly confused. The two speak to very different notions of equality. When we focus on the distribution of well-being, we are concerned primarily with the end result of a massive process of distribution and redistribution. Summary statistics, such as the Gini coefficient or the poverty rate, provide a snapshot of inequality at any given time. Such snapshots are problematic for many reasons. For one, they lump together people at very different phases of their life course, from students to retirees. Hence a rise in, say, poverty may simply be an effect of there being more students living in independent households. For another, they easily misrepresent real inequality if there is a lot of movement over time. A snapshot measure bundles together people with transient (and thus trivial) low or high incomes and those with persistent (and thus 'real') low or high incomes. It is well established that year-to-year changes in income are uncorrelated with changes in consumption or social deprivation.

People smooth their consumption over time and, in any case, the lion's share of deprivation is usually transient and short-lived (Bowlus and Robin 2003; Whelan et al. 2004).

In contrast, when we study opportunities, our concern is with mobility and life chances. Hence the focus is on the welfare dynamics throughout peoples' lives and, most importantly, across generations. Theory claims a direct causal connection between income inequalities and opportunities. Becker (1981) and Becker and Tomes (1986) posit a simple *money->investment->money* theory of inter-generational mobility: parental investment in their children's human capital dictates importantly their destiny and this explains why the offspring of moneyed parents will systematically attain more schooling. It follows that adult achievements will end up correlating with factors related to social origins (for an overview, see Solon 1999 and Corak 2004). It also follows that this correlation will depend on how much inequality there is in the parental generation.

We can illustrate the logic via a cross-national comparison of inter-generational income mobility and levels of income inequality. Table 10.1 presents Gini coefficients of disposable household income and the intensity of inter-generational income 'inheritance', ranking countries according to the latter.[2] As the data suggest there is a close – albeit not perfect – fit between overall levels of income inequality and the strength of the inheritance effect. This suggests that there exists an important relationship between the shape of the income distribution and the opportunity structure. Of course, it says nothing about the actual causal direction between the two.

The optimism of postwar social science can be traced to the fact that both dimensions of inequality seemed to move in a positive direction. There was clear evidence of declining wealth concentration, of wage compression, and of a more equal distribution of household incomes (Levy 1998; Davies and Shorrocks 1999; Lindert 2003; Morrisson 2003). To illustrate, the share of wealth owned by the top 1 per cent in Britain fell from 55 per cent in 1938 to 20 per cent in 1980, and in the US from 36 to 25 per cent (Lindert 2003, tables 1 and 3). The trend was identical with regard to household incomes where the top of the income pyramid experienced relative losses and the bottom vice versa (Brandolini 2005; Morrison, 2003). As Karoly and Burtless (1995) show, 40 per cent of the reduction in income inequality in the 1960s was due to declining earnings inequality among male heads of families. The tide lifted all boats but gave the little boats an extra lift.

With the benefit of hindsight it is now clear that the Golden Age income compression was aided by welfare state redistribution, the stable nuclear family and, perhaps most decisively, by the improved labour market prospects of low-skilled workers (see, e.g. Levy 1998 and

Table 10.1 Income inequality and inter-generational income mobility		
	Gini (mid-1990s)	**Parent–child income elasticities**
Denmark	0.236	0.15
Norway	0.238	0.17
Finland	0.217	0.18
Canada	0.284	0.19
Sweden	0.221	0.27
Germany	0.272	0.32
France	0.288	0.41
United States	0.355	0.47
United Kingdom	0.344	0.50

Source: Ginis are from Luxembourg Income Study (LIS), Key Figures; parent–child income correlations from Corak (2005)

Gustafsson and Johansson 1997). Social scientists at the time saw the coming of a 'middle-class' society or, as British sociologists put it, 'the affluent worker'. This view spilled over to social mobility theory that argued that, with the United States as the vanguard, advanced societies were embarking upon an era of diminishing ascription and rising meritocracy. Skills, knowledge and talent would prevail over social origins and the luck of birth and, hence, the old class divide would dissolve (Bell 1976). The argument was persuasive in so far as sons systematically did better than their fathers, be it in terms of educational attainment, incomes or occupational destiny (Levy 1998). The traditional family enterprise gave way to the modern corporation and with technological advance this conspired to favour skills and expertise over family of origin in hiring and promotion decisions. The occupational structure was changing in favour of more white-collar jobs and, no less important, the expansion and democratization of education meant that parental riches should have less effect on children's life chances. In brief all the vital elements of social change seemed to favour more equality and, hence, the Golden Age income compression appeared to confirm the theory (Lenski 1966).

The recent U-turn seems to directly invalidate the postwar theoretical consensus. But so also does comparative research on inter-generational mobility. With the exception of Sweden, research has concluded that the importance of social origins for educational attainment or for class mobility did not diminish appreciably over the past half century (Shavit and Blossfeld 1993; Erikson and Goldthorpe 1992). The Golden Age may have lifted all boats but it did not seriously equalize the opportunity structure. To use Erikson and Goldthorpe's expression, we live in a *constant flux*. These pessimistic conclusions are based on fairly old data and there is some recent evidence that mobility has increased among younger generations – at least in some countries. Esping-Andersen (2004) examines educational attainment and concludes that the *constant flux* does seem to prevail in the US, the UK and Germany, but that there has been a substantial equalization of opportunities in all three Scandinavian countries. Breen and Salazar's (2004) extraordinarily rigorous comparative study suggests, likewise, that there has been some improvement in class mobility for the youngest cohorts in a few countries.

The question we now face is whether mobility and opportunities will be adversely affected by widening income inequalities – as standard theory would predict. An unequivocal answer to this question is probably impossible to furnish. A closer scrutiny of, firstly, what hides behind the new burst of inequality and, secondly, of contemporary mobility dynamics, may help us along the way.

The Changing Income Distribution

A perusal of recent trends in income distribution invites gloom. Research shows a remarkable increase in income inequality and poverty. The surge began in the UK and the US (Gottschalk and Smeeding 1997; Atkinson 1999). The most recent data at our disposal suggest that most countries – but not all – are following suit. Table 10.2 presents a synthetic overview of Gini coefficients for household income over the past two decades.

With the notable exception of France and the Netherlands, all nations have experienced anywhere from modest to sharp jumps in *market income* dispersion.[3] What mainly distinguishes countries is the onset of the jump, beginning a decade earlier in the UK and the US and subsequently in the 1990s elsewhere (Gottschalk and Smeeding 2003). Market inequalities are, to a greater or lesser extent, ameliorated by welfare state redistribution, as the last three columns show. Kenworthy and Pontusson (2005) make a strong argument that most welfare states have increased their redistributive efforts in response to widening inequalities. Table 10.2 suggests that this is less true for Sweden and the US than for most other countries.

Although the trend seems general, there are important deviants that cast some doubt on a purely structural explanation. It is, for example, hard to imagine that Denmark, France and the Netherlands are far more sheltered against the cold winds of globalization than is Sweden or Germany. We need therefore to disentangle the inegalitarian thrust.[4] A first step is to pinpoint *where* in the income pyramid the main changes occur. Most studies agree that the top incomes are

Table 10.2 Changes in household income inequality over the 1980s and 1990s

	Market incomes			Disposable incomes		
	Gini c.1980	Gini c.2000	Change (%)	Gini c.1980	Gini c.2000	Change (%)
Denmark	0.331	0.355	+6	0.254	0.266	+4
Norway	0.284	0.337	+19	0.223	0.251	+13
Sweden	0.293	0.375	+28	0.197	0.252	+28
France	0.395	0.403	+1	0.270	0.273	0
Germany	0.285	0.360	+26	0.244	0.264	+8
Italy	0.434	0.456	+7	0.306	0.333	+9
Netherlands	0.378	0.339	−12	0.260	0.248	−5
Spain	n/a	0.574	n/a	0.318	0.323	+2
UK	0.332	0.450	+36	0.270	0.345	+28
US	0.359	0.436	+21	0.301	0.368	+22

Italian and Danish data are OECD estimates for 1985 and 2000 and derive from Forster and d'Ercole (2005), table 4. The Spanish 2000 estimates are from the European Community Household Panel (ECHP).

Sources: Luxembourg Income Study (LIS) data, and Kenworthy and Pontusson (2005), table A2

pulling ahead of the rest (Katz and Autor 1999; Gottschalk and Smeeding 1997; Piketty and Saez 2001). This is no doubt the main story. The ratio between the top- and middle-income decile has widened substantially just about everywhere. The UK ratio jumped from 1.8 in 1980 to 2.2 in 2000; the American from 2.6 to 3.0; and the Swedish from 1.5 to 1.7. But more recent evidence shows that the bottom is now losing ground. Besides the US, also Finland, Germany, Italy, Sweden and the UK have experienced deterioration at the bottom of the pyramid. So far, however, it is only in the UK and the US that we witness anything that approximates de facto polarization. [5]

Unravelling the New Inequalities

There is one group that clearly has suffered deterioration in a major way, namely young adults, who face an erosion of relative wages at all skill levels and who, especially in Europe, are hugely over-represented among the unemployed and those with precarious, short-term employment contracts (Wasmer 2002; Polavieja 2003). Juhn et al. (1993) show that young American workers have suffered a 70 per cent wage decline compared to mature workers. Similar, albeit less dramatic, trends have been identified across the OECD (Bover et al. 2002; Brandolini et al. 2002). Forster and d'Ercole (2005, Annex Table A6) show that the relative disposable income of young adults (18–25) has declined by

7 percentage points on average in the OECD countries. We observe especially sharp income erosion in the Nordic countries.[6] The deteriorating economic position of young workers in combination with heightened family instability and lone parenthood helps explain why there has been a virtually uniform, across-the-board rise in child poverty in the last decades.

Income distributions are measured at the household level and represent, therefore, the sum total of individual members' earnings, capital income, private and public transfers plus taxation. As far as the welfare state is concerned, we already saw that public redistribution appears effective in stemming market inequalities. Gottschalk and Smeeding (1997), the OECD (1999, table 3.3) and, most recently, Smeeding (2004) review the evidence and find that some welfare states may have become less effective in upholding the incomes of bottom decile households, due in part to less progressive taxation and, in part, to reductions in transfers to low-income households. Nevertheless, the trend is very nation specific and nowhere very strong. Any notion that welfare states are sliding towards the lowest common denominator is simply false and it would be impossible to attribute rising inequality to welfare state erosion. Indeed, in Scandinavia less progressive taxation has been offset by more redistributive spending, and countries like Germany and the UK have intensified efforts via the introduction of generous family allowances and of an array of anti-poverty measures, respectively. The Netherlands is a rare case where, indeed, family benefits have declined noticeably.

Wages and Incomes in Changing Labour Markets

There is broad agreement that the new inequalities are driven by ongoing labour market transformation (OECD 2000). On one hand, high unemployment and rising job precariousness contribute to inequality and help in particular account for the eroding status of young adults. On the other hand, fuelled by technological change and the rising knowledge intensity of production, skill requirements are intensifying. This should, in theory, raise the wage premium for skills and punish the less skilled.[7] In practice, the wage effect will depend on institutions (such as wage minima), labour demand and supply.

The rising skills premium is evident when we examine recent male wage trends. The top decile earners are leaping ahead in many countries – although clearly more in unregulated labour markets like the British and American where the top–middle decile ratio rose by 15 and 21 percentage points, respectively. But the gains at the top seem unrelated to labour market regulation since Italy (with 13 per cent), the

Netherlands and Sweden (with 8 per cent) and Germany (with 7 per cent) are clearly following suit. Wage erosion at the bottom is generally less severe and also less common. The bottom decile wages have remained stable in France, Italy, Norway and Finland, but have lost some ground in Germany and Sweden (a 6–7 percentage point decline relative to the middle) and, more substantially so, in the Netherlands, the UK and the US (a 9–11 percentage point decline).[8]

The trend may be clear but the substantial international variation tells us that a purely skills-based explanation will not suffice. Worker protection and industrial relations systems help explain why workers at the low end of the European labour market have lost less ground (OECD 2003; Wallerstein 1999). But still, recent data suggest that the gulf is now widening in Europe, too (Acemoglu 2002; Bover et al. 2002). Most countries have witnessed an, albeit slow, rise of low-wage employment, defined as wages below two-thirds the median (Lucifora et al. 2005). In 2001, a quarter of American workers and 20 per cent of British workers were low wage, compared to 13 in Germany and 15 in the Netherlands. In other words, we may expect that more and more countries will experience a continued rise in wage differentials – or, alternatively, of unemployment (OECD 2003, p. 63).

Acemoglu (2002) adds a supply-side dimension to Europe's less dramatic wage trends, arguing that the strong growth of highly educated workers in Europe over the past decades has suppressed wages at the top of the skill pyramid. This may also help explain why even skilled younger workers fare relatively poorly. But in general, the European 'youth-penalty' is more visible in terms of pervasive job precariousness and the wage erosion that is associated with unemployment (Gallie and Paugham 2000; Wasmer 2002). To illustrate, the *involuntary* share of temporary workers dominates among youth in Finland, Portugal and Spain (at rates between 50 and 70 per cent), is significant in the UK (26 per cent) and moderately high in the rest of Europe (15–20 per cent). In terms of earnings there is also a clear over-representation of young workers within the low-wage population. Lucifora et al. (2005) show that about 60 per cent of youths (under 25) are low wage in the Netherlands, UK, and the US, with a somewhat lower incidence (about 40 per cent) in France and Germany. These are very large numbers, however interpreted. Moreover, in many countries, in Southern Europe especially, virtually all unemployment is concentrated among young and female workers.

Yet not all news is gloomy. Surprisingly – and contradicting the prevailing feminist view – women are making important wage gains relative to men across all skill levels. The erosion of wages at the bottom is far worse among low-skilled men while highly skilled women enjoy major earnings gains relative to similar men (Blau and

Kahn 2003; Waldfogel and Mayer 1999). Also, it seems clear that the 'youth-penalty' is far greater for men than for women. In the US the earnings of 25 to 34-year-old men declined by 23 per cent compared to only 4.5 per cent among women during the 1980s and 1990s (Schrammel 1998). The gender wage gap is narrowing in Europe, too, although there are important national differences (Blau and Kahn 1995, table 11.4; Blau and Kahn 2003, table 7.2; OECD 2002, tables 2.15 and 2.16).[9] The latest Eurostat data show that the (hourly based) gender wage gap is narrowing substantially in the UK, the Netherlands, Ireland and Italy. It has remained basically stable in Denmark, France and Germany, but it has also widened – and appreciably so – in Spain and even Sweden.[10] If women enjoy relative pay gains while, simultaneously, increasing their labour supply we would expect an increase in women's contribution to total household income. In fact, this has happened during the 1990s in most countries. In France, the Netherlands and Spain their relative income contribution rose by a full 5 percentage points. The result is that the gender composition of total household income is becoming less asymmetric, in Denmark approaching parity (women's share is 42 per cent). In countries with lower female labour supply, like the Netherlands and Spain, their share hovers around 25 per cent.[11]

It is accordingly evident that not *all* trends move in the same inegalitarian direction. But whether women's gains can offset the general trend depends, firstly, on whether females' wage differentials are widening in tandem with males' and, secondly, on demographic behaviour and, in particular, on changes in household structure. Since all indications are that rising wage inequality occurs for both sexes rather similarly, the question boils down to the effect of demographic change.

Demographic Change and Household Structure

There are three great demographic transformations under way that all affect income distributions. Firstly, couples are increasingly unstable and ever more people opt for prolonged single-hood. This translates into a far more heterogeneous household structure with a growing share of vulnerable units – lone parent families in particular. The share of children in single mother households has risen everywhere, now ranging between a low of about 5 per cent in Southern Europe to a high of 15–20 per cent in Scandinavia and North America.[12] Fertility has, in the meantime, fallen sharply and this implies of course that there are fewer mouths to feed. Yet, its distributive impact depends on the correlation between fertility and family income. Most countries continue to adhere to the classical pattern with higher birth rates among less educated women. But in the Nordic countries the reverse is now the case. If high-income households increase their relative fertility rate this should, all else constant, help narrow differentials in family consumption power. But all told, ongoing change in household structure is likely to *widen* income inequality.

Secondly, marital homogamy is intensifying, in particularly at the high end. Partnerships and marriages are increasingly based on similarities in educational attainment and, accordingly, in potential earnings power (Blossfeld and Drobnic 2001; Burtless 1999).[13] The more that the strong and the weak bundle, the more we should expect *heightened* income inequalities. But this will, in turn, depend very much on the third transformation, namely on patterns of female labour supply.

Since women's earnings are improving relative to men's, their intensity of employment can have very powerful effects on household income distributions. But the precise direction of the effect is conditional on the actual composition of women's labour supply. If the intensity of labour supply (hours worked) is positively correlated with education, the impact of female employment will end up being inegalitarian. When women are mostly coupled with men of similar education and skill levels, the income effect from women's earnings will be attenuated at the household level. To put it simply, the high-skilled double earner couple will race ahead of the rest, be they single earner units or low-skilled double earner couples. The gap will widen additionally if unemployment and joblessness are more widespread at the bottom. In contrast, if female labour supply grows disproportionally among women at the 'bottom', the net long-run effect should be declining income inequality. The future of our income distribution depends, in other words, very much on the precise contours of women's employment.

The transformation of women's preferences is indeed quite revolutionary. Yet, a bird's-eye historical panorama shows that the vanguards of the revolution were higher status, educated women. Working class women are much slower to follow suit. In most affluent countries, the participation rate of less educated women is half that of their more educated sisters in Southern Europe, and about three-quarters in Scandinavia, the US and the UK.[14]

In short, if female participation is concentrated 'at the top' it will help widen household inequalities. If, in contrast, there is a substantial catch up among less educated women – as has occurred in the Nordic countries, the UK and the US – there ought to be an equalizing effect. But participation and actual employment do not necessarily coincide. For one, female unemployment tends to be far higher than male and it is especially pronounced among less educated women (OECD 2000, Annex Table D).

Joblessness among less educated women is part and parcel of the contemporary preoccupation with social polarization. There is strong evidence that unemployment comes in couples, thereby distancing the bottom even further from work-rich couples (de Graaf and Ultee 2000; Gregg and Wadsworth 2001). Iacovou (2003) argues, additionally, that work polarization between households contributes to the consolidation of worklessness since women in more polarized environments (like the UK) are less likely to compensate with more work when their husbands are unemployed. The data also suggest that the failure of women to compensate is far more likely among the less educated. Obviously the impact of worklessness depends a great deal on its magnitude and persistency. The share of working age *couples* with no employed adult varies between 6–8 per cent in Scandinavia, Germany and the US and 13–15 per cent in the UK and the Netherlands.[15] All told, we would expect substantial income gaps between work-poor and work-rich households, in particular in countries – like the Southern European – where dual career couples are mainly found at the top. In fact, OECD (2000, table 3.4) shows that workless household incomes are typically around half those of work-rich households, but the gap widens to a third in Italy and the US and narrows to 60 per cent in Denmark and Sweden.[16]

Even if less educated women increase their participation, an equalizing effect may still fail to materialize if there are major asymmetries in the *intensity* of labour supply. To illustrate, a two-career couple may potentially supply 80 or perhaps even 100 hours per week; the single earner half that; and the lone mother, realistically far less.[17] Empirical trends in labour supply suggest that such asymmetries are actually widening (Juhn and Murphy 1997; Hyslop 2001; Aaronson 2002; Karoly and Burtless 1995). Smeeding's (2004) data for Europe and North America show that couples in the top quintile work roughly 2–3 times as many annual hours as do the lowest, and about 20–30 per cent more hours than does the middle quintile. Hyslop (2001) shows that assortative mating accounts for 28 per cent of (permanent) household inequality and for 23 per cent of its increase. Marital homogamy manifests itself also in couples' intensity of work and it is therefore unclear how much wives can offset the falling earnings of less skilled males.

A key empirical question, therefore, is whether education-based marital homogamy translates into selective patterns of labour supply and convergence of earnings. We can estimate this by simple couple-correlations of (weekly) hours worked and of (annual) work income (see table 10.3).[18]

As one would expect, labour supply homogamy is far more pronounced in countries with high female participation, such as Denmark and Sweden, and correspondingly weaker in Italy and Spain.[19] But the data also show that similarities of work intensity do

Table 10.3 Homogamy of marital labour supply and earnings: couple correlations for 1993 and 2001

	1993 pLabour supply	1993 pEarnings	2001 pLabour supply	2001 pEarnings
Denmark	0.39	0.20	0.41	0.16
France	0.26	0.19	0.22	0.17
Germany	0.19	−0.13	0.20	−0.12
Italy	0.17	0.15	0.17	0.18
Spain	0.12	0.18	0.18	0.20
Sweden	n/a	n/a	0.52	0.17
UK	0.31	0.16	0.32	0.07
US	0.27	0.10	0.29	0.07

Source: ECHP, panels 1994 and 2001 and, for the US, Panel Study of Income Dynamics (PSID) panels for same years

not necessarily produce high earnings correlations. There are numerous reasons for this, one being, simply, that earnings are annual while hours are measured on a weekly basis. Hence, if women's annual level of work intensity is substantially lower than men's this alone would explain the divergence. But the discrepancy is surely also due to male–female earnings differentials *conditional* on work intensity. In Spain, for example, wives' employment rates are low overall but this coincides with a surprisingly high rate among women in top-level occupations married to men in similar high status jobs (Smith 2005). We note that Germany is an exception to the extent that spouses' earnings are negatively correlated, suggesting that wives of very high-income men tend to earn very little.

Of considerable importance for the female earnings effect is the relative gender wage gap across the earnings distribution. As noted, the average Danish gender gap (comparatively modest) has not declined further over the past decade, but this average hides huge differences: a marked rise in the gap within the top deciles and a narrowing at the bottom. In the US the opposite has happened, and it is mainly at the top that the gap has narrowed (Smith 2005). Data on conditional wage gaps (controlling for relevant human capital, experience, region, size of firm, contract status) sheds additional light on the potentially equalizing effect of female employment (Arulampalam et al. 2004). Consistent with Smith (2005), there is unusually large variation in the Danish wage gaps. The private sector wage gap at the top (24 per cent) is more than twice as large as at the bottom (10 per cent), and for the public sector there is a similar, if more modest, difference. This contrasts with most other EU countries where the wage gap at the top and bottom is pretty much identical – in Spain and Germany, the gap is actually larger at the bottom.

Table 10.4 Decomposition of household income inequality by husbands' and wives' earnings contribution (couple households only)

	I CovT	II CovH	III CovW	IV %ΔCovT-CovH (×100)
Denmark				
1993	0.364	0.327	0.374	0.10
2001	0.261	0.313	0.316	−0.20
Sweden				
1997	0.650	0.933	1.093	−0.43
2001	0.736	1.127	1.129	−0.48
France				
1993	0.685	0.612	1.242	0.19
2001	0.464	0.348	0.702	0.16
Germany				
1993	0.373	0.349	0.684	0.06
2001	0.402	0.351	0.796	0.13
Italy				
1994	0.455	0.290	0.533	0.36
2001	0.427	0.300	0.472	0.30
Spain				
1994	0.669	0.594	1.075	0.11
2001	0.526	0.404	0.866	0.23
UK				
1993	0.650	0.455	0.763	0.30
2001	0.459	0.358	0.639	0.22
US				
1993	0.741	0.933	1.221	−0.26
2001	0.554	0.626	1.006	−0.13

CovT/CovH/CovW are the coefficients of variance for, respectively total, husbands' and wives' earnings.

%Δ CovT-CovH is the percentage difference between total household and husbands' earnings (note that we also include cohabiting couples).

Source: Estimated from ECHP, all waves, US estimates are based on PSID

Table 10.4 presents one simple way to examine how the combination of women's employment and earnings affects household inequality. The approach is to decompose total household income variance into that attributable to the two partners' respective earnings.[20] Calculating the percentage difference between total household and husband's (or male partner's) earnings (in the last column) will indicate whether women's earnings augment or abate intra-household inequality (Lam 1997). Where the sign is *negative*, women's earnings have an egalitarian impact. Columns 1–3 present, respectively, the coefficient of variance for total household earnings, for husbands' and for wives' earnings. The estimates cover the 1990s, a decade of substantial growth in female labour supply, especially in countries with traditionally low levels of participation. For reasons of space I present only estimates for the first and last years (1993 and 2001).

It is important to remember that we estimate only earnings (including cases with *zero* earnings) within couples. The data are therefore not comparable with previous tables. The comparisons over time are, furthermore, sensitive to business cycle effects: the early 1990s were bad economic times while 2001 represents the tail end of a long boom. A comparison of the coefficients in columns 2 and 3 confirm the substantial cross-national differences in gender asymmetries: in Scandinavia, the earnings variance for men and women is almost identical, which implies gender convergence in labour supply and wages. As one would expect, the gender asymmetries are pronounced in Spain and Italy – and also in Germany and the UK.

The data in the final column tell us how women's employment affects household inequalities. The negative sign that we observe for Denmark, Sweden and the US represents an *equalizing* effect. Clearly the egalitarian impact of wives' earnings is most pronounced in Sweden. In Denmark we notice a shift in favour of equalization during the 1990s. This is probably due to two concomitant effects. As we saw earlier, during the 1980s and 1990s, the Danish gender pay gap narrowed for low-income women and widened for those at the top. In addition, female unemployment was substantially higher during recession years.[21] For all three cases, the coefficients mirror patterns of female labour supply and, especially, a disproportionate rise in employment at the bottom of the income hierarchy.

For the other countries women's employment is, in contrast, a source of more household inequality. In the UK, the effect has abated during the 1990s while in Germany and especially in Spain a significant rise in women's employment during the decade has actually translated into a parallel rise in inequality. In fact, the Spanish labour supply correlation jumped sharply during the 1990s – another confirmation that female employment growth was predominantly concentrated at the 'top'. And we also saw that both the German and the Spanish gender wage gap is greater at the bottom than at the top.

The rise of lone parent households is surely an additional source of household inequality, mainly because they are highly concentrated in the low end of the income distribution. This is evident in comparative poverty data. With the exception of Scandinavia, where virtually all lone mothers work, single mother employment rates and earnings tend to be low. In Continental Europe lone mother poverty rates hover around 30 per cent; in the UK and the US, it is substantially higher (about 50 per cent in the latter).[22] In dynamic terms, the *rise* of female-headed households explains about half of the total increase in the US Gini during the 1970s and 1980s (Karoly and Burtless 1995, p. 398).

All told, even if women's wages are improving relative to men's, the revolution in women's behaviour is more likely to heighten than to abate inequality. The conditions required for an equalizing effect are quite steep: namely near universal, Nordic-type female employment levels wherein the labour supply of 'low end' women grows more rapidly than at the 'high end'. Pasqua (2002) presents counterfactual income distributions that illustrate the point very well. If all women did indeed work more or less like in Denmark, Spain's inequality would decrease by 15 per cent. Or, if the Spanish earnings distribution among women were identical to the Danish, yet again Spain's inequality would drop by 16 per cent.

Life Course Dynamics and the Opportunity Structure

An apparent paradox presents itself when we look at inequality from a lifetime perspective: namely, inequality at once both increases and decreases. It becomes greater because most citizens at one time in their life have experienced economic hardship, usually during education and in the early career years. Lifetime income estimates produce therefore a massive incidence of (transient) poverty. To illustrate, a recent study shows that virtually all Danes (93 per cent) experienced some poverty at some point in time during their lives (Okonomisk Raad 2001). And Denmark, as is well known, boasts one of the world's lowest poverty rates! Of course, Danish youth abandon the parental home early and usually spend a number of years with few means. Mobility data, however, demonstrate that such poverty is overwhelmingly of brief duration and essentially trivial in nature. The same study shows that, on a lifetime income basis, only 1 per cent of Danes have experienced a life dominated by poverty.

The other side of the paradox is that lifetime-based income distributions are substantially *less* unequal than are cross-sections. On the basis of ten-year permanent income estimates, the inequality reduction is 8–9 per cent for Denmark and the US and almost 14 per cent for Sweden (Aaberge et al. 1996). Taking much longer periods, American studies suggest that Ginis for lifetime income distributions are about 40–50 per cent lower, a figure that is quite consistent with findings from Sweden (Haider 2001; Bowlus and Robin 2003; Björklund 1998; Björklund and Palme 2002). In Denmark a government study using simulations shows that the lifetime Gini coefficient is only 0.124 compared to the cross-section Gini of 0.239, that is only half as large (Okonomisk Raad 2001, table II, p. 10).

The fall in inequality occurs because the cross-section lumps together people at very different phases of their life course while, over time, most citizens are mobile.[23] If we are interested in opportunities and life chances it is clearly lifetime income that will tell the true story. The extent of lifetime income inequality in a country is mainly a function of two factors: the overall income spread and the degree of *mobility*. In table 10.1 we saw that countries' inter-generational mobility pretty much matches overall inequality levels. This may be a spurious relationship if high-inequality levels are offset by a lot of mobility or if, vice versa, there is little mobility in low-inequality countries.[24] Put differently, the tidal wave of rising income inequality that we now witness must primarily be judged in terms of mobility rates.

To assess the connection between income distributions and mobility, the logical approach would be to examine whether mobility rates co-vary with changes in the income distribution. This requires very long time series of data. A number of US studies have attempted to answer this question by comparing more truncated 'lifetime' income distributions over periods in which levels of inequality changed (Gittleman and Joyce 1999; Haider 2001; Aaronson 2002; Bowlus and Robin 2003). Based on age–wage curves, Lucifora et al. (2005) conclude very similarly for the UK. The picture that emerges is that, yes, lifetime inequality rises in tandem with cross-sectional inequality. In other words, mobility does not offset rises in income inequality. Indeed, there is also evidence that the strength of inter-generational inheritance abates during periods of less inequality only to intensify again as inequality rises (Harding et al. 2005).

Since the big leap in American inequality occurred in the 1980s and then stabilized in the 1990s, a comparison of mobility across these two decades would be informative. Using the PSID data I estimate that the likelihood of being persistently poor for 3+ years drops from 0.38 in the 1980s to 0.30 in the 1990s.[25] That poverty persistency abated in the US during the 1990s can, no doubt, be ascribed to the booming full employment economy and to less-educated wives' increased participation. In this sense, Sweden provides an important orthogonal test since both unemployment and income inequalities rose sharply during the 1990s. Yet, the Fritzell and Henz (2001) survey of the data concludes that, in fact, Swedish poverty persistency continued to decline. Hills' (1998; 2004) examination of the British evidence suggests, however, that rising income inequality has spilled over to mobility chances, concluding that there has occurred a significant reduction in income mobility and a rise in poverty persistency since the 1980s.

What do we make of these rather contradictory findings? For one, we clearly lack sufficiently robust data for enough countries and over enough time. Hence, we can do little more than venture informed guesses. Two, some of the puzzling differences can perhaps be attributed to prevailing economic conditions, such as the unemployment rate. The 1990s were indeed good years for the American economy – but so they were for the British. And in Sweden, bad times did no harm to mobility chances. And three, this suggests that the welfare state may also be quite important in terms of sustaining mobility under conditions of rising income inequality.

But aside from welfare state effects, most studies of income dynamics and mobility converge in the view that growing wage dispersion is key to not only cross-sectional inequality but also to lifetime income opportunities (Gittleman and Joyce 1999; Bowlus and Robin 2003). The logic is straightforward because even if mobility rates remain stable a rise in differentials will produce more inequality in terms of lifetime income. But here we return, once again, to the dual nature of contemporary wage behaviour, namely that concomitant with wider earnings differentials there is also a narrowing of the gender wage gap. In dynamic lifetime terms, the question then boils down to whether women's relative gains in *cross-sectional* earnings are paralleled in cumulative lifetime earnings.

Everything we know about demographic and family change points in exactly that direction. Women have fewer children, postpone fertility, and they interrupt their careers far less than earlier. This means not just less foregone income during maternity but also far less long-term depreciation due to eroded human capital and loss of experience caused by lengthy interruptions. In other words, the revolution in women's behaviour ought to help narrow the lifetime-based gender earnings gap – particularly so when the gender wage gap closes and when fertility differences by social class narrow. In the Nordic countries now women with higher education actually have more children than the less educated (Hoem 2005; Romsen 2004).

Early studies of the lifetime income loss due to childbearing and interruptions presented rather dramatic effects, basically because interruptions were very long (ten years over the lifetime on average). Applying the standard Mincer–Polacheck benchmark estimator, the lifetime income loss due to the 'missing ten years' would have been about 5 per cent while the additional loss due to human capital depreciation would be another 20 per cent (Polacheck 2003).[26]

In most advanced countries fertility rates are now half those that obtained in the 1960s, first births are delayed substantially, and childcare is, at least in some countries, now the norm. Hence, we would anticipate that interruptions around births are fewer and shorter, in particular among educated women and in countries with ample provision of day care. This is certainly the case in the US where the share of mothers that returned to work within nine months of birth doubled in the 1970s–1980s, reaching 46 per cent in 1987 (Browning 1992).[27] Sigle-Rushton and Waldfogel (2004) show that mothers' lifetime income loss is less than what obtained in the 1960s – but only for some countries.[28] For medium-educated mothers with two children, the gross income loss up to age 45 ranges from 23–5 per cent in Scandinavia and the US to 40 per cent in Germany and the Netherlands. Extending the estimate up to age 60 suggests that an important part of the child-penalty is eventually recuperated if, that is, women remain in uninterrupted employment until retirement. In this latter scenario, the Danish mother will have lost only 8 per cent of her potential income, and the German and British about 25 per cent.

Britain and Scandinavia provide a fruitful contrast considering that the Nordic countries boast practically universal participation in day care while this is scarce in Britain. One study that simulates lifetime incomes for the 1958 British birth cohort shows that a typical British woman will forego about half of her potential lifetime income if she has two children (Joshi et al. 1996). This estimate is very consistent with recent German and Dutch findings – but not with Danish or Swedish (Davies and Joshi 2001; Datta Gupta and Smith 2002). The great difference lies in the duration of employment interruptions and in subsequent part-time work. Whereas British, Dutch and German women interrupt for longer periods and then resume with reduced working hours, Scandinavian women return relatively quickly and are less likely to opt for prolonged part-time work.[29] Later British research has attempted to see whether more recent female cohorts have altered their behaviour. Rake (2000) and Davies and Joshi (2001) suggest a potentially polarizing trend because higher educated women are beginning to emulate the Nordic pattern while less educated women are, in fact, reducing even further their post-birth labour supply.

This translates directly into a household income effect of significant proportions. Rake estimates that a childless, low-skilled woman will contribute 41 per cent to the couple's lifetime income. But her contribution drops to only 24 per cent if she has two children. For the high-skilled woman the difference is trivial (49 and 47 per cent, respectively). When, as in Britain, birth-induced interruptions are very highly correlated with education then we will witness heightened inegalitarian effects also in terms of lifetime *household* incomes. If, in contrast, the behavioural differences narrow, as is the case in Denmark, the lifetime based inegalitarian impulse will be weaker. In fact, up-to-date data show almost no significant lifetime income loss for the average Danish woman (Okonomisk Raad 2001).[30]

Since the revolution in women's behaviour accelerated in the 1990s, in particular in Southern Europe, one would expect a process of convergence towards the Nordic pattern among younger women. For these we can obviously not estimate lifetime incomes but data on birth-related interruptions can be used to achieve a rough prediction

Table 10.5 Estimated lifetime income penalties for women with two children in the 1990s		
	Average birth interruption (months)	Estimated total lifetime income penalty (assuming 2 children) in %[a]
Denmark		
All women	9	5.0
Less educated	20	9.0
Spain		
All women	46	20.0
Less educated	50	21.0

[a] Estimated by applying the Mincer–Polacheck benchmark coefficients (as above).

of what will come to pass among those who are mothers today. Using the ECHP panels, 1994–2001, table 10.5 compares two prototypical extremes within Europe–Denmark and Spain. The estimated lifetime income penalty applies the Mincer–Polacheck coefficients to the empirically observed birth-related interruptions of all women (averaged) and of less educated women (less than upper secondary).

We note that the interruption gap between the less educated and average woman is wider in Denmark than in Spain. But since interruptions among less educated Danes are fairly brief, their impact on lifetime income is modest. In contrast, all Spanish women interrupt for far longer periods and, hence, the lifetime income penalties are far greater for Spanish women across levels of education.

Thus we would expect that women will help equalize household lifetime income only if less educated women were to emulate the life course behaviour of higher educated British, or of most Scandinavian, women. In other words, the way that women influence lifetime inequalities is essentially identical to that for cross-sectional inequalities.

Inter-generational Inheritance and Inequality

The persistency of social inheritance (the *constant flux*) suggests that the underlying mechanisms that dictate our opportunity structure have remained largely unchanged over the past half century. Those, like T. H. Marshall, who believed that the welfare state and education reform would undo the class divide were, accordingly, overly optimistic.

Standard theory explains the social origins effect in terms of parents' investment in their children's human capital. Economists, unsurprisingly, highlight the importance of monetary investments but this can, in principle, be extended to all forms of investment, including time dedicated to nurturing, caring and stimulation. Sociologists also emphasize the transmission of cultural capital and its beneficial influence on cognitive development and on children's adaptation to the typically middle-class biased school milieu (Bourdieu 1983). The argument actually dates back to Plato, who advocated that gifted children of uncultured parents be removed from their family.

Beginning with the narrower monetary model, the logic is straightforward. Unequal life chances exist because parents are unequally able (or possibly unwilling) to invest in their offspring's human capital. This reasoning suggests that patterns of social inheritance will change under two conditions. One, more income inequality between families will strengthen inheritance – in particular if the rise in inequality implies that the poorest families are losing ground.[31] Two, social inheritance should abate to the extent that education and, more generally, human capital acquisition, is publicly financed – simply because this will diminish the importance of parental resources for children's educational attainment.[32]

Empirical research provides some, albeit rather limited, evidence in favour of this thesis. There is firstly evidence that parental expenditure on children becomes more unequal as a result of rising income inequality. Bianchi et al. (2003, table 2.2) show an 8 percentage point increase in the Gini of household child expenditure in the US over the past decade. And Harding et al. (2005) show that inter-generational income mobility rose in the US during the years of narrowing income differentials only to decline again in the recent decades of more inequality. There are also arguments that Sweden's unique success in diminishing the importance of social origins for educational attainment is, at least to some extent, owed to an extraordinarily concerted effort to equalize access to education (Erikson and Jonsson 1996). But there is also evidence that shows why, in general, postwar education reforms did little to equalize the opportunity structure (Shavit and Blossfeld 1993).

While virtually all agree that education is the main link between social origins and subsequent life chances it is also evident that the key mechanism does not lie in the educational system per se. This conclusion emerges from the OECD's (2001) huge Programme for International Student Assessment (PISA) study from which it is possible to distinguish school effects from family effects on youth's literacy skills. As a rule of thumb the relative weight of the two factors is in the order of 1:5. It also emerges from a huge body of evaluation research that shows that later adult remedial programmes have little effect because the preconditions for learning, training and skill acquisition lie very early in childhood (Haveman and Wolfe 1995; Danziger and Waldfogel 2000; Heckman and Lochner 2000).

Since it is in early childhood that the family effect is most intense and also of greatest potential consequence for a child's school performance and later life chances, this is where we should focus our analytical lens. Social scientific research is in broad agreement that the main family effects boil down to parental incomes and cultural-cognitive stimulation. But there is very little clarity regarding the relative importance of the two and, in any case, income and culture are very likely to co-vary.

It is now well established that poverty and economic insecurity in (early) childhood has severely adverse consequences. American research shows that poor children will have two years less schooling than the non-poor and will, subsequently, earn far lower wages (Mayer 1997; Duncan and Brooks-Gunn 1997). European studies provide similar, if generally less dramatic, results (Vleminckx and Smeeding 2001; Maurin 2002; CERC 2004). But why does poverty have such negative effects? There are essentially two, non-rival, explanations. Firstly, deprivation and economic insecurity mean that parents lack resources to invest in their children's schooling. Secondly, low-income families are likely to be risk-adverse and will therefore shun the risks of school failure (Breen 2001). In both cases the end result is similar: children are likely to curtail education at an earlier date.

In fact, several studies explain Sweden's success in reducing social inheritance with reference to its very low child poverty rates (Erikson and Jonsson 1996). It follows that any measure that effectively combats child poverty will pay off in terms of improved equality of opportunities. Welfare state redistribution in favour of families is crucial here but there is little doubt that mothers' employment is the single most effective antidote to child poverty (Esping-Andersen 2002; Rainwater and Smeeding 2004). The child poverty rate drops by a factor of 3 or 4 when mothers work. In other words, the rise in female employment combined with fewer and shorter interruptions around births will in all likelihood reduce social inheritance effects.

But if 'cultural capital' and cognitive stimulation are key to children's life chances then the positive income effect of mothers' employment may jeopardize the quality of child rearing if parent–child interaction diminishes in proportion to mothers' labour supply. The income dividend from mothers' work may accordingly be offset by inferior stimulus. Empirical research on this question fails to produce unequivocal answers. Overview studies suggest that, generally speaking, maternal employment does not have harmful effects and that it may even be positive (Duncan and Brooks-Gunn 1997; Haveman and Wolfe 1995; Gregg et al. 2005; James-Burduny 2005). But this depends very much on the quality of the mother's job and even more on the quality of childcare. Ermisch and Francesconi's (2002) study of Britain comes to rather more pessimistic conclusions. They find that full-time employment is decidedly negative for children's learning while part-time employment has no clear effects. Their findings are difficult to generalize because quality childcare is very scarce in the UK.

The PISA data provide an excellent opportunity to sort out these effects on children's cognitive performance. Using the literacy test scores for 15–16 year olds, we can examine the relative impact of parental education, socioeconomic status, 'cultural capital', and of mothers' employment intensity on child outcomes. The results are shown in table 10.6. Since girls systematically outshine boys in reading comprehension, the model includes a gender dummy. I also include a dummy for the child's immigrant status since this is likely to influence reading abilities. Fathers' education is measured in terms of years of education and, to avoid multi-colinearity, I measure mothers' education with dummies (the reference is less than secondary level). Socioeconomic status is the standard SEI-score that weights the occupational status and income of the head of household. The cultural capital variable is a composite of three items, two of which (number of books and frequency of discussing cultural issues in the family) measure the general 'everyday' level of culture, and one (attending opera, theatre and the like) that taps elite culture. Finally, the regressions include dummies for mother's employment status (reference is not employed).

The importance of family cultural capital is evident. As theory would suggest, income and cultural capital are both significant and strong predictors of child outcomes. But when we estimate the standardized Beta coefficients it emerges that the explanatory power of the culture variable is roughly twice as strong as the socioeconomic status variable.

It is chiefly mothers' education that matters for their children's development and this is plentifully confirmed in our analyses. There is good news on this front in the sense that, everywhere, women are making great strides – and are surpassing men – in terms of educational attainment. But there is also bad news because intensified marital educational homogamy implies potential polarization across families.

What matters is that mothers have at least upper secondary level schooling.[33] The additional 'child-returns' to tertiary education are quite marginal. Since mothers' education is of vital importance for child outcomes, their embrace of paid employment may imply reduced child stimulation. But the regressions in table 10.6 suggest that this is not necessarily the case. The effect of maternal employment is generally insubstantial, statistically insignificant and, in the case of part-time work, the impact is basically *positive*. Full-time employment has a significant negative effect in the US, Spain and (not shown) also in the Netherlands. Our findings do not confirm Ermisch and Francesconi's (2002) British results.[34]

Table 10.6 Family characteristics and literacy scores among 15-year-olds (OLS regressions)

	USA	UK	Germany	Spain	Denmark	Norway	Sweden
Constant	421.34***	444.86***	375.97***	425.09***	388.85***	406.06***	433.92***
Gender	18.68***	15.53***	25.57***	16.08***	20.24***	27.51***	27.51***
Immigrant	−15.98*	−14.01**	−40.92***	−20.65***	−25.48***	−35.25***	−35.66***
Father education	3.57*	0.76	7.52***	1.84*	8.19***	2.98*	−0.27
Mother education (secondary)	13.79*	10.31	43.61***	45.57***	37.87***	30.83***	20.59*
Mother education (tertiary)	13.88*	15.42*	50.01***	41.79***	52.72***	20.44**	17.07*
Socio-economic status	1.10***	1.17***	0.90***	0.52***	0.50***	1.01***	1.06***
Cultural capital	34.21***	40.65***	36.39***	38.53***	34.17***	38.73***	30.84***
Mother part-time	16.84**	12.92***	5.00	−18.26***	8.24	4.76	5.05
Mother full-time	−8.91*	5.99**	−3.09	−7.63***	−0.77	2.91	7.41
R^2	0.182	0.200	0.247	0.231	0.199	0.170	0.170
N	2571	7458	3933	4780	3933	3470	3836

Reference for mothers' education is less than secondary (ISCED 0-2). Reference for mothers' part-time/full-time employment is not employed. To improve upon comparability of education systems, for the United States we include 'some college' (usually two years) with upper secondary education. The asterisks imply statistical significance and 0.01 level or better.

Source: Data from OECD PISA study

Table 10.7 The impact of maternal employment on the reading abilities of girls and boys (coefficients taken from full model above)

	Part-time employed		Full-time employed	
	Boys	**Girls**	**Boys**	**Girls**
USA	8.46	23.18***	−19.20**	−0.53
UK	12.12**	13.55***	3.13	8.42**
France	9.31	8.88	9.06*	12.16**
Germany	−1.92	11.61**	−9.08	3.11
Spain	−22.62***	−13.06***	−9.26**	−2.83
Netherlands	8.50	11.27*	−20.19**	−1.60
Denmark	10.44	6.52	2.84	3.73
Norway	4.27	4.60	1.01	5.15
Sweden	8.42	1.47	11.49	3.03

The asterisks imply statistical significance and 0.01 level or better.

Source: OECD PISA (2000) data base

Very few studies disaggregate the maternal employment effect by the child's sex. Doing so, as table 10.7 shows, results in strong orthogonality: the negative consequences of mothers' employment seem limited to boys while, in contrast, girls seem to benefit. Here we are most probably witnessing the different role that mothers occupy vis-à-vis their children; that of role model for the girls and that of nurturing for boys. Spain, again, is the only country in which maternal employment has negative consequences across the board.

Mothers' employment may surely have adverse consequences for children's development – and hence cancel out the beneficial income effect of their earnings – but this clearly depends on the alternatives available to the family. One is that fathers may augment the time they devote to children. There is evidence from the US and Scandinavia that *total* parental time dedicated to caring for children is actually increasing because fathers – especially the higher educated – have doubled their caring hours over the past decade (Bianchi et al. 2003; Esping-Andersen et al. 2005).

The second alternative lies in external care. The large literature that evaluates the impact of early childcare on children's later outcomes shows quite consistently that participation in quality day care contributes very positively to school attainment and subsequent adult life chances (Currie 2001; Waldfogel 2002; Corak 2005). The key issue has to do with quality rather than simply participation. Care arrangements for working mothers vary tremendously between countries and this is likely to spill over to child outcomes. If, as in most of Continental, and especially in Southern, Europe, care is primarily delegated to grandmothers, this will imply that early childhood stimulus comes to mirror inequalities in families' cultural capital. If, as in the United States and Britain, care is mainly purchased in the market, this means very uneven quality that will be related to family income. In both groups of countries it is therefore quite understandable that maternal employment, especially if full-time, may have negative effects.

The Nordic countries, with virtually universal enrolments in high quality day care, should theoretically weaken both the family income and 'cultural capital' effect. This is supported by analyses of the PISA data, since the per cent variance explained by the combined cultural and social economic status variables is substantially lower in Denmark, Finland and Sweden than in most other OECD countries.[35] Since almost all children, *irrespective of social background*, are enrolled very early, and in institutions of similar pedagogical standards, one would expect an important levelling effect in terms of early cognitive stimulus. In such a scenario even full-time maternal employment will have no adverse effect while children from less privileged milieux will draw the relatively greatest cognitive benefit. In other words, when universal maternal employment is coupled with universal day care, we would expect that children are far more homogenous in terms of learning abilities at the moment they start formal education. This should, in turn, help boost inter-generational mobility.

This is a question that awaits systematic research. In an earlier study I examined the impact of parental social background on children's educational attainment across five postwar cohorts (Esping-Andersen 2004). For most countries the results are consistent with the *constant flux* thesis. In Germany, Italy, the UK and the US there has been absolutely no significant increase in educational mobility from the earliest cohort, born in the 1940s, to the latest, born in the 1970s. But in Denmark, Norway and Sweden the impact of social origins begins to fall noticeably for the youngest cohorts. To illustrate, the (log) odds of attaining upper secondary education for children with less educated parents doubled in Denmark (from 0.213 to 0.450) and tripled in Sweden (from 0.100 to 0.320).

Since there is little doubt that 'money' and 'culture' both count, a concomitant levelling of both of these – as has happened in Scandinavia – represents a very persuasive explanation for why opportunities have been equalized there. Since, however, the distribution of income – but not of childcare – is becoming more unequal in these same countries, the future will provide us with a perfect test of their relative salience for inter-generational mobility and equality of opportunities.

Conclusions

The sudden U-turn in income distributions is, in the spirit of Pareto and Kuznets, mainly explained as a structural feature of advanced economies. If true, we would conclude – similar to Pareto – that there is little we can do to stem the tide. The question I posed in this chapter is whether there is any scope for human agency. To answer this question I have deliberately shifted the analytical lens from individual wages to household incomes. This is more likely to capture the impact of two rival processes underway in our societies, namely demographic change and the revolution in women's roles. I have also sought to shift our attention from static snapshots of the income distribution to a more dynamic approach to inequality. Our understanding of worsening income distributions depends essentially on their impact on citizens' life chances.

There is no doubt a strong demographic component behind the rise of inequality. Changing patterns of household formation result in greater instability and in more vulnerable family types. This may have second-order consequences for mobility patterns, too, since hardship in lone mother households can translate into inferior life chances for their offspring (McLanahan and Sandefur 1994). Increased marital homogamy is a second powerful source of heightened inequalities. It will reinforce the impact of wage dispersion if educational homogamy is matched by similarities in partners' labour supply. And it may also have adverse effects on mobility and the opportunity structure if homogamy leads to a widening of the distance between the top and bottom – be it in terms of parental education, cultural capital, or income. The fact that educational selection is most pronounced 'at the top' points in this direction. We have also seen that couples' labour supply is very skewed in favour of the top and that the trend appears to be worsening. All in all, it is most likely that such demographic trends will add additional fuel to the inequalities that come from greater individual wage dispersion.

The final outcome depends, however, very much on women's behaviour. For one, the most vulnerable households tend to be female headed and the intensity of labour supply is therefore very decisive here. The same holds for poverty more generally and within families with children in particular. There is little doubt that those worst hit by rising wage inequality are young workers – who coincidentally are also parents. The evidence again is very clear: the risk of poverty declines dramatically when single and coupled mothers work. The conventional male-breadwinner family is losing terrain because young and lower skilled men are the primary losers in the evolving wage distribution.

It is for this reason that two ongoing trends c*an be truly decisive. Firstly, the gender gap in pay is narrowing and this means that the marginal effect of additional female labour supply can be quite important for household income. If it decreases more among the less skilled this should have a beneficial effect on their labour supply and, hence, on the relative position of low-income households. Secondly, the net effect of women's employment depends on *which women* increase their supply most. As we have seen, in most of Europe the burst in female employment has been skewed towards the top and this will reinforce inequalities – as is happening in Germany and Spain. Women's employment can have an egalitarian impact only if the labour supply of women 'at the bottom' grows faster than 'at the top'. This is what we saw happening in Scandinavia and in the United States during the 1990s. But, and this is important to add, these conditions are quite fragile because women 'at the bottom' are disproportionally at risk of unemployment – as are their husbands. Hence, gains made in good economic times can easily be undone during recessions.

Most of the pieces in the inequality puzzle line up in favour of more inequality, not less. This does not bode well for the future, especially if it implies less mobility and a hardening of social inheritance across generations. Here we must first recognize that mobility needs to *increase* if it is to offset rising income inequality. The evidence we need to address this question is hard to come by and it is, accordingly, difficult to go much beyond speculative inference. What data we do have does, alas, not provide a particularly rosy picture. The evidence suggests that mobility is inferior in the most inegalitarian countries like the UK and the US and that, furthermore, it is even declining. If this is so, life chances are adversely affected at least in terms of inequalities of lifetime income. But by and large there are no signs that mobility is decreasing in other countries – but neither that it is increasing. In other words, if inequalities are mounting while mobility remains stable the long-term outcome will still be greater lifetime inequalities.

Mobility and life chances are powerfully governed by the luck of birth. If inter-generational mobility does not increase it is less likely that lifetime mobility will. The key, then, lies in the mechanisms that drive social inheritance. Unfortunately there is mainly bad news on this front. In the majority of countries, inter-generational mobility appears very stable. Scandinavia is an exception because inter-generational mobility is far greater than elsewhere and has risen importantly over the past decades.

It is tempting to explain the Scandinavian enigma in terms of generous welfare state support for families and the beneficial income effect of maternal employment. But there are two important qualifiers to this argument. One is that mothers' employment may have negative consequences for children's development; another that family cultural capital is possibly of greater importance than 'money'.

My analyses suggest that in some countries maternal employment, if full-time, does have adverse effects on children's cognitive skills but that this is certainly not the case in any of the Nordic countries. This may have to do with the nature of mothers' jobs but most likely with the main alternative, namely good quality childcare. The universality of childcare attendance that is now a mainstay of Scandinavian society is – if perhaps not intentionally so – an instrument of considerable importance in equalizing children's intellectual and motivational preparedness for subsequent schooling.

If true, this is an important finding since it suggests, firstly, that more mobility and greater equality of opportunities can be stimulated via policy and, secondly, that it is potentially possible to counter the rise of income inequality with enhanced mobility chances, both on a lifetime basis and inter-generationally. Unfortunately we will not really know until, sometime in the future, we can ascertain whether the leap in mobility that has occurred – thanks to childcare and low family poverty – will be undone by heightened income inequalities.

And this brings me to the gist of my conclusions. If there is one variable that connects across all the facets of inequality here examined it is the class-specific asymmetry of women's labour supply. Extending the 'revolution in women's behaviour' to those women that still remain wedded to the traditional female role is, all considered, a potentially very powerful antidote to the new inequalities.

Notes

This paper is an outgrowth of the Ralph Miliband Lecture delivered at the London School of Economics, 2 December 2004. The research for the paper was financed by MCyT project no. SEC 2003–02699. I especially thank Berkay Ozcan for research assistance. I would also like to thank Anders Björklund, Julio Carabaña, Daniele Checchi, Brian Nolan, Nina Smith, Jane Waldfogel, and the members of the DemoSoc group at Universitat Pompeu Fabra for their very generous comments and suggestions.

1 For a recent detailed presentation of Pareto's theory of inequality, see Becker et al. (2000).
2 The correlation coefficient (elasticity) measures how much of the variance in offsprings' income is explained by the variance of parents' income. A value of 0.5 (as for the UK) implies that 50 per cent of the differences in parental incomes were inherited by the children's generation.
3 Using different data sources, Forster and d'Ercole (2005) arrive at the same conclusion. In the OECD as a whole, the market income Gini rose by a little more than 4 percentage points since the mid-1980s.
4 Breen and Salazar (2004) show, for the UK, that most of the rise in inequality is due to 'between-group' effects, i.e. to changes in household structure and composition.

5   Smeeding (2004, table 1) shows that between 1979 and 2000, the lowest fifth in the US gained a total of $1.100 (or 9 per cent) in real terms while the top fifth gained a whopping $576.400 (or 201 per cent).

6   In Denmark their share fell by 11 percentage points, in Finland and Norway by 9, and in Sweden by 10 percentage points. In Southern Europe the erosion has been minor, in large part because young adults remain in the parental home. Thus, in Spain their relative decline was only about 2 percentage points.

7   For an overview, see Katz and Autor (1999), Card (1999) and Bowles et al. (2001).

8   Calculated from OECD's Labour Market Statistics Data (updated 15 July 2003).

9   The reasons for women's comparably superior wage performance include fewer and briefer interruptions around childbirth (thus reducing the child penalty), the demand for typically feminal skills and attributes in the new service economy, and a decline in gender job segregation (Waldfogel and Mayer 1999; OECD 2002).

10 Eurostat data from NewCronos. Disaggregating the Danish gender wage gap by deciles shows that the gap has widened substantially for higher income women but that it has, simultaneously, narrowed for women with low earnings. In the US the opposite occurred (Datta Gupta et al. 2002).

11 The only exceptions to this are Germany and the UK. Calculations are based on the ECHP waves 1994–2001.

12 Estimates from Luxembourg Income Study (LIS) Key Figures, at www.lisproject. org/keyfigures.htm.

13 The correlation for couples' level of education ranges from 0.5 in Denmark, Germany and the UK, to 0.6+ in Italy, Sweden and the US (estimated from Canada Statistics IALS micro-data files).

14 Calculated from OECD (2000, Annex Table D). The ratio measures participation rates of women with less than upper secondary schooling over women with at least an upper secondary degree.

15 The figures would be far higher were we to include also single person and lone parent households (see OECD 1998, table 1.7).

16 Here, of course, also the generosity and coverage of social benefits will make a large difference.

17 Smeeding (2004, table 9) shows dramatic differences in poverty rates between households that supply less or more than 1,000 hours per year.

18 The correlations include all couple households and also persons with zero earnings and/or zero hours worked.

19 Marital earnings homogamy is bound to be weaker than educational homogamy because of gender differences in the intensity of labour supply. Marital educational homogamy correlations hover between 0.5 and 0.7 in the advanced nations (with Germany, Norway and the UK at the lower end and Sweden and the US at the high end).

20 Note that I use 'husbands' and 'wives' as shorthand. The discussion and all the data presented refer to all types of couple households that include a male and a female.

21 We notice that the Danish labour supply correlation rises between 1993 and 2001 – yet another indication that unemployment was disproportionally higher among women in 1993. Re-estimating the US (PSID) data for the longer period, 1980–2001, does not change the conclusion. In all years the sign remains negative but the equalizing effect of wives' earnings fluctuates substantially across the business cycle, diminishing in periods of higher unemployment.

22 These rates derive from Luxembourg Income Study (LIS) Key Figures.

23 We should also not forget that public income transfers redistribute heavily across people's life cycles.

24 Technically speaking, the link between inequality at one point in time and permament inequality depends on the full covariance structure of incomes. The variance of incomes over time is a function of the average variance and the average of the covariances. This implies that an increase in cross-sectional inequality can only be offset if there is an *increase* in income mobility over time. For a discussion, see Gottschalk and Smeeding (2003, pp. 294–5).

25 Estimated from Kaplan Meyer survival rate analyses.

26 The estimated coefficient for each 'missing year' is −0.5 and the depreciation coefficient is between 1.5 and 2.0 (Polacheck 2003, p. 18). These coefficients derive from life cycle data that are capped at 17 years of possible employment. Hence, they may very well change if total years of employment are greater.

27 It is also the case for the Netherlands and the UK, but in Germany interruptions have actually become longer (Gustafsson et al. 2002; Kenjoh 2003; Gutierrez-Domenech 2005). In the 1990s, the average number of interrupted months ranges from 32 in Germany to 9 in the Netherlands (13 in Sweden). The UK has undergone a dramatic change in just one decade since the average declined from 25 in the 1980s to 14 in the 1990s (Gustafsson et al. 2002).

28 The Sigle-Rushton and Waldfogel study is not directly comparable since their estimations derive from cross-section data.

29 In the mid-1990s, the difference in labour supply among mothers with 2+ young children in Europe is very large. The percentage in full-time employment was 60 per cent in Denmark compared to only about 20 per cent in Germany and the UK (estimated from the 1995 wave of the ECHP).

30 Björklund (1998) shows that in Sweden lifetime income inequality is lower for couples than for individuals which also suggests that Swedish women's impact is positive for equality on a lifetime basis.

31 Erikson and Goldthorpe (1992) argue similarly in terms of how income distributions affect class mobility.

32 For an overview see Solon (1999).

33 The coefficient for secondary-educated women is twice as large as for less-educated women in Denmark and Germany, and 45 per cent larger in Spain. This implies a gain in children's literacy test score equivalent to 21 (a 5 per cent gain) in Germany, 38 (a 10 per cent gain) in Denmark, and 14 (a 4 per cent gain) in Spain.

34 Gregg et al. (2005) find that negative effects of full-time maternal employment are limited to higher educated women and only if they work during the first 18 months after birth.

35 The two variables explain 15 per cent of the variance in Denmark, 9 per cent in Finland and 11 per cent in Sweden compared to an OECD average of 20 per cent.

References

Aaberge, R., Bjorklund, A., Jantti, M., Pedersen, P., Smith, N., and Wennemo, T. 1996. 'Income Inequality and Income Mobility in the Scandinavian Countries Compared to the US.' Research Department Discussion Paper, no. 168. Statistics Norway.

Aaronson, S. 2002. 'The Rise in Lifetime Earnings Inequality Among Men.' Finance and Economic Discussion Paper 2002–21. Washington, DC: The Federal Reserve Board.

Acemoglu, D. 2002. 'Cross-Country Inequality Trends.' Luxembourg Income Study (LIS) Working Paper, no. 296, March.

Arulampalam, W., Booth, A. and Bryan, M. 2004. 'Is There a Glass Ceiling Over Europe? Exploring the Gender Pay Gap Across the Wage Distribution.' Institute for the Study of Labour (IZA) Working Paper, no. 1373, October.

Atkinson, A. B. 1999. 'Is Rising Income Inequality Inevitable? A Critique of the Transatlantic Consensus.' Annual Lecture, United Nations University.

Becker, G. 1981. *A Treatise on the Family*. Cambridge, Mass: Harvard University Press.

Becker, G. and Tomes, N. 1986. 'Human Capital and the Rise and Fall of Families.' *Journal of Labor Economics*, 4: 1–39.

Becker, G., Murphy, K. and Werning, I. 2000. 'Status, Lotteries and Inequality.' MS, University of Chicago, Department of Economics.

Bell, D. 1976. *The Coming of Postindustrial Society*. New York: Basic Books.

Bianchi, S., Cohen, P., Riley, S. and Nomaguchi, K. 2003. 'Inequalities in Parental Investment in Childrearing.' Russell Sage Foundation Working Paper, February.

Björklund, A. 1998. 'Income Distribution in Sweden.' *Swedish Economic Policy Review*, 5: 39–80.

Björklund, A and Jäntti, M. 1997. 'Intergenerational Income Mobility in Sweden Compared to the United States.' *American Economic Review*, 87: 1009–18.

Björklund, A. and Palme, M. 2002. 'Income Redistribution Within the Life Cycle Versus Between Individuals.' In D. Cohen, T. Piketty and G. Saint-Paul (eds), *The Economics of Rising Inequalities*. Oxford: Oxford University Press, pp. 171–204.

Blau, F. and Kahn, L. 1995. 'The Gender Earnings Gap.' In R. Freeman and L. Katz (eds), *Differences and Change in Wage Structure*. Chicago, Ill. University of Chicago Press.

Blau, F. and Kahn, L. 2003. 'Understanding International Differences in the Gender Pay Gap.' *Journal of Labor Economics*, 21 (1): 106–44.

Blossfeld, H. P. and Drobnic, S. 2001. *Careers of Couples in Contemporary Society*. Oxford: Oxford University Press.

Bourdieu, P. 1983. 'The Forms of Capital.' In J. Richardson (ed), *Handbook of Theory and Research in the Sociology of Education*. Westport, Conn.: Greenwood.

Bover, O., Bentolila, S. and Arellano, M. 2002. 'The Distribution of Earnings in Spain during the 1980s.' In D. Cohen, T. Pikkety and G. Saint-Paul (eds), *The Economics of Rising Inequalities*. Oxford: Oxford University Press, pp. 3–54.

Bowles, S., Gintis, H. and Osborne, M. 2001. 'The Determinants of Earnings: A Behavioural Approach.' *Journal of Economic Literature*, 39: 1137–76.

Bowlus, A. J. and Robin, J. M. 2003. 'Twenty Years of Rising Inequality in U.S. Lifetime Labor Income Values.' Formerly at www.restud.org.uk.

Bradbury, B., Jenkins, S. and Micklewright, J. 2001. *The Dynamics of Child Poverty in Industrialized Countries*. Cambridge: Cambridge University Press.

Brandolini, A. 2005 'A Bird's-eye View of Long-run Changes in Income Inequality.' Research Department Paper, Banca d'Italia.

Brandolini, A., Cipollone, P. and Sestito, P. 2002. 'Earnings Dispersion, Low Pay and Household Poverty in Italy, 1977–98.' In D. Cohen, T. Pikkety and G. Saint-Paul (eds), *The Economics of Rising Inequalities*. Oxford: Oxford University Press. pp. 225–64.

Breen, R. 2001. 'A Rational Choice Model of Educational Inequality.' Instituto Juan March Working Paper, no. 166, October: 1–29.

Breen, R. and Salazar, L. 2004. 'Has Increased Women's Educational Attainment

Led to Greater Earnings Inequality in the UK?' Paper, 21 December, Nuffield College.

Browning, M. 1992. 'Children and Household Behavior.' *Journal of Economic Literature*, XXX: 1434–75.

Burtless, G. 1999. 'Effects of Growing Wage Disparities and Changing Family Composition on the U.S. Income Distribution.' *European Economic Review*, 43: 853–65.

Cancian, M., Danziger, S. and Gottschalk, P. 1993. 'Working Wives and Family Income Inequality Among Married Couples.' In S. Danziger and P. Gottschalk (eds), *Uneven Tides: Rising Inequality in America*. New York: Russell Sage Foundation, pp. 195–221.

Cancian, M. and Reed, D. 1999. 'The Impact of Wives' Earnings on Income Inequality.' *Demography*, 36: 173–84.

Card, D. 1999. 'The Causal Effect of Education on Earnings.' In O. Ashenfelter and D. Card (eds), *Handbook of Labor Economics*, vol. 3. Amsterdam: North Holland.

CERC. 2004. *Child Poverty in France*. Report no. 4. Paris: Conseil de l'emploi, des revenus et de la cohésion sociale.

Corak, M. 2004. 'Do Poor Children Become Poor Adults?' Paper prepared for the Centro di Ricerca Inter-Universitario sullo Stato Sociale (CRISS) Workshop, Siena, 25–6 September.

Currie, J. 2001. 'Early Childhood Intervention Programs.' *Journal of Economic Perspectives*, 15: 213–38.

Danziger, S. and Waldfogel, J. (eds) 2000. *Securing the Future*. New York: Russell Sage Foundation.

Datta Gupta, N. and Smith, N. 2002. 'Children and Career Interruptions: The Family Gap in Denmark.' *Economica*, 69: 609–29.

Davies H. B. and Joshi, H. 2001. 'Who Bears the Cost of Britain's Children in the 1990s?' In K. Vleminckx and T. M. Smeeding (eds), *Child Well-being in Modern Nations*. Bristol: The Policy Press.

Davies, J. and Shorrocks, A. 1999. 'The Distribution of Wealth.' In A. Atkinson and F. Bourguignon (eds), *Handbook of Income Distribution*, vol. 1. Amsterdam: Elsevier, pp. 605–75.

De Graff, P. and Ultee, W. 2000. 'United in Employment, United in Unemployment.' In D. Gallie and S. Paugam (eds), Welfare Regimes and the Experience of Unemployment in Europe. Oxford: Oxford University Press.

Duncan, G. and Brooks-Gunn, J. 1997. *Consequences of Growing Up Poor*. New York: Russell Sage Foundation.

Duncan, G. and Rodgers, W. 1991. 'Has Children's Poverty Become More Persistent?' *American Sociological Review*, 56: 538–50.

Duncan, G., Yeung, W. J., Brooks-Gunn, J. and Smith, J. R. 1998. 'How Much Does Childhood Poverty Affect the Life Chances of Children.' *American Sociological Review*, 63: 406–23.

Erikson, R. and Goldthorpe, J. 1992. *The Constant Flux*. Oxford: Clarendon Press.

Erikson, R. and Jonsson, J. 1996. *Can Education be Equalized? The Swedish Case in Comparative Perspective*. Boulder, Colo.: Westview Press.

Ermisch, J. and Francesconi, M. 2002. 'The Effect of Parents' Employment on Children's Educational Attainment.' Institute for Social and Economic Research (ISER) Working Paper, no. 21. Colchester: University of Essex.

Esping-Andersen, G. 2002. *Why We Need a New Welfare State*. Oxford: Oxford

University Press.

Esping-Andersen, G. 2004. 'Untying the Gordian Knot of Social Inheritance.' *Research in Social Stratification and Mobility*, 21: 115–39.

Esping-Andersen, G., Guell, M. and Brodmann, S. 2005. 'When Mothers Work and Fathers Care. Joint Households Fertility Decisions in Denmark and Spain.' DemoSoc Working Paper, 5. Barcelona: Universitat Pompeu Fabra.

Forster, M. and d'Ercole, M. 2005. 'Income Distribution and Poverty in OECD Countries in the Second Half of the 1990s.' OECD Social, Employment and Migration Working Paper, no. 22.

Fritzell, J. and Henz, U. 2001. 'Household Income Dynamics.' In J. Jonsson and C. Mills (eds), *Cradle to Grave. Life Course Change in Sweden*. Durham: Sociology Press, pp. 184–210.

Gallie, D. and Paugam, S. 2000. *Welfare Regimes and the Experience of Unemployment in Europe*. Oxford: Oxford University Press.

Gittleman, M. and Joyce, M. 1999. 'Have Family Income Mobility Patterns Changed?' *Demography*, 36: 299–314.

Goldin, C. 2004. 'From the Valley to the Summit: The Quiet Revolution that Transformed Women's Work.' NBER Working Paper, no. 10335.

Gottschalk, P. and Smeeding, T. 1997. 'Cross-national Comparisons of Earnings and Income Inequality.' *Journal of Economic Literature*, XXXV: 633–87.

Gottschalk, P. and Smeeding, T. 2003. 'Empirical Evidence on Income Inequality in Industrial Countries.' In A. B. Atkinson and F. Bourguignon (eds), *Handbook of Income Distribution*, vol. 1. Amsterdam: Elsevier, pp. 261–308.

Gregg, P. and Wadsworth, J. 2001. 'Everything You Ever Wanted to Know About Worklessness and Polarization at the Household Level but Were Afraid to Ask.' *Oxford Bulletin of Economics and Statistics*, 63.

Gregg, P., Washbrook, E., Propper, C. and Burgesse, S. 2005. 'The Effects of Mothers' Return to Work Decision on Child Development in the U.K.' *Economic Journal*, 115:48–80.

Gustafsson, B. and Johansson, M. 1997. 'In Search of a Smoking Gun: What Makes Inequality Vary Over Time in Different Countries?' Luxembourg Income Study (LIS) Working Paper, no. 172.

Gustafsson, S., Kenjoh, E. and Wetzels, C. 2002. 'Postponement of Maternity and the Duration of Time Spent at Home After First Birth.' OECD-DEELSA Occasional Paper, no. 59.

Gutierrez-Domenech, M. 2005. 'Employment and Motherhood: A European Comparison.' *Labour Economics*, 12: 99–123.

Haider, S. 2001. 'Earnings Instability and Earnings Inequality of Males in the United States, 1967–1991.' *Journal of Labor Economics*, 19: 799–836.

Harding, D., Jencks, C., Lopoo, L. and Mayer, S. 2005. 'The Changing Effects of Family Background on the Incomes of American Adults.' In S. Bowles, H. Gintis and M. Osborne (eds), *Unequal Chances*. New York: Russell Sage.

Haveman, R. and Wolfe, B. 1995. *Succeeding Generations*. New York: Russell Sage Foundation.

Heckman, J. and Lochner, L. 2000. 'Rethinking Education and Training Policy: Understanding the Sources of Skill Formation in a Modern Economy.' In S. Daniziger and J. Waldfogel (eds), *Securing the Future*. New York: Russell Sage Foundation, pp. 47–86.

Hills, J. 1998. 'Does Income Mobility Mean That We Do Not Need to Worry About

Poverty?' In A. B. Atkinson and J. Hills (eds), *Exclusion, Employment and Opportunity*. London: London School of Economics, Centre for Analysis of Social Exclusion (CASE).

Hills, J. 2004. *Inequality and the State*. Oxford: Oxford University Press.

Hoem, J. 2005. 'Why Does Sweden Have Such High Fertility?' Max Planck Institute for Demographic Research (MPIDR) Working Paper, 2005–009.

Hyslop, D. 2001 'Rising U.S. Earnings Inequality and Family Labor Supply: The Covariance Structure of Intrafamily Earnings.' *American Economic Review*, 91 (4): 755–77.

Iacovou, M. 2003. 'Work-rich and Work-poor Couples: Polarisation in 14 countries in Europe.' European Panel Analysis Group (EPAG) Working Paper, 45. Colchester: University of Essex.

James-Burduny, S. 2005. 'The Effect of Maternal Labor Force Participation on Child Development.' *Journal of Labor Economics*, 23 (1): 177–211.

Joshi, H., Davies, H. and Land, H. 1996. *The Tale of Mrs Typical*. London: Family Policy Studies Centre.

Juhn, C. and Murphy, K. 1997. 'Wage Inequality and Family Labor Supply.' *Journal of Labor Economics*, 15 (1): 72–97.

Juhn, C., Murphy, K. and Pierce, B. 1993. 'Inequality and Rise in Returns to Skills.' *Journal of Political Economy*, 101: 410–42.

Karoly, L. and Burtless, G. 1995. 'Demographic Change, Rising Earnings Inequality, and the Distribution of Personal Well-being, 1959–1989.' *Demography*, 32 (3): 379–405.

Katz, L. and Autor, D. 1999. 'Changes in the Wage Structure and Earnings Inequality.' In O. Ashenfelter and D. Card (eds), *Handbook of Labor Economics*, vol. 3A. Amsterdam: Elsevier, pp. 1464–1555.

Kenjoh, E. 2003. 'Women's Employment Around Birth of the First Child.' Institute for Social and Economic Research (ISER) Working Paper, no. 16.

Kenworthy, L. and Pontusson, J. 2005. 'Rising Inequality and the Politics of Redistribution in Affluent Countries.' Luxembourg Income Study (LIS) Working Paper, no. 400.

Kuznets, S. 1955. 'Economic Growth and Income Inequality.' *American Economic Review*, 45: 1–28.

Lam, D. 1997. 'Demographic Variables and Income Inequality.' In M. Rosenzweig and O. Stark (eds), *Handbook of Population and Family Economics*. Amsterdam: Elsevier, pp. 1015–62.

Lenski, G. 1966. *Power and Privilege: A Theory of Social Stratification*. New York: McGraw-Hill.

Levy, F. 1998. *The New Dollars and Dreams*. New York: Russell Sage.

Lindert, P. H. 2003. 'Three Centuries of Inequality in Britain and America.' In A. B. Atkinson and F. Bourguignon (eds), *Handbook of Income Distribution*, vol. 1. Amsterdam: Elsevier, pp. 167–216.

Lucifora, C., McKnight, A. and Salverda, W. 2005. 'Low Wage Employment in Europe.' *Socio-Economic Review*, 3: 293–310.

Luxembourg Income Study (LIS) at www.lisproject.org/.

Machin, S. 1998. 'Childhood Disadvantage and Intergenerational Transmissions of Economic Status.' In A. Atkinson and J. Hills (eds), *Exclusion, Employment and Opportunity*. London: London School of Economics, Centre for Analysis of

Social Exclusion (CASE).

Maurin, E. 2002. 'The Impact of Parental Income on Early Schooling Transitions.' *Journal of Public Economics*, 85: 301–32.

Mayer, S. 1997. *What Money Can't Buy*. Cambridge, Mass.: Harvard University Press.

McLanahan, S. and Sandefur, G. 1991. *Growing Up With a Single Parent*. Cambridge, Mass.: Harvard University Press.

Morrison, C. 2003. 'Historical Perspectives on Income Distribution: The Case of Europe.' In A. B. Atkinson and F. Bourguignon (eds), *Handbook of Income Distribution*, vol. 1. Amsterdam: Elsevier, pp. 217–60.

OECD 1998. *Employment Outlook*. Paris: OECD.

OECD 1999. *A Caring World*. Paris: OECD.

OECD 2000. *Literacy in the Knowledge Society*. Paris: OECD.

OECD 2001. *Employment Outlook*. Paris: OECD.

OECD 2002. *Knowledge and Skills for Life*. Paris: OECD.

OECD 2003. *Employment Outlook*. Paris: OECD.

OECD PISA 2000. Database at www.pisa.oecd.org/

Okonomisk, Raad 2001. *Dansk Okonomi*. Copenhagen: Det Okonomiske Raads Formandsskab.

Oxley, H., Dang, T., Forster, M. and Pellazari, M. 1999. 'Income Inequalities and Poverty Among Children and Households with Children in Selected OECD Countries.' Luxembourg Income Study (LIS) Working Paper Series.

Panel Study of Income Dynamics (PSID) at http://psidonline.isr.umich.edu/.

Pasqua, S. 2002. 'Wives' Work and Income Distribution in European Countries.' University of Torino, Centre for Household, Income, Labour and Demographic Economics (CHILD) Working Paper, no. 1.

Piketty, T. 2003. 'Theories of Persistent Inequality and Intergenerational Mobility.' In A. B. Atkinson and F. Bourguignon (eds), *Handbook of Income Distribution*, vol. 1. Amsterdam: Elsevier, pp. 429–476.

Piketty, T. and Saez, E. 2001. 'Income Inequality in the United States, 1913–1998.' NBER Working Paper, no. 8467.

Polacheck, S. 2003. 'How the Human Capital Model Explains Why the Gender Wage Gap Narrowed.' Maxwell School of Citizenship and Public Affairs Working Paper, no. 375. Syracuse University.

Polavieja, J. 2003. 'Temporary Contracts and Labour Market Segmentation in Spain.' *European Sociological Review*, 19 (5): 501–18.

Rake, K. 2000. *Women's Incomes over the Lifetime*. London: HMSO.

Romsen, M. 2004. 'Fertility and Family Policy in Norway.' *Demographic Research*, 10: 266–86.

Schrammel, K. 1998. 'Comparing the Labor Market Success of Young Adults from Two Generations.' *Monthly Labor Review*, February: 3–9.

Sigle-Rushton, W. and Waldfogel, J. 2004. 'Family Gaps in Income: A Cross-National Comparison.' Maxwell School of Citizenship and Public Affairs Working Paper, no. 382. Syracuse University.

Shavit, Y. and Blossfeld, H. P. 1993. *Persistent Inequality*. Boulder: Colo.: Westview Press.

Smeeding, T. 2004. 'Government Programs and Social Outcomes. The United States in Comparative Perspective.' Paper presented at the Smolensky Conference, University of California, Berkeley, 12–13 December.

Smith, M. 2005. 'Dual Earning in Europe: Time and Occupational Equity.' *Work,*

Employment and Society, 19: 131–39.

Solon, G. 1999. 'Intergenerational Mobility in the Labor Market.' pp. 1761–1800. In O. Ashenfelter and D. Card (eds), *Handbook of Labor Economics*, vol. 3A. Amsterdam: Elsevier Science.

Vleminckx, K. and Smeeding, T. 2001. *Child Well-being, Child Poverty and Child Policy in Modern Nations*. Bristol: The Policy Press.

Waldfogel, J. 2002. 'Child Care, Women's Employment, and Child Outcomes.' *Journal of Population Economics*, 15: 527–48.

Waldfogel, J. and Mayer, S. 1999. 'Male–Female Differences in the Low-wage Labor Market.' Paper presented at the American Economics Association Meetings, New York, January.

Wallerstein, M. 1999. 'Wage-setting Institutions and Pay Inequality in Advanced Industrial Societies.' *American Journal of Political Science*, 43: 649–80.

Warren, J., Hauser, R. and Sheridan, J. 2002. 'Occupational Stratification Across the Life Course.' *American Sociological Review*, 67: 432–55.

Wasmer, E. 2002. 'The Causes of the Youth Employment Problem.' In D. Cohen, T. Pikkety and G. Saint-Paul (eds), *The Economics of Rising Inequalities*. Oxford: Oxford University Press, pp. 133–46.

Whelan, C., Layte, R. and Maitre, B. 2004. 'Understanding the Mismatch Between Income Poverty and Deprivation: A Dynamic Comparative Analysis.' *European Sociological Review*, 20: 287–302.

11

Reframing Justice in a Globalizing World

Nancy Fraser

GLOBALIZATION is changing the way we argue about justice. Not so long ago, in the heyday of social democracy, disputes about justice presumed what I shall call a 'Keynesian-Westphalian frame'. Typically played out within modern territorial states, arguments about justice were assumed to concern relations among fellow citizens, to be subject to debate within national publics, and to contemplate redress by national states. This was true for each of two major families of justice claims, claims for socioeconomic redistribution and claims for legal or cultural recognition. At a time when the Bretton Woods system of international capital controls facilitated Keynesian economic steering at the national level, claims for redistribution usually focused on economic inequities within territorial states. Appealing to national public opinion for a fair share of the national pie, claimants sought intervention by national states in national economies. Likewise, in an era still gripped by a Westphalian political imaginary, which sharply distinguished 'domestic' from 'international' space, claims for recognition generally concerned internal status hierarchies. Appealing to the national conscience for an end to nationally institutionalized disrespect, claimants pressed national governments to outlaw discrimination and accommodate differences among citizens. In both cases, the Keynesian-Westphalian frame was assumed. Whether the matter concerned redistribution or recognition, class differentials or status hierarchies, it went without saying that the unit within which justice applied was the modern territorial state.[1]

To be sure, there were always exceptions. Occasionally, famines and genocides galvanized public opinion across borders. And some cosmopolitans and anti-imperialists sought to promulgate globalist views.[2] But these were exceptions that proved the rule. Relegated to the sphere of 'the international', they were subsumed within a problematic that was focused primarily on matters of security, as opposed to justice. The effect was to reinforce, rather than to challenge, the Keynesian-Westphalian frame. That framing of disputes about justice generally prevailed by default from the end of World War II through until the 1970s.

Although it went unnoticed at the time, the Keynesian-Westphalian frame gave a distinctive shape to arguments about social justice. Taking for granted the modern territorial state as the appropriate unit, and its citizens as the pertinent subjects, such arguments turned on *what* precisely those citizens owed one another. In the eyes of some, it sufficed that citizens be formally equal before the law; for others, equality of opportunity was also required; for still others, justice demanded that all citizens gain access to the resources and respect they needed in order to be able to participate on a par with others, as full members of the political community. The argument focused, in other words, on *what* should count as a just ordering of social relations within a society. Engrossed in disputing the 'what' of justice, the contestants apparently felt no necessity to dispute the 'who'. With the Keynesian-Westphalian frame securely in place, it went without saying that the 'who' was the national citizenry.

Today, however, the Keynesian-Westphalian frame is losing its aura of self-evidence. Thanks to heightened awareness of globalization, and to post-Cold War geopolitical instabilities, many observe that the social processes shaping their lives routinely overflow territorial borders. They note, for example, that decisions taken in one territorial state often impact on the lives of those outside it, as do the actions of transnational corporations, international currency speculators and large institutional investors. Many also note the growing salience of supranational and international organizations, both governmental and non-governmental, and of transnational public opinion, which flows with supreme disregard for borders through global mass media and cybertechnology. The result is a new sense of vulnerability to transnational forces. Faced with global warming, the spread of AIDS, international terrorism and superpower unilateralism, many believe that their chances for living good lives depend at least as much on processes that trespass the borders of territorial states as on those contained within them.

Under these conditions, the Keynesian-Westphalian frame no longer goes without saying. For many, it is no longer axiomatic that the modern territorial state is the appropriate unit for thinking about issues of justice. Nor that the citizens of such states are the pertinent subjects. The effect is to destabilize the previous structure of political claims making – and therefore to change the way we argue about social justice.

This is true for both major families of justice claims. In today's world, claims for redistribution increasingly eschew the assumption of national economies. Faced with transnationalized production, the outsourcing of jobs and the associated pressures of the 'race to the bottom', once nationally focused labour unions look increasingly for allies abroad. Inspired by the Zapatistas, meanwhile, impoverished peasants and indigenous peoples link their struggles against despotic local and national authorities to critiques of transnational corporate predation and global neoliberalism. Finally, WTO protestors directly target the new governance structures of the global economy, which have vastly strengthened the ability of large corporations and investors to escape the regulatory and taxation powers of territorial states.

In the same way, movements struggling for recognition increasingly look beyond the territorial state. Under the umbrella slogan 'women's rights are human rights', for example, feminists throughout the world are linking struggles against local patriarchal practices to campaigns to reform international law. Meanwhile, religious and ethnic minorities, who face discrimination within territorial states, are reconstituting themselves as diasporas and building transnational publics from which to mobilize international opinion. Finally, transnational coalitions of human-rights activists are seeking to build new cosmopolitan institutions, such as the International Criminal Court, which can punish state violations of human dignity.

In such cases, disputes about justice are exploding the Keynesian-Westphalian frame. No longer addressed exclusively to national states or debated exclusively by national publics, claimants no longer focus solely on relations among fellow citizens. Thus, the grammar of argument has altered. Whether the issue is distribution or recognition, disputes that used to focus exclusively on the question of *what* is owed as a matter of justice to community members now turn quickly into disputes about *who* should count as a member and *which* is the relevant community. Not just 'the what' but also 'the who' is up for grabs.

Today, in other words, arguments about justice assume a double guise. On the one hand, they concern first-order questions of substance, just as before: how much economic inequality does justice permit, how much redistribution is required and according to which principle of distributive justice? What constitutes equal respect, which kinds of differences merit public recognition and by which means? But above and beyond such first-order questions, arguments about justice today also concern second-order, meta-level questions: what is the proper frame within which to consider first-order questions of justice? Who are the relevant subjects entitled to a just distribution or reciprocal recognition in the given case? Thus, it is not only the substance of justice, but also the frame, which is in dispute.[3]

The result is a major challenge to our theories of social justice. Preoccupied largely with first-order issues of distribution and/or recognition, these theories have so far failed to develop conceptual resources for reflecting on the meta-issue of the frame. As things stand, therefore, it is by no means clear that they are capable of addressing the double character of problems of justice in a globalizing age.[4]

In this chapter, I shall propose a strategy for thinking about the problem of the frame. I shall argue, first, that in order to deal satisfactorily with this problem, the theory of justice must become three-dimensional, incorporating the political dimension of *representation*, alongside the economic dimension of distribution and the cultural dimension of recognition. I shall also argue, second, that the political dimension of representation should itself be understood as encompassing three levels. The combined effect of these two arguments will be to make visible a third question, beyond those of the 'what' and the 'who', which I shall call the question of the 'how'. That question, in turn, inaugurates a paradigm shift: what the Keynesian-Westphalian frame cast as the theory of social justice must now become a theory of *post-Westphalian democratic justice*.

For a Three-Dimensional Theory of Justice: On the Specificity of the Political

Let me begin by explaining what I mean by justice in general and by its political dimension in particular. In my view, the most general meaning of justice is parity of participation. According to this radical-democratic interpretation of the principle of equal moral worth, justice requires social arrangements that permit all to participate as peers in social life. Overcoming injustice means dismantling institutionalized obstacles that prevent some people from participating on a par with others, as full partners in social interaction. Previously, I have analysed two distinct kinds of obstacles to participatory parity, which correspond to two distinct species of injustice (Fraser 2003). On the one hand, people can be impeded from full participation by economic structures that deny them the resources they need in order to interact with others as peers; in that case they suffer from distributive injustice or maldistribution. On the other hand, people can also be prevented from interacting on terms of parity by institutionalized hierarchies of cultural value that deny them the requisite standing; in that case they suffer from status inequality or misrecognition.[5] In the first case, the problem is the class structure of society, which corresponds to the economic dimension of justice. In the second case, the problem is the status order, which corresponds to the cultural dimension.[6] In modern capitalist societies, the class structure and the status order do not neatly mirror each other, although they interact causally. Rather, each has some autonomy vis-à-vis the other. As a result, misrecognition cannot be reduced to a secondary effect of maldistribution, as some economistic theories of distributive justice appear to suppose. Nor, conversely, can maldistribution be reduced to an epiphenomenal expression of misrecognition, as some culturalist theories of recognition tend to assume. Thus, neither recognition theory alone nor distribution theory alone can provide an adequate understanding of justice for capitalist society. Only a two-dimensional theory, encompassing both distribution and recognition, can supply the necessary levels of social-theoretical complexity and moral-philosophical insight (for a full argument see Fraser 2003).

That, at least, is the view of justice I have defended in the past. And this two-dimensional understanding of justice still seems right to me as far as it goes. But I now believe that it does not go far enough. Distribution and recognition could appear to constitute the sole dimensions of justice only insofar as the Keynesian-Westphalian frame was taken for granted. Once the question of the frame becomes subject to contestation, the effect is to make visible a third dimension of justice, which was neglected in my previous work – as well as in the work of many other philosophers.[7]

The third dimension of justice is *the political*. Of course, distribution and recognition are themselves political in the sense of being contested and power-laden; and they have usually been seen as requiring adjudication by the state. But I mean political in a more specific, constitutive sense, which concerns the constitution of the state's jurisdiction and the decision rules by which it structures contestation. The political in this sense furnishes the stage on which struggles over distribution and recognition are played out. Establishing criteria of social belonging, and thus determining who counts as a member, the political dimension of justice specifies the reach of those other dimensions: it tells us who is included, and who excluded, from the circle of those entitled to a just distribution and reciprocal recognition. Establishing decision rules, likewise, the political dimension sets the procedures for staging and resolving contests in both the economic and the cultural dimensions: it tells us not only who can make claims for redistribution and recognition, but also how such claims are to be mooted and adjudicated.

Centered on issues of membership and procedure, the political dimension of justice is concerned chiefly with *representation*. At one level, which pertains to the boundary-setting aspect of the political, representation is a matter of social belonging; what is at issue here is inclusion in, or exclusion from, the community of those entitled to make justice claims on one another. At another level, which pertains to the decision-rule aspect, representation concerns the procedures that structure public processes of contestation; what is at issue here are the terms on which those included in the political community air their claims and adjudicate their disputes.[8] At both levels, the question can arise as to whether the relations of representation are just. One can ask: do the boundaries of the political community wrongly exclude some who are actually entitled to representation? Do the community's decision rules accord equal voice in public deliberations and fair representation in public decision-making to all members? Such issues of representation are specifically political. Conceptually distinct from both economic and cultural questions, they cannot be reduced to the latter, although, as we shall see, they are inextricably interwoven with them.

To say that the political is a conceptually distinct dimension of justice, not reducible to the economic or the cultural, is also to say that it can give rise to a conceptually distinct species of injustice. Given the view of justice as participatory parity, this means that there can be distinctively political obstacles to parity, not reducible to maldistribution or misrecognition, although (again) interwoven with them. Such obstacles arise from the political constitution of society, as opposed to the class structure or status order. Grounded in a specifically political mode of social ordering, they can only be adequately grasped through a theory that conceptualizes representation, along with distribution and recognition, as one of three fundamental dimensions of justice.

If representation is the defining issue of the political, then the characteristic political injustice is *misrepresentation*. Misrepresentation occurs when political boundaries and/or decision rules function to wrongly deny some people the possibility of participating on a par with others in social interaction – including, but not only, in political arenas. Far from being reducible to maldistribution or misrecognition, misrepresentation can occur even in the absence of the latter injustices, although it is usually intertwined with them.

At least two different levels of misrepresentation can be distinguished. Insofar as political decision rules wrongly deny some of the included the chance to participate fully, as peers, the injustice is what I call *ordinary-political* misrepresentation. Here, where the issue is intraframe representation, we enter the familiar terrain of political science debates over the relative merits of alternative electoral systems. Do single-member district, winner-takes-all, first-past-the-post systems unjustly deny parity to numerical minorities? And if so, is proportional representation or cumulative voting the appropriate remedy? (Guinier 1994; Ritchie and Hill 2001). Likewise, do gender-blind rules, in conjunction with gender-based maldistribution and misrecognition, function to deny parity of political participation to women? And if so, are gender quotas an appropriate remedy? (Phillips 1995; Rai 2002; Gray 2003; Htun 2004). Such questions belong to the sphere of ordinary-political justice, which has usually been played out within the Keynesian-Westphalian frame.

Less obvious, perhaps, is a second level of misrepresentation, which concerns the boundary-setting aspect of the political. Here the injustice arises when the community's boundaries are drawn in such a way as to wrongly exclude some people from the chance to participate *at all* in its authorized contests over justice. In such cases, misrepresentation takes a deeper form, which I shall call *misframing*. The deeper character of misframing is a function of the crucial importance of framing to every question of social justice. Far from being of marginal importance, frame-setting is among the most consequential of political decisions. Constituting both members and non-members in a single stroke, this decision effectively excludes the latter from the universe of those entitled to consideration within the community in matters of distribution, recognition and ordinary-political representation. The result can be a serious injustice. When questions of justice are framed in a way that wrongly excludes some from consideration, the consequence is a special kind of meta-injustice, in which one is denied the chance to press first-order justice claims in a given political community. The injustice remains, moreover, even when those excluded from one political community are included as subjects of justice in another – as long as the effect of the political division is to put some relevant aspects of justice beyond their reach. Still more serious, of course, is the case in which one is excluded from membership in any political community. Akin to the loss of what Hannah Arendt called 'the right to have rights', that sort of misframing is a kind of 'political death' (Arendt 1973, pp. 269–84).[9] Those who suffer it may become objects of charity or benevolence. But deprived of the possibility of authoring first-order claims, they become non-persons with respect to justice.

It is the misframing form of misrepresentation that globalization has recently begun to make visible. Earlier, in the heyday of the postwar welfare state, with the Keynesian-Westphalian frame securely in place, the principal concern in thinking about justice was distribution. Later, with the rise of the new social movements and multiculturalism, the center of gravity shifted to recognition. In both cases, the modern territorial state was assumed by default. As a result, the political dimension of justice was relegated to the margins. Where it did emerge, it took the ordinary-political form of contests over the decision rules internal to the polity, whose boundaries were taken for granted. Thus, claims for gender quotas and multicultural rights sought to remove political obstacles to participatory parity for those who were already included in principle in the political community.[10] Taking for granted the Keynesian-Westphalian frame, they did not call into question the assumption that the appropriate unit of justice was the territorial state.

Today, in contrast, globalization has put the question of the frame squarely on the political agenda. Increasingly subject to contestation, the Keynesian-Westphalian frame is now considered by many to be a major vehicle of injustice, as it partitions political space in ways that block many who are poor and despised from challenging the forces that oppress them. Channelling their claims into the domestic political spaces of relatively powerless, if not wholly failed, states, this frame insulates offshore powers from critique and control (Pogge 1999 and 2001; Forst 2001 and 2005). Among those shielded from the reach of justice are more powerful predator states and transnational private powers, including foreign investors and creditors, international currency speculators and transnational corporations (Harris and Seid 2000). Also protected are the governance structures of the global economy, which set exploitative terms of interaction and then exempt them from democratic control (Cox 1996 and 1997; Gill 1998; Helleiner 1994; Storm and Rao 2004; Boyce 2004). Finally, the Keynesian-Westphalian frame is self-insulating; the architecture of the interstate system protects the very partitioning of political space that it institutionalizes, effectively excluding transnational democratic decision-making on issues of justice (Dryzek 1999; Bohman 1999; Held 1995, pp. 99–140; 1999; 2000).

From this perspective, the Keynesian-Westphalian frame is a powerful instrument of injustice, which gerrymanders political space at the expense of the poor and despised. For those persons who are denied the chance to press transnational first-order claims, struggles against maldistribution and misrecognition cannot proceed, let alone succeed, unless they are joined with struggles against misframing. It is not surprising, therefore, that some consider misframing the defining injustice of a globalizing age.

Under these conditions, of heightened awareness of misframing, the political dimension of justice is hard to ignore. Insofar as globalization is politicizing the question of the frame, it is also making visible an aspect of the grammar of justice that was often neglected in the previous period. It is now apparent that no claim for justice can avoid presupposing some notion of representation, implicit or explicit, insofar as none can avoid assuming a frame. Thus, representation is always already inherent in all claims for redistribution and recognition. The political dimension is implicit in, indeed required by, the grammar of the concept of justice. Thus, no redistribution or recognition without representation.[11]

In general, then, an adequate theory of justice for our time must be three-dimensional. Encompassing not only redistribution and recognition, but also representation, it must allow us to grasp the question of the frame as a question of justice. Incorporating the economic, cultural and political dimensions, it must enable us to identify injustices of misframing and to evaluate possible remedies. Above all, it must permit us to pose, and to answer, the key political question of our age: how can we integrate struggles against maldistribution, misrecognition and misrepresentation within a *post-Westphalian* frame?

On the Politics of Framing: From State-Territoriality to Social Effectivity?

So far I have been arguing for the irreducible specificity of the political as one of three fundamental dimensions of justice. And I have identified two distinct levels of political injustice: ordinary-political misrepresentation and misframing. Now, I want to examine the politics of framing in a globalizing world. Distinguishing affirmative from transformative approaches, I shall argue that an adequate politics of representation must also address a third level: beyond contesting ordinary-political misrepresentation, on the one hand, and misframing, on the other, such a politics must also aim to democratize the process of frame-setting.

I begin by explaining what I mean by 'the politics of framing'. Situated at my second level, where distinctions between members and non-members are drawn, this politics concerns the boundary-setting aspect of the political. Focused on the issues of who counts as a subject of justice, and what is the appropriate frame, the politics of framing comprises efforts to establish and consolidate, to contest and revise, the authoritative division of political space. Included here are struggles against misframing, which aim to dismantle the obstacles that prevent disadvantaged people from confronting the forces that oppress them with claims of justice. Centred on the setting and contesting of frames, the politics of framing is concerned with the question of the 'who'.

The politics of framing can take two distinct forms, both of which are now being practised in our globalizing world.[12] The first approach, which I shall call the *affirmative* politics of framing, contests the boundaries of existing frames while accepting the Westphalian grammar of frame-setting. In this politics, those who claim to suffer injustices of misframing seek to redraw the boundaries of existing territorial states or in some cases to create new ones. But they still assume that the territorial state is the appropriate unit within which to pose and resolve disputes about justice. For them accordingly, injustices of misframing are not a function of the general principle according to which the Westphalian order partitions political space. They arise, rather, as a result of the faulty way in which that principle has been applied. Thus, those who practise the affirmative politics of framing accept that the principle of state-territoriality is the proper basis for constituting the 'who' of justice. They agree, in other words, that what makes a given collection of individuals into fellow subjects of justice is their shared residence on the territory of a modern state and/or their shared membership in the political community that corresponds to such a state. Thus, far from challenging the underlying grammar of the Westphalian order, those who practise the affirmative politics of framing accept its state-territorial principle.[13]

Precisely that principle is contested, however, in a second version of the politics of framing, which I shall call the *transformative* approach. For proponents of this approach, the state-territorial principle no longer affords an adequate basis for determining the 'who' of justice in every case. They concede, of course, that that principle remains relevant for many purposes; thus, supporters of transformation do not propose to eliminate state-territoriality entirely. But they contend that its grammar is out of synch with the structural causes of many injustices in a globalizing world, which are not territorial in character. Examples include the financial markets, 'offshore factories', investment regimes and governance structures of the global economy, which determine who works for a wage and who does not; the information networks of global media and cybertechnology, which determine who is included in the circuits of communicative power and who is not; and the bio-politics of climate, disease, drugs, weapons and biotechnology, which determine who will live long and who will die young. In these matters, so fundamental to human well-being, the forces that perpetrate injustice belong not to 'the space of places', but to 'the space of flows'.[14] Not locatable within the jurisdiction of any actual or conceivable territorial state, they cannot be made answerable to claims of justice that are framed in terms of the state-territorial principle. In their case, so the argument goes, to invoke the state-territorial principle to determine the frame is itself to commit an injustice. By partitioning political space along territorial lines, this principle insulates extra- and non-territorial powers from the reach of justice. In a globalizing world, therefore, it is less likely to serve as a remedy for misframing than as a means of inflicting or perpetuating it.

In general, then, the transformative politics of framing aims to change the deep grammar of frame-setting in a globalizing world. This approach seeks to supplement the state-territorial principle of the Westphalian order with one or more *post-Westphalian* principles. The aim is to overcome injustices of misframing by changing not just the boundaries of the 'who' of justice, but also the mode of their constitution, hence the way in which they are drawn.[15]

What might a post-Westphalian mode of frame-setting look like? Doubtless it is too early to have a clear view. Nevertheless, the most promising candidate so far is the 'all-affected principle'. This principle holds that all those affected by a given social structure or institution have moral standing as subjects of justice in relation to it. On this view, what turns a collection of people into fellow subjects of justice is not geographical proximity, but their co-imbrication in a common structural or institutional framework, which sets the ground rules that govern their social interaction, thereby shaping their respective life possibilities, in patterns of advantage and disadvantage.

Until recently, the all-affected principle seemed to coincide in the eyes of many with the state-territorial principle. It was assumed, in keeping with the Westphalian world picture, that the common framework that determined patterns of advantage and disadvantage was precisely the constitutional order of the modern territorial state. As a result, it seemed that in applying the state-territorial principle, one simultaneously captured the normative force of the all-affected principle. In fact, this was never truly so, as the long history of colonialism and neocolonialism attests. From the perspective of the metropole, however, the conflation of state-territoriality with social effectivity appeared to have an emancipatory thrust, as it served to justify the progressive incorporation, as subjects of justice, of the subordinate classes and status groups who were resident on the territory but excluded from active citizenship.

Today, however, the idea that state-territoriality can serve as a proxy for social effectivity is no longer plausible. Under current conditions, one's chances to live a good life do not depend wholly on the internal political constitution of the territorial state in which one resides. Although the latter remains undeniably relevant, its effects are mediated by other structures, both extra- and non-territorial, whose impact is at least as significant (Pogge 2002, especially pp. 112–16 and pp. 139–44). In general, globalization is driving a widening wedge between state territoriality and social effectivity. As those two principles increasingly diverge, the effect is to reveal the former as an inadequate surrogate for the latter. And so the question arises: is it possible to apply the all-affected principle directly to the framing of justice, without going through the detour of state-territoriality?[16]

This is precisely what some practitioners of transformative politics are seeking to do. Seeking leverage against offshore sources of maldistribution and misrecognition, some globalization activists are appealing directly to the all-affected principle in order to circumvent the state-territorial partitioning of political space. Contesting their exclusion by the Keynesian-Westphalian frame, environmentalists and indigenous peoples are claiming standing as subjects of justice in relation to the extra- and non-territorial powers that impact on their lives. Insisting that effectivity trumps state-territoriality, they have joined development activists, international feminists and others in asserting their right to make claims against the structures that harm them, even when the latter cannot be located in the space of places. Casting off the Westphalian grammar of frame-setting, these claimants are applying the all-affected principle directly to questions of justice in a globalizing world (Castells 1997; Guidry et al. 2000; Khagram et al. 2002; Keck and Sikkink 1998; St Clair 2000).

In such cases, the transformative politics of framing proceeds simultaneously in multiple dimensions and on multiple levels.[17] On one level, the social movements that practise this politics aim to redress first-order injustices of maldistribution, misrecognition and ordinary-political misrepresentation. On a second level, these movements seek to redress meta-level injustices of misframing by reconstituting the 'who' of justice. In those cases, moreover, where the state-territorial principle serves more to indemnify than to challenge injustice, transformative social movements appeal instead to the all-affected principle. Invoking a post-Westphalian principle, they are seeking to change the very grammar of frame-setting – and thereby to reconstruct the meta-political foundations of justice for a globalizing world.

But the claims of transformative politics go further still. In addition to appealing to a post-Westphalian principle, this politics is also inaugurating a post-Westphalian *process* of frame-setting. Above and beyond their other claims, these movements are also claiming a say in the process of frame-setting. Rejecting the standard view, which deems frame-setting the prerogative of states and transnational elites, they are effectively aiming to democratize the process by which the frames of justice are drawn and revised. Asserting their right to participate in constituting the 'who' of justice, they are simultaneously transforming the 'how' – by which I mean the accepted procedures for determining the 'who'.[18] At their most reflective and ambitious, accordingly, transformative movements are demanding the creation of new democratic arenas for entertaining arguments about the frame. In some cases, moreover, they are creating such arenas themselves. In the World Social Forum, for example, some practitioners of transformative politics have fashioned a transnational public sphere where they can participate on a par with others in airing and resolving disputes about the frame (Bohman 1998; Guidry et al. 2000; Pomiah 2004; Lara 2003; Fraser 2005b). In this way, they are prefiguring the possibility of new institutions of *post-Westphalian democratic justice*.[19]

The democratizing dimension of transformative politics points to a third level of political injustice, above and beyond the two previously discussed. Previously, I distinguished first-order injustices of ordinary-political misrepresentation from second-order injustices of misframing. Now, however, we can discern a third-order species of political injustice, which corresponds to the question of the 'how'. Exemplified by undemocratic processes of frame-setting, this injustice consists in the failure to institutionalize parity of participation at the meta-political level, in deliberations and decisions concerning the 'who'. Because what is at stake here is the process by which first-order political space is constituted, I shall call this injustice *meta-political misrepresentation*. Meta-political misrepresentation arises when states and transnational elites monopolize the activity of frame-setting, denying voice to those who may be harmed in the process, and blocking creation of democratic fora where the latter's claims can be vetted and redressed. The effect is to exclude the overwhelming majority of people from participation in the meta-discourses that determine the authoritative division of political space. Lacking any institutional arenas for such participation, and submitted to an undemocratic approach to the 'how', the majority is denied the chance to engage on terms of parity in decision-making about the 'who'.

In general, then, struggles against misframing are revealing a new kind of democratic deficit. Just as globalization has made visible injustices of misframing, so transformative struggles against neoliberal globalization are making visible the injustice of meta-political misrepresentation. Exposing the lack of institutions where disputes about the 'who' can be democratically aired and resolved, these struggles are focusing attention on the 'how'. By demonstrating that the absence of such institutions impedes efforts to overcome injustice, they are revealing the deep internal connections between democracy and justice. The effect is to bring to light a structural feature of the current conjuncture: struggles for justice in a globalizing world cannot succeed unless they go hand in hand with struggles for *meta-political democracy*. At this level, too, then, no redistribution or recognition without representation.

Paradigm Shift: Post-Westphalian Democratic Justice

I have been arguing that what distinguishes the current conjuncture is intensified contestation concerning both the 'who' and the 'how' of justice. Under these conditions, the theory of justice is undergoing a paradigm shift. Earlier, when the Keynesian-Westphalian frame was in place, most philosophers neglected the political dimension. Treating the territorial-state as a given, they endeavoured to ascertain the requirements of justice theoretically, in a monological fashion. Thus, they did not envision any role in determining those requirements for those who would be subject to them, let alone for those who would be excluded by the national frame. Neglecting to reflect on the question of the frame, these philosophers never imagined that those whose fates would be so decisively shaped by framing decisions might be entitled to participate in making them. Disavowing any need for a dialogical democratic moment, they were content to produce monological theories of social justice.

Today, however, monological theories of social justice are becoming increasingly implausible. As we have seen, globalization cannot help but problematize the question of the 'how', as it politicizes the question of the 'who'. The process goes something like this: as the circle of those claiming a say in frame-setting expands, decisions about the 'who' are increasingly viewed as political matters, which should be handled democratically, rather than as technical matters, which can be left to experts and elites. The effect is to shift the burden of argument, requiring defenders of expert privilege to make their case. No longer able to hold themselves above the fray, they are necessarily embroiled in disputes about the 'how'. As a result, they must contend with demands for meta-political democratization.

An analogous shift is currently making itself felt in normative philosophy. Just as some activists are seeking to transfer elite frame-setting prerogatives to democratic publics, so some theorists of justice are proposing to rethink the classic division of labour between theorist and *demos*. No longer content to ascertain the requirements of justice in a monological fashion, these theorists are looking increasingly to dialogical approaches, which treat important aspects of justice as matters for collective decision-making, to be determined by the citizens themselves, through democratic deliberation. For them, accordingly, the grammar of the theory of justice is being transformed. What could once be called the 'theory of social justice' now appears as the 'theory of *democratic justice*'.[20]

In its current form, however, the theory of democratic justice remains incomplete. To complete the shift from a monological to dialogical theory requires a further step, beyond those most envisioned proponents of the dialogical turn.[21] Henceforth, democratic processes of determination must be applied not only to the 'what' of justice, but also to the 'who' and the 'how'. In that case, by adopting a democratic approach to the 'how', the theory of justice assumes a guise appropriate to a globalizing world: dialogical at *every* level, meta-political as well as ordinary-political, it becomes a theory of *post-Westphalian democratic justice*.

The view of justice as participatory parity lends itself easily to such an approach. This principle has a double quality that expresses the reflexive character of democratic justice. On the one hand, the principle of participatory parity is an outcome notion, which specifies a substantive principle of justice by which we may evaluate social arrangements: the latter are just if and only if they permit all the relevant social actors to participate as peers in social life. On the other hand, participatory parity is also a process notion, which specifies a procedural standard by which we may evaluate the democratic legitimacy of norms: the latter are legitimate if and only if they can command the assent of all concerned in fair and open processes of deliberation, in which all can participate as peers. By virtue of this double quality, the view of justice as participatory parity has an inherent reflexivity. Able to problematize both substance and procedure, it renders visible the mutual entwinement of those two aspects of social arrangements. Thus, this approach can expose both the unjust background conditions that skew putatively democratic decision-making and the undemocratic procedures that generate substantively unequal outcomes. As a result, it enables us to shift levels easily, moving back and forth as necessary between first-order and meta-level questions. Making manifest the co-implication of democracy and justice, the view of justice as participatory parity supplies just the sort of reflexivity that is needed in a globalizing world.

Let me conclude by recalling the principal features of the theory of justice that I have sketched here. An account of post-Westphalian democratic justice, this theory encompasses three fundamental dimensions: economic, cultural and political. As a result, it renders visible, and criticizable, the mutual entwinement of maldistribution, misrecognition and misrepresentation. In addition, this theory's account of political injustice encompasses three levels. Addressing not only ordinary-political misrepresentation, but also misframing and meta-political misrepresentation, it allows us to grasp the problem of the frame as a matter of justice. Focused not only on the 'what' of justice, but also on the 'who' and the 'how', it enables us to evaluate the justice of alternative principles and alternative processes of frame-setting. Above all, as I noted before, the theory of post-Westphalian democratic justice encourages us to pose, and hopefully to answer, the key political question of our time: how can we integrate struggles against maldistribution, misrecognition, and misrepresentation within a post-Westphalian frame?

Notes

This essay originally appeared in *New Left Review*, 36 (November–December 2005), 1–19 and is reprinted with permission. First delivered as a 2004 Spinoza Lecture at the University of Amsterdam, the text was revised at the Wissenschaftskolleg zu Berlin 2004–5, then delivered as a Miliband Lecture at the London School of Economics in March 2005. Thanks to all three institutions for their support of this work, to James Bohman for bibliographical advice, to Kristin Gissberg and Keith Haysom for research assistance, and to Amy Allen, Seyla Benhabib, Bert van den Brink, Alessandro Ferrara, Rainer Forst, John Judis, Ted Koditschek, María Pía Lara, David Peritz and (especially) Eli Zaretsky for helpful comments and stimulating discussions.

1 The phrase 'Keynesian-Westphalian frame' is meant to signal the national-territorial underpinnings of justice disputes in the heyday of the postwar democratic welfare state, roughly 1945 through the 1970s. In this period, struggles over distribution in North America and Western Europe were premised on the assumption of state steering of national economies. And national Keynesianism, in turn, was premised on the assumption of an international state system that recognized territorial state sovereignty over domestic affairs, which included responsibility for the citizenry's welfare. Analogous assumptions also governed disputes about recognition in this period. The term 'Westphalian' refers to the Treaty of 1648, which established some key features of the international state system in question. However, I am concerned neither with the actual achievements of the Treaty nor with the centuries-long process by which the system it inaugurated evolved. Rather, I invoke 'Westphalia' as a political imaginary that mapped the world as a system of mutually recognizing sovereign territorial states. My claim is that this imaginary undergirded the postwar framing of debates about justice in the First World. For the distinction between Westphalia as 'event', as 'idea/ideal', as 'process of evolution', and as 'normative scoresheet', see Falk (2002).

2 It might be assumed that, from the perspective of the Third World, Westphalian premises would have appeared patently counterfactual. Yet it is worth recalling that the great majority of anti-colonialists sought to achieve independent Westphalian states of their own. In contrast, only a small minority consistently championed justice within a global frame – for reasons that are entirely understandable.

3 This situation is by no means unprecedented. Even the most cursory reflection discloses historical parallels – for example, the period leading up to the Treaty of Westphalia and the period following World War I. In these moments, too, not just the substance of justice, but also the frame, was up for grabs.

4 I have discussed the elision of the problem of the frame in mainstream theories of justice in my first Spinoza Lecture, 'Who Counts? Thematizing the Question of the Frame.' See also Fraser (2005a).

5 This 'status model' of recognition represents an alternative to the standard 'identity model'. For a critique of the latter and a defence of the former, see Fraser (2000).

6 Here I assume quasi-Weberian conceptions of class and status (see Weber 1958).

7 The neglect of the political is especially glaring in the case of theorists of justice who subscribe to liberal or communitarian philosophical premises. In contrast, deliberative democrats, agonistic democrats, and republicans have sought to theorize the political. But most of these theorists have had relatively little to say about the relation between democracy and justice; and none has conceptualized the political as one of three dimensions of justice. Deliberative democratic accounts of the political include Habermas (1996) and Gutmann and Thompson (1996). Agonistic accounts of the political include Connolly (1991), Honig (1993), Mouffe (1993) and Tully (1995). Republican accounts of the political include Skinner (1990) and Pettit (1996). In contrast to these thinkers, a handful of others have linked the political directly to justice, although not in the way I do here. See, for example, Walzer (1983), Young (1990), Sen (1999) and Benhabib (2004).

8 Classic works on representation have dealt largely with what I am calling the decision-rule aspect, while ignoring the membership aspect. See, for example, Pitkin (1967) and Manin (1997). Works that do treat the membership aspect

include Walzer (1983) and Benhabib (2004). However, both Walzer and
Benhabib arrive at conclusions that differ from the ones I draw here.

9 'Political death' is my phrase, not Arendt's.

10 Among the best accounts of the normative force of these struggles are
Kymlicka (1995) and Williams (1998).

11 I do not mean to suggest that the political is the master dimension of justice,
more fundamental than the economic and the cultural. Rather, the three
dimensions stand in relations of mutual entwinement and reciprocal
influence. Just as the ability to make claims for distribution and recognition
depends on relations of representation, so the ability to exercise one's political
voice depends on the relations of class and status. In other words, the capacity
to influence public debate and authoritative decision-making depends not
only on formal decision rules but also on power relations rooted in the
economic structure and the status order, a fact that is insufficiently stressed
in most theories of deliberative democracy. Thus, maldistribution and
misrecognition conspire to subvert the principle of equal political voice for
every citizen, even in polities that claim to be democratic. But of course the
converse is also true. Those who suffer from misrepresentation are vulnerable
to injustices of status and class. Lacking political voice, they are unable to
articulate and defend their interests with respect to distribution and recognition, which in turn exacerbates their misrepresentation. In such cases, the
result is a vicious circle in which the three orders of injustice reinforce one
another, denying some people the chance to participate on a par with others
in social life. In general, then, the political is not the master dimension. On the
contrary, although they are conceptually distinct and mutually irreducible,
the three sorts of obstacles to parity of participation are usually intertwined.
It follows that efforts to overcome injustice cannot, except in rare cases,
address themselves to one such dimension alone. Rather, struggles against
maldistribution and misrecognition cannot succeed unless they are joined
with struggles against misrepresentation – and vice versa. Where one puts the
emphasis, of course, is both a tactical and strategic decision. Given the current
salience of injustices of misframing, my own preference is for the slogan, 'No
redistribution or recognition without representation.' But even so, the politics
of representation appears as one among three interconnected fronts in the
struggle for social justice in a globalizing world.

12 In distinguishing 'affirmative' from 'transformative' approaches, I am adapt-
ing terminology I have used in the past with respect to redistribution and
recognition (see Fraser 1995 and 2003).

13 For the state-territorial principle, see Baldwin (1992). For doubts about the
state-territorial principle (among other principles), see Whelan (1983).

14 I borrow this terminology from Castells (1996).

15 I owe the idea of a post-territorial 'mode of political differentiation' to John G.
Ruggie. See his immensely suggestive essay, 'Territoriality and Beyond:
Problematizing Modernity in International Relations' (1993). See also
Pangalangan (2001).

16 Everything depends on finding a suitable interpretation of the all-affected
principle. The key issue is how to narrow the idea of 'affectedness' to the point
that it becomes a viable operationalizable standard for assessing the justice of
various frames. The problem is that, given the so-called butterfly effect, one
can adduce evidence that just about everyone is affected by just about everything. What is needed, therefore, is a way of distinguishing those levels and
kinds of effectivity that are sufficient to confer moral standing from those that

are not. One proposal, suggested by Carol Gould, is to limit such standing to those whose human rights are violated by a given practice or institution. Another proposal, suggested by David Held, is to accord standing to those whose life expectancy and life chances are significantly affected. My own view is that the all-affected principle is open to a plurality of reasonable interpretations. As a result, its interpretation cannot be determined monologically, by philosophical fiat. Rather, philosophical analyses of affectedness should be understood as contributions to a broader public debate about the principle's meaning. (The same is true for empirical social-scientific accounts of who is affected by given institutions or policies.) In general, the all-affected principle must be interpreted dialogically, through the give and take of argument in democratic deliberation. That said, however, one thing is clear. Injustices of misframing can be avoided only if moral standing is not limited to those who are already accredited as official members of a given institution or as authorized participants in a given practice. To avoid such injustices, standing must also be accorded to those non-members and non-participants significantly affected by the institution or practice at issue. Thus, Sub-Saharan Africans, who have been involuntarily disconnected from the global economy, count as subjects of justice in relation to it, even if they do not participate officially in it. For the human-rights interpretation, see Gould (2004). For the life expectancy and life-chances interpretation, see Held (2004, p. 99ff). For the dialogical approach, see below, as well as Fraser (2005a and 2006). For the involuntary disconnection of Sub-Saharan Africa from the official global economy, see Ferguson (1999, pp. 234–54).

17 For a useful account, which differs from the one presented here, see Chin and Mittelman (1997).

18 For further discussion of the 'how', see Fraser (2005a and 2006).

19 For the time being, efforts to democratize the process of frame-setting are confined to contestation in transnational civil society. Indispensable as this level is, it cannot succeed so long as there exist no formal institutions that can translate transnational public opinion into binding, enforceable decisions. In general, then, the civil-society track of transnational democratic politics needs to be complemented by a formal-institutional track. For further discussion of this problem, see Fraser (2005a and 2006). Also Bohman (1999).

20 The phrase comes from Shapiro (1999). But the idea can also be found in Habermas (1996), Benhabib (2004) and Forst (2002).

21 None of the theorists cited in the previous note has attempted to apply the 'democratic justice' approach to the problem of the frame. The thinker who comes closest is Rainer Forst, as he appreciates the importance of framing. But even Forst does not envision democratic processes of frame setting.

References

Arendt, Hannah 1973. *The Origins of Totalitarianism.* New York: Harcourt Brace.

Baldwin, Thomas 1992. 'The Territorial State.' In H. Gross and T. R. Harrison (eds), *Jurisprudence: Cambridge Essays.* Oxford: Clarendon Press, pp. 207–30.

Benhabib, Seyla 2004. *The Rights of Others: Aliens, Residents, and Citizens.* Cambridge: Cambridge University Press.

Bohman, James 1998. 'The Globalization of the Public Sphere: Cosmopolitanism Publicity and Cultural Pluralism.' *Modern Schoolman*, 75 (2): 101–17.

Bohman, James 1999. 'International Regimes and Democratic Governance.' *International Affairs*, 75 (3): 499–513.

Boyce, James K. 2004. 'Democratizing Global Economic Governance.' *Development and Change*, 35: 593–99.

Castells, Manuel 1996. *The Rise of the Network Society*. Oxford: Blackwell Publishers.

Castells, Manuel 1997. *The Power of Identity*. Oxford: Blackwell Publishers.

Chin, Christine and Mittelman, James H. 1997. 'Conceptualizing Resistance to Globalisation.' *New Political Economy*, 2 (1): 25–37.

Connolly, William 1991. *Identity/Difference: Negotiations of Political Paradox*. Ithaca, NY: Cornell University Press.

Cox, Robert W. 1996. 'A Perspective on Globalization.' In James H. Mittelman (ed.), *Globalization: Critical Reflections*. Boulder, Colo.: Lynne Rienner, pp. 21–30.

Cox, Robert W. 1997. 'Democracy in Hard Times: Economic Globalization and the Limits to Liberal Democracy.' In Anthony McGrew (ed.), *The Transformation of Democracy?* Cambridge: Polity Press, pp. 49–72.

Dryzek, John 1999. 'Transnational Democracy.' *Journal of Political Philosophy*, 7 (1): 30–51.

Falk, Richard 2002. 'Revisiting Westphalia, Discovering Post-Westphalia.' *Journal of Ethics*, 6 (4): 311–52.

Ferguson, James 1999. 'Global Disconnect: Abjection and the Aftermath of Modernism.' In James Ferguson (ed.), *Expectations of Modernity: Myths and Meanings of Urban Life on the Zambian Copperbelt*. Berkeley: University of California Press, pp. 234–54.

Forst, Rainer 2001. 'Towards a Critical Theory of Transnational Justice.' In Thomas Pogge (ed.), *Global Justice*. Oxford: Blackwell Publishers, pp. 169–87.

Forst, Rainer 2002. *Contexts of Justice: Political Philosophy Beyond Liberalism and Communitarianism*, trans. J. M. M. Farrell. Berkeley: University of California Press.

Forst, Rainer 2005. 'Justice, Morality and Power in the Global Context.' In Andreas Follesdal and Thomas Pogge (ed.), *Real World Justice*. Dordrecht: Springer.

Fraser, Nancy 1995. 'From Redistribution to Recognition? Dilemmas of Justice in a "Postsocialist" Age.' *New Left Review*, 212: 68–93.

Fraser, Nanccy 2000. 'Rethinking Recognition: Overcoming Displacement and Reification in Cultural Politics.' *New Left Review*, 3 (May/June): 107–20.

Fraser, Nancy 2003. 'Social Justice in the Age of Identity Politics: Redistribution, Recognition and Participation.' In Nancy Fraser and Axel Honneth, *Redistribution or Recognition? A Political-Philosophical Exchange*, trans. Joel Golb, James Ingram and Christiane Wilke. London: Verso.

Fraser, Nancy 2005a. 'Democratic Justice in a Globalizing Age: Thematizing the Problem of the Frame.' In Nathalie Karagiannis and Peter Wagner (eds), *Varieties of World-Making: Beyond Globalization*. Liverpool: Liverpool University Press.

Fraser, Nancy 2005b. 'Transnationalizing the Public Sphere.' In Max Pensky (ed.), *Globalizing Critical Theory*. Totowa, NJ: Rowman & Littlefield.

Fraser, Nancy 2006. 'Abnormal Justice.' *Critical Inquiry*, 32 (3).

Gill, Stephen 1998. 'New Constitutionalism, Democratisation and Global Political Economy.' *Pacifica Review*, 10 (1): 23–38.

Gould, Carol C. 2004. *Globalizing Democracy and Human Rights*. Cambridge: Cambridge University Press.

Gray, Tricia 2003. 'Electoral Gender Quotas: Lessons from Argentina and Chile.' *Bulletin of Latin American Research*, 21 (1): 52–78.

Guidry, John A., Kennedy, Michael D. and Zald, Mayer N. 2000. *Globalizations and Social Movements: Culture, Power and the Transnational Public Sphere*. Ann Arbor: University of Michigan Press.

Guinier, Lani 1994. *The Tyranny of the Majority*. New York: The Free Press.

Gutmann, Amy and Thompson, Dennis 1996. *Democracy and Disagreement*. Cambridge, Mass.: Belknap Press.

Habermas, Jürgen 1996. *Between Facts and Norms: Contributions to a Discourse Theory of Law and Democracy*. Cambridge, Mass.: MIT Press.

Harris, Richard L. and Seid, Melinda J. 2000. *Critical Perspectives on Globalization and Neoliberalism in the Developing Countries*. Boston: Leiden.

Held, David 1995. *Democracy and the Global Order: From the Modern State to Cosmopolitan Governance*. Cambridge: Polity Press.

Held, David 1999. 'Transformation of Political Community: Rethinking Democracy in the Context of Globalization.' In Ian Shapiro and Cassiano Hacker-Cordón (eds), *In Democracy's Edges*. Cambridge: Cambridge University Press, pp. 84–111.

Held, David 2000. 'Regulating Globalization?' *International Journal of Sociology*, 15 (2): 394–408.

Held, David 2004. *Global Covenant: The Social Democratic Alternative to the Washington Consensus*. Cambridge: Polity Press.

Helleiner, Eric 1994. 'From Bretton Woods to Global Finance: A World Turned Upside Down.' In Richard Stubbs and Geoffrey R. D. Underhill (eds), *Political Economy and the Changing Global Order*. New York: St. Martin's Press, pp. 163–75.

Honig, Bonnie 1993. *Political Theory and the Displacement of Politics*. Ithaca, NY: Cornell University Press.

Htun, Mala 2004. 'Is Gender Like Ethnicity? The Political Representation of Identity Groups.' *Perspectives on Politics*, 2 (3): 439–58.

Keck, Margaret E. and Sikkink, Kathryn 1998. *Activists Beyond Borders: Advocacy Networks in International Politics*. Ithaca, NY: Cornell University Press.

Khagram, Sanjeev, Sikkink, Kathryn and Riker, James V. (eds) 2002. *Restructuring World Politics: Transnational Social Movements, Networks, and Norms*. Minnesota: University of Minnesota Press.

Kymlicka, Will 1995. *Multicultural Citizenship: A Liberal Theory of Minority Rights*. Oxford: Oxford University Press.

Lara, María Pía. 2003. 'Globalizing Women's Rights: Building a Public Sphere.' In Robin N. Fiore and Hilde Lindemann Nelson (eds), *Recognition, Responsibility, and Rights: Feminist Ethics and Social Theory*. Totowa, NJ: Rowman & Littlefield, pp. 181–93.

Manin, Bernard 1997. *The Principles of Representative Government*. Cambridge: Cambridge University Press.

Mouffe, Chantal 1993. *The Return of the Political*. London: Verso.

Pangalangan, Raul C. 2001. 'Territorial Sovereignty: Command, Title, and Expanding the Claims of the Commons.' In David Miller and Sohail H. Hashmi (eds), *Boundaries and Justice: Diverse Ethical Perspectives*. Princeton, NJ: Princeton University Press, pp. 164–82.

Pettit, Philip 1996. 'Freedom as Antipower.' *Ethics*, 106 (3): 576–604.

Phillips, Anne 1995. *The Politics of Presence*. Oxford: Clarendon Press.

Pitkin, Hannah Fenichel 1967. *The Concept of Representation*. Berkeley: University of California Press.

Pogge, Thomas W. 1999. 'Economic Justice and National Borders.' *Revision*, 22 (2): 27–34.

Pogge, Thomas W. 2001. 'The Influence of the Global Order on the Prospects for Genuine Democracy in the Developing Countries.' *Ratio Juris*, 14 (3): 326–43.

Pogge, Thomas W. 2002. *World and Poverty and Human Rights: Cosmopolitan Responsibilities and Reforms*. Cambridge: Polity Press.

Pomiah, Thomas 2004. 'Democracy vs Empire: Alternatives to Globalization Presented at the World Social Forum.' *Antipode*, 36 (1): 130–33.

Rai, Shirin M. 2002. 'Political Representation, Democratic Institutions and Women's Empowerment: The Quota Debate in India.' In Jane L. Parpart, Shirin M. Rai and Kathleen Staudt (eds), *Rethinking Empowerment: Gender and Development in a Global/Local World*. New York: Routledge, pp. 133–45.

Ritchie, Robert and Hill, Steven 2001. 'The Case for Proportional Representation.' In Robert Ritchie and Steven Hill, *Whose Vote Counts?* Boston: Beacon Press, pp. 1–33.

Ruggie, John G. 1993. 'Territoriality and Beyond: Problematizing Modernity in International Relations.' *International Organization*, 47: 139.

Sen, Amartya 1999. *Development as Freedom*. New York: Anchor Books.

Skinner, Quentin 1990. 'The Republican Ideal of Political Liberty.' In Gisela Bock, Quentin Skinner and Maurizio Viroli (eds), *Machiavelli and Republicanism*. Cambridge: Cambridge University Press.

St Clair, Alexander 2000. 'Seattle Diary.' In Alexander Cockburn and Jeffrey St. Clair (eds), *Five Days That Shook the World: The Battle for Seattle and Beyond*. London: Verso.

Storm, Servaas and Rao, J. Mohan 2004. 'Market-Led Globalization and World Democracy: Can the Twain Ever Meet?' *Development and Change*, 35 (3): 567–81.

Tully, James 1995. *Strange Multiplicity: Constitutionalism in an Age of Diversity*. Cambridge: Cambridge University Press.

Walzer, Michael 1983. *Spheres of Justice*. New York: Basic Books.

Weber, Max 1958. 'Class, Status, Party.' In Hans H. Gerth and C. Wright Mills (eds), *From Max Weber: Essays in Sociology*. Oxford: Oxford University Press.

Whelan, Frederick 1983. 'Democratic Theory and the Boundary Problem.' In J. R. Pennock and R. W. Chapman (eds), *Nomos XXV: Liberal Democracy*. New York and London: New York University Press, pp. 13–47.

Williams, Melissa 1998. *Voice, Trust, and Memory: Marginalized Groups and the Failings of Liberal Representation*. Princeton, NJ: Princeton University Press.

Young, Iris Marion 1990. *Justice and the Politics of Difference*. Princeton, NJ: Princeton University Press.

Index